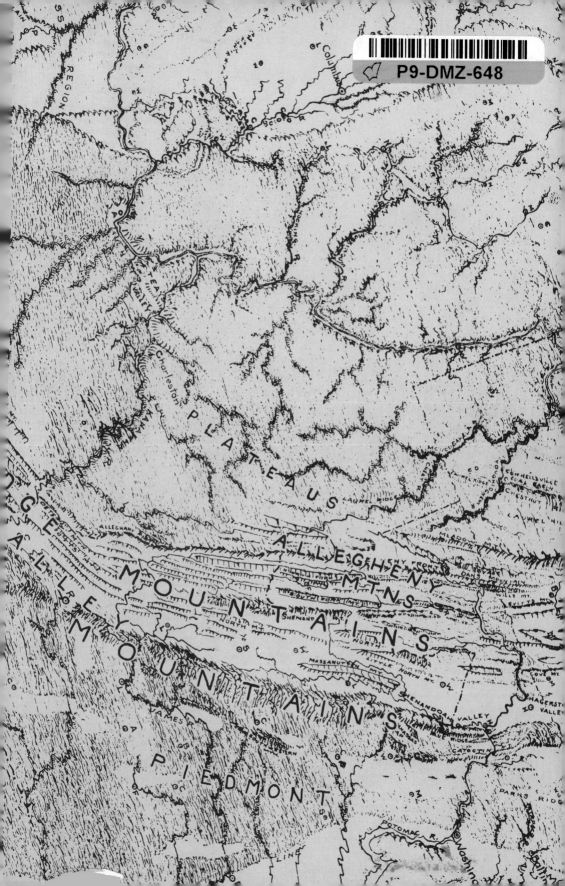

THE SOUTHERN APPALACHIANS

A Wilderness Quest

THE SOUTHERN

Other books by Charlton Ogburn

THE WHITE FALCON

THE BRIDGE

BIG CAESAR

THE MARAUDERS

SHAKE-SPEARE—THE MAN BEHIND THE NAME (co-author)

THE GOLD OF THE RIVER SEA

THE WINTER BEACH

THE FORGING OF OUR CONTINENT *(Smithsonian Library)*

THE CONTINENT IN OUR HANDS

WINESPRING MOUNTAIN

APPALACHIANS

A Wilderness Quest

CHARLTON OGBURN

William Morrow & Company, Inc. NEW YORK 1975

Title page photograph, Raven, credit: Luther Goldman.

Printed in the United States of America.

1 2 3 4 5   79 78 77 76 75

Designed by Margaret Dodd

Library of Congress Cataloging in Publication Data

Ogburn, Charlton (date)
The southern Appalachians.

Bibliography: p.
Includes index.
1. Appalachian Mountains, Southern. I. Title
F217.A65O32   917.4   74-34293
ISBN 0-688-00341-9

To Ede and Winnie Eskrigge, Malc Monroe, Charlie Wagner,
Nhoj White, Lint Young and, in memory, to Raburn Monroe,
all of Highlands, in whose illustrious company
an ever-to-be-grateful, very adolescent contemporary
grew in devotion to the Southern mountains.

Scale

25   0   25   50   75   100 MILES

COPYRIGHT BY A.K. LOBECK

Acknowledgments

The author wishes to express his entirely inadequate thanks to Time-Life Books, Inc., for financial support that made this book feasible.

The author is also indebted for help to:
   Thelma Howell, Richard C. Bruce and Bill Floyd of the Highlands Biological Station, Inc., Highlands, N.C.;
   Mabel and Arthur Cronquist, New York Botanical Garden, New York City;
   Robert S. Dietz, National Oceanographic and Atmospheric Administration, Miami, Fla.;
   Harry G. M. Jopson, Bridgewater College, Virginia;
   Sidney S. Horenstein, American Museum of Natural History, New York City;
   Ernest M. Dickerman, Wilderness Society, Washington, D.C.;
   Harold Robinson, National Museum of Natural History, Washington, D.C.;
   Larry Grand, James W. Hardin and John Mange, North Carolina State University, Raleigh, N.C.;
   Lewis Anderson, Duke University, Durham, N.C.;
   Norton Miller, University of North Carolina, Chapel Hill, N.C.;
   Wayne C. Cloward, V. H. Hofield, Alan J. Lamb, David W. Scott and W. E. Waters, United States Forest Service;
   Frederick R. Bell, Granville B. Liles, Paul F. McCrary and Edwin N. Winge, National Park Service;
   C. F. Shaffer, Commission of Game and Inland Fisheries, Commonwealth of Virginia;
   John Rauschenberger, State and Private Forests, State of North Carolina; and
   John H. Kern, Fort Dix, N.J., United States Army.

Contents

I   The Range of Shadow   3
II   The Discoverers   9
III The High Road   24
IV   The Great Smokies   38
V   The Progeny of Time   59
VI   Virginia's Greatest and the Complete Mountain   73
VII Depth and Heights of the Blue Ridge   96
VIII The Last Ramparts Southward   119
IX   Something About the Mammals   139
X   The Forest   151
XI   Long Ridges, Cumberlands and a Valedictory   172
XII A Prayer, and the West Virginia Alleghenies   190
XIII The Round of Seasons   213
     Appendix   229
     Bibliography   237
     Index   241

List of Maps

Topography of the Southern Appalachians	vi and vii
Map A	25
Map B	35
Map C	76
Map D	122

Unless otherwise credited, the photographs, both color and black-and-white, appearing in these pages are the work of the author.

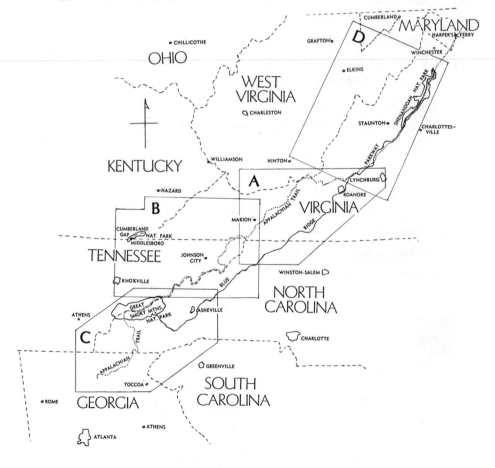

THE SOUTHERN APPALACHIANS

A Wilderness Quest

I *The Range of Shadow*

If I were called upon to introduce a newcomer to the East to our Appalachian Mountains, I should take him to the lowlands south and east of Knoxville drained by the tributaries of the Tennessee. Here, on the inland side of the range, there would rise before him on the horizon a blue silhouette which as he approached would break up into individual mountain ramparts of between four and five thousand feet from base to ridge. The Atali Unega of the Cherokees, or White Mountains—for frosts and snows begin early and recur late on the dark crests—they have acquired for us the name of Great Smoky Mountains. Their forms often, indeed, recede into mists and by Eastern standards they are large. Seen from the Tennessee side they do not, moreover, suffer much when compared in stature with the granite peaks above Colorado's South Park or Estes Park. The spectacle thus puts a somewhat different light on the statistics, which show that summits exceeding Denver's elevation above sea-level—and Denver is a city of the Plains—are high for the Appalachians; the Rockies are a mile high at their base. Nothing I have seen of other ranges has caused me to look with any less respect on the mountains that acquired a hold on me in my boyhood, I suppose through my susceptibility to Nature and a human impressionability before nobility and grandeur.

They do not, it is true, smite the vision. Though each time I see them they move me as much as ever, they have never wrung a gasp from me as I have gasped at the sight of the Alps, the Rockies, the Sierra Nevada and the Tetons. They are not Shining Mountains as the Rockies were to the first white men to reach them. They are not a Range of Light, as the Sierra Nevada was to John Muir and is to all who have seen it through his eyes. By contrast they are rather a range of shadow. They lie in the shadow of the clouds that form in their valleys by night and visit their summits by day, and the shadow of the forest that subdues the light on most of their highest elevations, as in their deepest gorges. For one whose views are colored by history, shadows of human origin fall upon them too. These are cast by the

3

The Appalachians.

dark deeds of violence and the bloodshed they have witnessed since the white men began to invade them, and by the sadness of the fate suffered by the two peoples who in historic times have had their roots in them—the Cherokees and other Indian tribes, and the white settlers who became the Southern Mountaineers.

It took a long time for our forebears to come into possession of the range. In their westward migration no barrier between the Atlantic and the Pacific stood more forbidding than the Appalachians. In 1728, defeated by

their steep slopes and tangled declivities as he sought to run the boundary line between Virginia and North Carolina, Colonel William Byrd declared that "Our country has now been inhabited more than 130 years by the English, and still we hardly know anything of the Appalachian Mountains, that are nowhere above 250 miles from the sea." Writing on the eve of World War I, Horace Kephart exclaimed, "A hundred and thirty years later, the same thing could have been said of the same mountains."

Kephart was a librarian who in 1904 had gone to live in the southern

Appalachians where life was most primitive—in the Smokies—to cure him—self of alcoholism and pursue a deep interest in the frontier, and was still there, writing eloquently of the mountain folk who were his neighbors and companions, eighteen years later. At the start he had found an amazing lack of information on the mountains. "In all the region north of Virginia and east of the Black Hills of Dakota there is but one summit (Mount Washington, in New Hampshire) that reaches above 6,000 feet above sea level, and there are only a dozen others that exceed 5,000 feet. By contrast, south of the Potomac there are 46 peaks, and forty-one miles of dividing ridges, that rise above 6,000 feet, and besides 288 mountains and some 300 miles of divide that stand more than 5,000 feet above the sea." And yet: "The Alps and Rockies, the Pyrenees and the Harz are more familiar to the American people, in print and picture, if not by actual visit." Something may be allowed Kephart's natural desire to dramatize his adventure. But lofty and still remote the southern Appalachians stood before him. In the succeeding sixty years their wildness has by no means been entirely lost. Much has even been regained.

At day's end, as the shadows of the ridges creep up the western flanks of their neighbors, it is not difficult to see in the mountains the barrier of darkness that earlier generations beheld in them. In the eyes of those to whom geological antiquity is real, or who drive their minds to grasp its reality, still another kind of shadow overlies the Appalachians. It is that of vanished eons. And the antiquity of these highlands is indeed great. Their memories go back to a very different earth. They saw the flowering of the age of reptiles in the hundred-million-year reign of the dinosaurs. Indeed, they saw its dawn. They looked down, presumably from peaks as high as any in North America today, on the birth of the Atlantic Ocean. The beds of Triassic, so-called red sandstone along their foot from the Connecticut River valley into North Carolina—source of much building material, including that of New York's famous brownstones—are composed of sediments from their erosion in deep basins created during the Atlantic's birth throes, when the earth's crust was rent and huge blocks of it imperceptibly subsided.

With maturity, human beings tend to become simpler and more consistent, as indeed do the languages that peoples speak; and so do the creations of geological change. The extravagances of feature of young mountains, from their jagged pinnacles skirted by glaciers to the canyons many thousands of feet below, cut by their perennially snow-fed torrents, together with the wide range of environments they offer flora and fauna, are things of the immeasurably long ago in the southern Appalachians. The range appears by Western and Alpine standards homogeneous and lacking in dramatic contrasts. The contrasts are there, and striking enough to its devotees, but they are not those of extremes. The variety is rich, only it is of a kind that causes one to look about with every step rather than press forward in anticipation of changes that, when they come, will be stunning. Except for the Spruce-Fir stands on the highest summits and the scattered pine barrens, there are none of those forests of two or three species only that are general in the West. It would not be surprising to find a dozen kinds of trees and as many of lesser woody plants on a few acres of Southern mountainside. It is an oft-rehearsed fact that the trees of the Great Smokies number no fewer species than those of all Europe. A day's hike in few other places in the Temperate Zones would discover as many as a hike from a 2,500-foot valley to a 6,000-foot height in the southern Appalachians.

Besides showing the range at its most impressive, the western approach to the Smokies has the advantage of bringing the motorist more or less naturally to Gatlinburg, the main Tennessee entrance to the Great Smoky Mountains National Park. From here, at an elevation below 1,300 feet, it is but six miles in a straight line to the near 6,600-foot summit of Mount LeConte. The trail, by which it is about twice as far, is probably the only one east of the Rockies on which you can climb a mile in vertical distance between sunup and sundown. For this and other reasons, if the newcomer to whom I was introducing our Eastern mountains could visit only one place in the range, I should set him on the hike up LeConte.

It was with that hike, which I shall get back to in due course, that I myself began two years ago. I was of a number invited to contribute a report on one of the nation's remaining wilderness areas and, given my choice of eight or ten of those areas, chose the southern Appalachians without hesitation. That was the start of what proved to be a rare and enviable experience for me. It called for my learning all I could about the range, justified my spending many days exploring it in a camping bus, dismounting continually, and led to my hiking and backpacking through it for some 350 miles, by my estimate—all memorable. The experience brought home to me, more than perhaps any had before, the power that mountains can exert over us. From the lowlands they seem to soar in imperturbable tranquility above the complexities of our lives, that confuse and vitiate us. They seem to stand warrant that there is that which lies beyond pettiness and frustration, expanding our spirit as the ocean does, too, in its way. They take possession of one.

Or they did of me. To help in planning my excursions, I tacked to the wall by my desk the four sheets of the Department of Commerce's Aeronautical Chart, covering the southern Appalachians in a scale of 1:500,000, or about 80 miles to the inch, and rendering its relief more clearly and attractively than any other map I know. (The version without navigational overprinting is the one to have.) A glance would put me at the mercy of those contours. I would sit gazing at some spot I did not know, my eye moving from the green of the lower elevations to the buff of the higher, from the initially pale buff to a darker shade and, where the terrain rose above 5,000 feet, to a darker still. And I would wonder what it was like on the way up, and where a dot with a figure beside it represented the mountaintop. While I was driving through the range itself, each form that reared against the sky—and there are tens of hundreds—left me dissatisfied and restless when, as was usually the case, I had to pass it unclimbed. Some persons speak of "conquering" a mountain; they are those, I suppose, to whom love is a matter of conquering a mate. What causes one to turn aspiring eyes to the summit is desire to know the mountain, to encompass it in one's life. In climbing a mountain you conquer yourself.

Here I should explain that the southern Appalachians were considered to begin (or end) at the Mason-Dixon Line—the southern border of Pennsylvania—and that I was to confine myself to those parts where the mountains rose to at least 3,000 feet. At the same time I might confess that I have found it hard to let go of the subject. The farther I have ventured in it the more my feelings have become involved with it and the more conscious I have become that I could devote the rest of my life to its study without coming near an end. When I was supposed to have written all I was going to, I could not forego a last trip down the range on the full tide of spring's arrival, this time with Vera, my wife; she had been done out of all but one of my previous trips by the necessity of providing a home for offspring. The effect was to open the field up all over again.

As for this account, I hope that those who know the southern Appalachians better than I may find in it a spur to memories that will be more vivid than any evocations I may attempt, and that others may be led to make or extend their own discovery of the range. Nothing could mean more to me than new accessions to the considerable body of those who hold the southern Appalachians in a high and jealous regard.

A last footnote:

To seek for wilderness in a range that extends as an archipelago through the most populous section of the country might seem an all but futile enterprise. And that is so if we take wilderness to mean pristine Nature unaffected by civilized man. By that definition no wilderness survives in the range outside a few pockets and certain reaches of the Great Smokies. I am content to think of it as wilds, which means to me any place where a lone individual with a sprained ankle would be in a serious plight. By that definition there is wilderness aplenty in the southern Appalachians. It comes to me, too, that there is wilderness wherever the cry of a hawk or owl is heard and, for that matter, in the most guileless face any flower ever opened to the light. There is wilderness in us, too, in our blood, to the degree that we are alive and not altogether instruments of thought, or creatures of passivity and convention.

II *The Discoverers*

"The wild Highlanders have loved their rugged mountains from before the days of Ossian," the British historian G. M. Trevelyan writes. "But those mountains were, until recently, a horror to the lowlander and above all to the Englishman." Observing that this antipathy toward mountains on the part of civilized man lasted until the latter part of the eighteenth century, Trevelyan quotes from a letter written by a Mr. Burt, an adviser to General George Wade, who opened the Highlands to the outside world with a system of hard-surfaced roads in the second quarter of that century:

> The summits of the highest [mountains] are mostly destitute of earth; and the huge naked rocks, being just above the heath, produce the disagreeable appearance of a scabbed head. Those ridges of the mountains that appear next to the ether, by their rugged, irregular lines, the heath and black rock, are rendered extremely harsh to the eye. But of all views, I think the most horrid, to look at the hills from east to west or *vice versa;* for then the eye penetrates far among them, and sees more particularly their stupendous bulk, frightful irregularity, and horrid gloom, made yet more sombrous, by the shades and faint reflections they communicate to one another.

Trevelyan believes it "quite possible that our ancestors were as fond of natural beauty as we are" and notes that Burt himself was by no means insensible to it, as witness what further he had to say:

> Now what do you think of a poetical mountain, smooth and easy of ascent, clothed with a verdant, flowery turf, where shepherds tend their flocks, sitting under the shade of tall poplars, etc?

In Burt's day, however, most mountains meant to outsiders venturing among them great hardships and danger from lawless bands. That is certainly what the southern Appalachians offered until late in the eighteenth century, though the Indians might well have argued that the interlopers' bands were more lawless than theirs. There is little reason to believe that the invaders found their countenance any more inviting than Burt did the Highlands'. It is known that Daniel Boone did not. Certainly the first white men to tackle the Appalachians seem to have experienced none of the feelings the mountains stir in us today. Hernando de Soto and his men, marching up from Florida in 1540, appear to have reached that river of odd name that winds among the high North Carolina mountains, the French Broad (so called because it flowed into French territory, to distinguish it from another Broad River). If they found anything to wonder at or admire, word of it has not come down to us. The Portuguese gentleman who accompanied the expedition and called himself the Fidalgo of Elvas wrote of it: "From Cutifa-Chiqui [thought to be Silver Bluff on the Savannah River] to Xuala [identified as a town of the Suali Indians southeast of the site of Asheville] are 250 [?] of mountainous country; thence to Guaxule [probably in the northeastern corner of Georgia] the way [is] over very rough and lofty ridges." The Fidalgo found more to comment on in the means of escape practised by an Indian queen de Soto had along as a guide and hostage, and who perhaps had led them on a wild goose chase in the mountains. After they had left Xuala, "the ladie of Cutifa-Chiqui (whom the Governor carried with him, as is aforesaid, with purpose to carry her to Guaxule, because her territory reached thither) . . . went out of the way and entered a wood, saying, she went to ease herself, and so she deceived them, and hid herself in the wood." But de Soto gave the range the name it has since borne, from the Appalache Indians of Florida.

The first white man after the Spanish to see the Southern mountains was probably John Lederer, a twenty-six-year-old German physician. From his statehouse in Jamestown in 1669 Governor William Berkeley had sent Lederer off to find a route to the western Indians, with whom the French had been enjoying a profitable trade from the north.

Lederer had ascended a river to its headwaters in the Blue Ridge. Darwin Lambert identifies the river as the South Anna. In his highly readable, ecological-historical account of the mountains of the Shenandoah National Park, *The Earth-man's Story*, he tells how he and his wife, 300 years later to the day, retraced what he believes to have been Lederer's approach to the range.

On March 14th Lederer "first descried the Apalataean Mountains, bearing due West to the place I stood upon; their distance from me was so great, that I could hardly discern whether they were Mountains or Clouds." On reaching the range he climbed a mountain Lambert thinks was probably Hightop, a summit looking down from 3,885 feet on Swift Run Gap, today the middle entrance to the Park. "The height of this mountain," Lederer wrote, "was very extraordinary; for notwithstanding I set out with the first appearance of light, it was late in the evening before I gained the top." From here "To the North and West, my sight was suddenly bounded by Mountains higher than I stood upon." These would

THE DISCOVERERS / 11

have been the Long Ridges and West Virginia Alleghenies. In the morning, he reported that he saw "The Atlantic-Ocean washing the Virginia shore." This observation is one of several that long led historians to doubt the young German's whole report. It could, however, be explained as occasioned by a low cloud bank and a trick of light. Lederer wandered about in the snow for some days, as he says, "hoping to find some passage through the Mountains; but the coldness of the Air and Earth together, seizing my Hands and Feet with numbness, put me to a *ne plus ultra,*" and he turned back the way he had come.

Lederer left no testimony to indicate that he found the mountains other than toilsome obstacles. Neither did the two gentlemen who two years later, acting also on Governor Berkeley's commission to find a western trade route, hit upon a passage through the range. Thomas Batts and Robert Fallam, having crossed the Blue Ridge via the gateway of the Roanoke River, soon reached the New, which rises in northern North Carolina, in part along the Blue Ridge Parkway, and flows north into the Great Kanawha, a tributary of the Ohio. Following it to the present West Virginia border, the explorers claimed for Charles II all the lands to the west in the drainage system—just three months after Simon St. Lusson at Sault Ste. Marie, 650 miles away, had claimed the same lands for Louis XIV. Their imaginations seizing upon a backwash of the New River and transforming it into a tidal flow, they announced on their return that they had found a route to the Pacific. In fact, three generations were yet to pass before the mountains would be other than an ominous wall of darkness and, to civilization, Lederer's *ne plus ultra*—the "let there not be any going beyond" said to have been inscribed on the Pillars of Hercules.

Still, in another expedition at another interval of two years, James Needham, journeying forth to seek trade with the Cherokees, reached a village of theirs probably on the same river de Soto is thought to have reached, the French Broad, a tributary of the Tennessee. Needham was killed by an Occaneechi guide, who, to show his defiance of the English, plucked out his heart and held it aloft. A young companion, Gabriel Arthur, was saved by the last-second arrival of Cherokees. Joining his rescuers for safety, he was taken by them on a amazing peregrination, all the way to the territory whence the name of the Appalachians had derived, the land of the Apalaches in western Florida. Thence, after unsuccessfully attacking a Spanish Mission, the Cherokee band returned Arthur to his people via the Great Kanawha, which he became the first white man to see. What account Arthur gave of his travels can only be imagined—he was illiterate—but it is unlikely to have made the mountains much more appealing; and the savage murder of Needham would have revived memories on the James, where, 50 years before, 357 colonists had been massacred by Indians on one grisly day.

The next Virginia governor who sought a route across the mountains went himself, in 1716. The expedition could hardly have differed more in character from its predecessors or from all other penetrations of the unknown. Governed by then from Williamsburg, the Old Dominion had entered upon its time of sword and gauntlet. It was a band of cavaliers, and their servants, that the gorgeously attired soldier-governor Alexander Spotswood led up the Rapidan to the foothills of the Blue Ridge, picking up a dozen frontier rangers en route. The party had enlivened the march with hunting and some carousal, but the range itself was a different matter. Three days were spent getting the horses up to the crest at Swift Run Gap, and the difficulty of descent on the other side proved even greater. Any apostrophization of the mountains was doubtless profane. But the Shenandoah and its bounty awaited them.

One learns with surprise from Samuel Kercheval's *A History of the Valley of Virginia* that "Much the greater part of the country . . . was one vast prairie and like the rich prairies of the west, afforded the finest possible pasturage for wild animals." Inasmuch as any part of the valley today would, if left to itself, quickly grow up in woods, it can only be that the Indians had the habit of burning it off, either as the accidental consequence of their "fire hunts," or on purpose to enhance its suitability for game and berry-bearing plants. Elsewhere, considerable parts of the great Eastern forest appear similarly to have been opened up by fires set by the Indians. Indeed, the pioneers are said to have found the smoke of these fires positively choking at times.

Be that as it may, the Shenandoah Valley in the early eighteenth century, according to Kercheval, "abounded in the larger kinds of game. The buffalo, elk, deer, bear, panther, wild cat, wolf, fox, beaver, otter, and all other kinds of animals, wild fowl, etc., common to forest countries, were abundantly plenty." Governor Spotswood and his party hunted, feasted and drank in turn the health of the King and all the members of the Royal Family from the extraordinary store of various spirituous liquors brought with them. These libations may have added glow to the reports of the Shenandoah's allure and promise emanating from the returning explorers. If so, they fitted in with the purpose the stage-play had had in the Governor's mind from the start. Even his presentation to each of the gentlemen adventurers of a golden horseshoe inscribed *Sic Juvat Transcendere Montes*—"So pleasant is it to cross the mountains"—played a part. Spotswood had fought the French at Blenheim and Malplaquet—and now he saw them in control of the upper Mississippi Valley. He must have foreseen the inevitable collision that would make the Appalachians a range of shadow indeed, one illumined by flames, and unquestionably he saw the value of western settlement.

It took time for the bait to produce results, but in 1726 a German immigrant followed the trail of the Knights of the Golden Horseshoe over Swift Run Gap and built a cabin on the beautiful river beyond. Within a few years his enthusiastic reports had drawn fifty others to the area. By then, too, the first of the Germans from the north had taken up land in the valley near the present site of Winchester. In the settlement of Appalachia Germans took the lead. Driven from their homes in the Rhenish Palatinate and Würtemberg by the recurrent ravages of French invaders, misrule at the hands of their own princes, and the terrible winter of 1708–9, which froze birds and wild animals and killed the vines, they crossed the ocean. Settling first in New York, where they were mercilessly abused and exploited, they found a promised land in central Pennsylvania. There the giant barns and rich fields testify today to their true peasant's feeling for the soil. Before long they were overflowing through passes in South Mountain—the beginning of the Blue Ridge—into the Great Valley. By 1760 they had reached the New River, "converting, as they advanced," says John A. Caruso in *The Appalachian Frontier,* "a trackless wilderness into a continuous agricultural paradise."

On the heels of the Germans came a much greater and continuing tide of immigrants from the British Isles. Much of it was made up of Scots-Irish, as they are called, though they numbered many English while the Scots had little Irish admixture. They were descendants of colonists settled in the two counties of northern Ireland wrested from their previous owners under Elizabeth and James, the Scots being mostly Presbyterian lowlanders. Hard-working, fearing their jealous, wrathful, Old Testament God, they had prospered on the fertile lands of their new home. Indeed, they had done so well that the Crown, to protect domestic agriculture and industry, banned the importation of products of Ireland. When the laws discriminating against the Presbyterian clergy were enacted, it was too much for the settlers. The consequences were to prove too much for the Crown, too; for when the Scots-Irish in 1718 commenced to flock to the American colonies, there to become in time the second most numerous element of the population, they brought the seeds of the American Revolution with them. In 1772 their descendants on the Watauga River, just north of the eastern end of the Great Smoky Mountains, were to form an association that John A. Caruso calls "the first free and independent government, democratic in spirit and representative in form, ever to be formed on the American continent." John Murray Lord Dunmore, new Governor of Virginia, saw it in much the same light, as a dangerous example "of forming governments distinct from and independent of His Majesty's Authority." Eight years later, in October 1780, the settlers were to avenge the wrongs suffered by their forebears. At King's Mountain, in the North Carolina Piedmont, 1,400 frontiersmen assembled from the mountain communities would bring a force of 1,000 "American volunteers" under British Major Patrick

Ferguson to bay and destroy it, forcing Major General Lord Charles Cornwallis with the main British force to retreat to South Carolina. What probably decided the battle was the superiority in range and accuracy of the Pennsylvania rifle, which threw a spinning projectile, to the smooth-bore British musket.

The Scots-Irish followed much the same path as the German immigrants. Landing at northeastern ports, they made their way to the hinterlands of New York and Pennsylvania, whence those who could not find land within their means turned south into the Great Valley. Filtering down through the mountains, they met other English and Scots Presbyterians from the Piedmont, whose experiences of the privileges enjoyed by the Anglican Church and the planter aristocracy of the lowlands had given them a similar outlook. These new Americans were fiercely independent, equalitarian and self-reliant, possessed of an indomitable will to survive and prevail, tough in mind and body. Stung by the slights and injuries they had taken from the advantaged class, their superiors in breeding, cultivation and wealth, they were hostile to all that class stood for. They were bound by no ties to the Old World or, like their German fellows, to the English Crown.

With a stern, fatalistic religion to keep their impetuosity in check, the Scots-Irish combined an intense and ingenious practicality, shrewdness and a long grasp for life's tangibles. From their habituation to clan warfare in the ancestral home and to battling the wild Celts in Ulster, they brought with them a fighting instinct and aggressiveness and a handiness with weapons. Given the nature of the American frontier and the general determination to advance it, regardless, they made ideal frontiersmen, the equal before long of the redmen, whose woodcraft and dress they adopted. They were not only the new Americans, they were to be the creators of the New America. This would formally succeed to the old when one of their number, Andrew Jackson, was elevated to the Presidency. And of this New America, which would sweep westward to the Pacific in the course of the next century, southern Appalachia was a prime staging area.

What did they think of it—the first pioneers? What must they have thought? The mountains were a world as far apart for them as those of Antarctica for us today. Farther. The range held the invader blindfolded within its forests and embrasures. Its valleys were choked with rhododendron, its slopes all but barred by the trunks of fallen trees requiring decades to decay, too big even to see over. Most of it was next to impossible to traverse except on trails made by the hoofed animals, bears and Indians. Its passes for a man and wife with children, a pack animal with gear and a cow or two were exhausting to surmount. Its rains compounded the other hardships it imposed. Its trees were of such girth that girdling them and waiting for the years to topple the corpses offered to many the only means

There are times, hiking a waterless ridge crest, when one is glad to have had a thoughtful predecessor.

of clearing a tract for planting. Its depths were unpitying of illness or injury, the peril of Indians unremitting.

Speaking of the mountains of the North Carolina and Tennessee border in the late eighteenth century, an Indian agent wrote: "Every spring, every ford, every path, every farm, every trail, every house, nearly, in its settlement, was once the scene of danger, exposure, attack, exploit, achievement, death." As one reads the harrowing record of betrayals, of pitched battles in the forest's shadows, of white men's cabins and Indians' villages descended upon in murderous forays, of hostages slain and vengeances exacted, one hardly knows which side gave the worse account of itself—but may reflect that the theme of it all was the displacement of the Indians by the whites. "In this swift tableau, barbarism was common on both sides," Michael Frome observes in his richly informative account of the Great Smoky Mountains, *Strangers in High Places.* "Even so, it is difficult to identify, among the many treaties signed with the Cherokee [whose tribal lands included most of southern Appalachia], one which the Indians violated, or one which the whites honored."

In the reckoning between France and Britain, whites set their Indian allies upon whites in a crescendo of horrors. Young George Washington, trying to hold an Appalachian frontier 350 miles long with 700 men, sometimes saw the mountains disappear from view behind the smoke of burning plantations. "What can I do?" he cried of the ferocity of the redmen. "If bleeding, dying! would glut their insatiate revenge, I would be a willing offering to savage fury, and die by inches to save a people!"

Appalachia had become home to the new Americans. On the whole, they took to it, with all its dangers. They could have echoed John Milton's "The mountain nymph, sweet Liberty." Here, finally, they were masters of their fates. Probably more than any other of their fellow countrymen before or since, they adapted themselves to their wilderness, from which they learned to extract nearly all the necessities of life. An early visitor, describing one of their settlements, wrote that "The clothes of the people consist of deer skins, their food of Johnycakes, deer and bear meat. A kind of white people are found here who live like savages. Hunting is their chief occupation."

The wilderness was a provider. Hoofed animals were plentiful, and while bison and elk were soon killed off, deer and bear remained for a time in scarcely diminished numbers, as did turkeys. For a marksman with the long-barreled rifle that was to prove itself at King's Mountain, there was seldom need for hunger in the cabin, however crude this might be, or dwarfed by its own chimney. Acorns, chestnuts and beechnuts showered down in the forest to fatten free-ranging hogs. The wilderness rewarded courage and energy—the wilderness of the bottomlands, where the game mostly was, and the fertile soil. The heights above them were another matter. As a rule these had little to offer. The Appalachians' invaders became mountain people only in the course of time and by necessity, as the good bottomlands filled up and newcomers and descendants of the old were forced farther and farther back up into the hills, into higher and narrowing valleys of shallower soil. To the pioneers the mountains must have appeared as adversaries—and intimidating ones, seen at best only as symbols of the awful power of a somber Deity. No siren ever sang to mariners more irresistibly than the wilderness to Daniel Boone, greatest of the Long Hunters—so called from the duration of their southward and westward forays for deerskins and beaver pelts. The Shawnees themselves accounted him their superior in the artfulness the wilds demanded. But as for those craggy summits on high, Boone spoke feelingly and probably for all when he exclaimed of the rock exposures high on Cumberland Mountain, through which the famous gap opened the way to Kentucky, "The aspect of these cliffs is so wild and horrid that it is impossible to behold them without terror."

Through the latter half of the eighteenth century the contest for the mountains raged. And in its blood-soaked chronicle one comes, as to an island of peace in a sea of turmoil, upon the figure of William Bartram. Son of John Bartram, the Quaker farmer of Philadelphia turned plant-collector and honored as such by distinguished fellow enthusiasts on both sides of the ocean, William became America's leading botanist. In 1775 he carried his plant-explorations from Charleston up the Savannah River and across the mountains of the Georgia and South Carolina border and of adjacent North Carolina to the valley of the Little Tennessee and the Cowee Mountains bordering it, and finally to the Nantahalas. Relations between the whites and the Cherokees were tense, and Bartram had been warned of the dangers he would face by the knowledgeable superintendent of Indian affairs of the southern colonies. He had gone anyway. Twice he had encounters on the trail that could well have proved fatal, one with a Cherokee murderer outlawed by his own people, the other with an illustrious Cherokee chief and his party; but in both cases the simplicity and transparent benevolence of the solitary plant-collector were his surety.

In Bartram's *Travels* we seem to discover another, vanished Polynesia:

> [We] began to ascend the hills of a range which we were under the necessity of crossing, and having gained its summit, enjoyed a most enchanting view, a vast expanse of green meadows and strawberry fields, a meandering river gliding through, saluting in its various turnings the swelling green, turfy knolls, embellished with parterres of flowers and fruitful strawberry beds; flocks of turkeys strolling about them; herds of deer prancing in the meads or bounding over the hills; companies of young, innocent Cherokee virgins, some busily gathering the rich fragrant fruit, others having already filled their baskets, lay reclined under the shade of

> floriferous and fragrant native bowers of Magnolia, Azalea, Philadelphus [Mock-orange], perfumed Calycanthus [Allspice], sweet Yellow Jessamine, and cerulian Glycine frutescens [American wisteria], disclosing their beauties to the fluttering breeze, and bathing their limbs in the cool, fleeting streams; whilst other parties, more gay and libertine, were yet collecting strawberries or wantonly chasing their companions, tantalizing them, staining their lips and cheeks with the rich fruit.

Wilderness is evidently how you see it. Today, our admiration of the heroic, land-hungry frontiersman with his ever-ready rifle and scalping knife, tamer of that wilderness, is less whole-souled than it used to be. We look back upon him from a land pillaged from sea to sea by his spiritual heirs, whose quick way with shooting irons reminds us of William Bartram's judgment of the Indians, that "as moral men they certainly stand in no need of European civilization." And Bartram and his way of seeing the wilderness look better and better.

In Bartram's *Travels* we first behold the mountains through modern eyes, as when, from "Occonne Mountain"—evidently in the northwestern corner of South Carolina—he

> ...enjoyed a view inexpressibly magnificent and comprehensive. The mountainous wilderness ... appearing regularly undulated as the great ocean after a tempest; ... the nearest ground to me of a perfect full green, next more glaucous, and lastly almost blue as the ether with which the most distant curve of the horizon seems to be blended.

Or again, when from Wine Spring Bald in the Nantahalas he

> ... beheld with rapture and astonishment, a world of mountains piled upon mountains, ... [an] amazing prospect of grandeur.

When William Bartram was born in 1739, settlement in the mountains had progressed no farther than the Shenandoah Valley. To the south it had nowhere even reached the Blue Ridge. Yet when he died in 1823, well-to-do Charlestonians were already traveling by horseback and carriage through the gap below 3,231-foot Mount Tryon to summer homes at Flat Rock; such is the tempo of American history. And here many in later years, arriving by train from the low country, must have had their first view of the mountains upon waking and been as riven by the spectacle as Roderick Peattie recalls being: "The morning was misty, and then suddenly, dramatically, through a cleft in the valley fog appeared Tryon Mountain, clean, washed by the air of the winter morning . . . I had never looked up before to see the earth."

After Flat Rock came the other resorts: Blowing Rock, Swannanoa, Lake Toxaway, High Hampton, Highlands—to the north, Hot Springs and White Sulphur Springs. One was even ahead of it: Berkeley Springs, to which George Washington repaired, and before the white man the Indians, the warring tribesmen burying the tomahawk on approaching the health-giving spa—which today retains much of the atmosphere of a nineteenth century watering-place. The high-water mark, in actual elevation, was reached when in 1877 a former Union Army general built a 20-room lodge of log construction on the crest of the Roan Mountain at 6,150 feet, just below the summit, replacing it in 1885 with Cloudland Hotel, of 166 rooms.

And the visitors to those resorts, women in white blouses and full, ankle-length skirts, men in their older business clothes—for sports attire had not been heard of—who transferred from panting railroad trains to lurching hackneys (I remember walking behind a buckboard at the age of six on a steep, gravelly road up from Franklin, North Carolina, fascinated by the mica to be picked up alongside): would they have spoken of the grandeur of mountains or beheld them with rapture as they observed the renowned spectacle of the sunrise from the Roan; or from Sunset Rocks above Highlands saw Standing Indian and Bartram's Wine Spring Bald turn black against a fiery western sky?

A century after Bartram's visit, many probably would have done so. They would have heard with understanding Wordsworth's confession that

> The sounding cataract
> Haunted me like a passion: the tall rock,
> The mountain, and the deep and gloomy wood,
> Their colours and their forms, were then to me
> An appetite . . .

William Cullen Bryant had spoken "To him who in love of Nature holds/ Communion with her visible forms" of "patriarchs of the infant world, . . . hoary seers of ages past, . . . rock-ribbed and ancient as the sun." Painters of the Hudson River School in the mountains to the north had depicted rocky crags plunging to darkening depths against farther summits aureate in the declining sun. And, in fact, two anonymous travelers, after ascending the Roan, had written in *Harper's New Monthly Magazine* for November 1857 of "the scene which meets the eye while standing on this summit" that "Any effort to convey to the reader the sensations experienced by the beholder would indeed be vain essay." They then went on to describe the panorama of the Appalachians by means of the same analogy Bartram had drawn on, and which probably cannot be bettered:

> The sweep of the vision in every direction is unlimited, except by the curvature of the earth or the haziness of the atmosphere. The first idea suggested is that you are looking over a vast blue ocean, whose monstrous billows, once heaving and pitching in wild disorder, have been suddenly arrested by some overruling power.

Six years earlier a woman carriage passenger had written of reaching Rockfish Gap (where the Skyline Drive and the Blue Ridge Parkway now join) that "we were all struck with admiration. We were, both literally and figuratively, *up in the clouds*. . . . Oh, if I could always behold such scenes, I think I could be better and purer—less selfish and worldly-minded."

A consciousness of nature was awakening in the American people, and a romantic view of the mountains, elevated or somber, had taken hold.

So had a commercial view. Appalachia "was an immensely rich timber world that contained the finest hardwoods that ever stood," M. A. Mattoon of the United States Forest Service wrote in 1949, going on to tell in few words what happened to it:

> During and after the Civil War, the railroads began to string the little villages together. Railroads crept up the valleys slowly. . . . As the little balloon-stacked engines rocked over the slender rails, the whistle warned of approaching doom. With assured rail shipment to the outside, where an expanding Nation demanded and got what it needed, the stage was set for the coming of the big sawmills into the mountains. They came, slowly at first, and then with logging railroads of their own, like locusts. Handsome timber in increasing amounts fell to the ax, but there always seemed to be more. Sawmill towns sprang up in their temporary ugliness, thrived, and vanished as the cutting moved on. Fire raged on the heels of loggers, and devastation over large areas seemed certain. When Europe burst into the horror of warfare in 1914, demands on the forest mounted and reconstruction saw no let-up. So the large sawmills, accompanied by many little sawmills, marched across the face of the remaining Appalachian wilderness, and its big timber disappeared. Today, after the second World War, a host of little mills is picking up the scraps and eating into thrifty young timber that will be needed in the future.

Motorists on the Blue Ridge Parkway can see at Yankee Horse Trail, Mile 34.4, a short, reconstructed section of a logging railroad. The original, built in 1919–20 and 50 miles long, a sign explains, carried more than a hundred million board feet to the mill. That would cover 2,300 acres with board an inch thick. Almost everywhere I have hiked in the mountains I have come on old logging railway roadbeds. Many miles have I followed them, always conscious of the difference between now and then; for those I hiked on go through forest that is now in the public domain. To quote again from Mr. Mattoon:

> Shortly after the turn of the century, a few far-seeing men in New England and the South noticed the disappearing forests, the damage to soil and young timber from fire, the effect on stream flow and the purity of water supplies. . . . After years of work with an apathetic public, success crowned their efforts, and in 1911 the Congress enacted legislation whereby it became possible for the Federal Government to purchase areas of wild lands

on the headwaters of navigable rivers, and the chain of national forests in the Appalachians was born. Purchase of land has been going on through the years until now there are about 6 million acres in public ownership.

One is justified in breathing more easily about the prospects of the mountains through which the old roadbeds wind than one otherwise could be—though how much more easily remains to be seen.

One of the far-seeing men Mattoon refers to was Gifford Pinchot, who, becoming Theodore Roosevelt's close consultant on forestry, did more than any other single person to save the nation's timberlands—what was left of them or could be restored. Another was Joseph A. Holmes, State Geologist of North Carolina, who suggested to Pinchot, then a young man lately returned from his studies under a pioneer British forester, that the Federal Government ought to acquire timberlands in the southern Appalachians and manage them in accordance with sound forestry principles. It was the germ of the National Forests idea, which would be enacted into law two decades later, and it was hatched in talks between the two men in the mansion built by George W. Vanderbilt on his estate near Asheville. Here Pinchot was engaged in managing the 100,000 acres of forest belonging to the estate. "Biltmore," as Vanderbilt called it, became the first large tract of managed forest in the nation and, in 1898, the site of the first school of forestry in the United States. Later the tract became the nucleus of the Pisgah National Forest. The Blue Ridge Parkway passes through it in climbing from the French Broad River at Asheville to the shoulder of Mount Pisgah—3,000 feet in 18 miles. Here, by the way, where Red Spruces suddenly reappear, the old Vanderbilt Inn, a contemporary of Cloudland Hotel, once stood, replaced today by one of the three handsome lodges along the Parkway.

The scalping of the southern Appalachians of their forests and the growth of their popularity with vacationers proceeded apace. Among the latter there can have been little objection to the former. The mountains afforded relief from summer heat and were scenic, their beauty a solace, their exalted stature even an inspiration. Many visitors were assuredly distressed to see the shambles the lumbermen left in their wake. But they could read, as in a newspaper of 1890, of "the great and inexhaustible virgin forest of the Blue Ridge." Felling timber was progress. It was good business and testimony to the nation's vitality, not to be questioned. As Pinchot remarked, "The man who could get his hands on the biggest slice of natural resources was the best citizen."

Even to their devotees, the mountains remained, one suspects, peripheral. The sentiment they prevailingly evoked was doubtless still that expressed by the distinguished botanist Thomas Nuttall in 1816: "How charmed have I been with the romantic and picturesque mountains of the

French Broad. I shall ever remember this awful chaste but magnificent scenery with pleasure." Asa Gray of Harvard, the most famous American botanist of the past century, was one of the keen collectors in the southern Appalachians; in three places I have come upon official state highway markers recording his visits. But one finds no sign in his writing that the mountains stirred him. He would probably, for that matter, have smiled a little patronizingly, as both scientist and churchman, at his fellow botanist William Bartram's ardent avowal that "Perhaps there is not any part of creation, within reach of our observations, which exhibits a more glorious display of the Almighty hand than the vegetable world." A conception of mountains as at the center of it all would have been foreign to the patrons of Vanderbilt Inn and to those of Cloudland, among them Asa Gray, with whom Roan Mountain was a favorite. Although there is Biblical warrant for the association of the Deity with the hills, most would probably have dismissed as heathen ritual the response of John Lederer's three Indian guides to the first appearance of the Blue Ridge on the horizon. This (Darwin Lambert relates) was to prostrate themselves and exclaim, *"Okaeepoeze!"*—"God is nigh!" They would have been puzzled if not alarmed by G. M. Trevelyan's suggestion that the mountain, standing above the arena of human strife, confusion and perplexity, "seems to have personality which says to us as we gaze on it . . . 'But there is a secret behind.' It will always be a secret."

Eighty years ago a Bostonian, Bradford Torrey, went traveling in the southern Appalachians. Especially because of the dearth of books on the range, I was excited at finding an account of the experiences of such an explorer in *A World of Green Hills* in the little public library when, just before going to college, I went to work at the equally small museum at Highlands, North Carolina, to help out with the local birds. I read it avidly. Torrey had headed first for Highlands and had come to it just as I had, from the railroad station at Seneca, South Carolina, and through Walhalla, thence into the mountains by winding gravel road, though this had taken him two days instead of two hours. He had lodged at the big, white clapboard Highlands Inn, which I passed daily and was to stay in myself for a bit the next summer and again forty-four years later.

Torrey was a bird man, and he had set out to canvas the avifauna in the very area of my own searchings; I was made to feel part of the community of high scientific endeavor. Uplifted, I read, "I was no sooner off the hotel piazza for my first ante-breakfast stroll at Highlands, than I was on the watch for Carolina snowbirds [juncos] and mountain solitary vireos, two varieties ('subspecies' is the more modern word) originally described a few years ago, by Mr. Brewster, taken at this very place." William Brewster, discoverer of the Brewster's Warbler, was a name to conjure with; I trod hallowed ground! But with all it revealed of nature and local folk, the book conveyed little emotion—little of the excitement at the mountains that I, their devout adherent, felt. Today I see in it where its author and I parted company. Recalling how with a single bend in the brook he was following into the hills he was at once out of the world, Torrey declared, "Life is such a path as this. The forest shuts behind us, and is open only at our feet, with here and there a flower or butterfly or a strain of music to take up our thoughts, as we travel toward the clearing at the end."

Bradford Torrey belonged to the generation of my grandparents. Since the texts they grew up on were written, man's universe has been transformed. It has been expanded in space and time far beyond the capacity of our imaginations to encompass it. The question of its purpose or meaning, which would have given my grandparents no trouble, is one we should today hardly even presume to raise. The theatre has grown too great, man been displaced too far from the center of the stage. But as man's relative significance has shrunk, his absolute power has correspondingly increased. For some time we found compensation for the former process in the latter. Now, however, it is borne in upon us that, so far as our planet is concerned, we have been using our prodigious power to despoil the theatre, just as we have been coming so much more fully to comprehend its antiquity, richness and wonder.

A terrible disquiet possesses us that there is a design in Creation —ecology is the biologist's term for its most immediate and organic manifestations—which we are violating to our grave danger. The soul-destroying ugliness we have produced in the grinding up of the earth and its garment of life brings our outlawry home to us. To escape it and regain relationship with the whole, through which, surely, the Creator is expressed rather than through us uniquely, we turn to that which we have not refashioned in our own image. This, in its pristine form, is wilderness. We do not regard the works of nature as suitable merely for taking up our thoughts as we travel toward a clearing at the end. On the contrary, we look to them for the clarification. The mountains among which the trail leads do, in our eyes, speak of a secret behind it all, and if the secret is ultimately unknowable, they seem to stand warrant for its greatness.

III *The High Road*

In 1946 I was driving south to revisit Highlands, where I had spent parts of several summers beginning when I was seventeen. Said to be the highest incorporated town east of the Rockies, Highlands is located just within the last high rim of the Blue Ridge to the southeast, from which one looks a few miles into Georgia and South Carolina. In 1928, the well-known Highlands Biological Station of today had barely been got under way by an indefatigable Atlantan, Clark Foreman, and shared a little white clapboard building with the public library. My having been imported, to see what my youthful enthusiasm for birds could discover about the area ornithologically, will give an idea of the modesty of the Station's beginnings. After those brief summers, I had seen no more of the mountains until, the war over, I set forth from Washington, D. C., to return.

It was while driving through North Carolina that I noticed a road on the map designated "Blue Ridge Parkway," and decided to see what it was. It turned out to be a modest highway that passed undulatingly around high, grassy domes, with wave on wave of forested mountains fading off into the west. (My memory is clearly of the sector around Doughton Park.) Shying away from settlements, passing over or under the infrequent transmontane roads, it was free of trucks, billboards and other blights of civilization. My spirits soared with it. I could hardly believe my eyes. Was this lilting, beckoning roadway, winding through the most glorious highlands without ulterior aim, seeming as lofty in purpose as in elevation, the work of a nation that turned the highway approach to its every city into an extravaganza of strident, gaudy, debased commercialism?

That it should be seems even more remarkable to me now, after many trips on the Blue Ridge Drive. That is my term for the combination of Skyline Drive and Blue Ridge Parkway. These are two segments of a single, continuous road sinuously threading the Blue Ridge Mountains, between vistas of almost uninterrupted loveliness or natural majesty, for an incredible 575 miles, from the upper end of the Shenandoah National Park

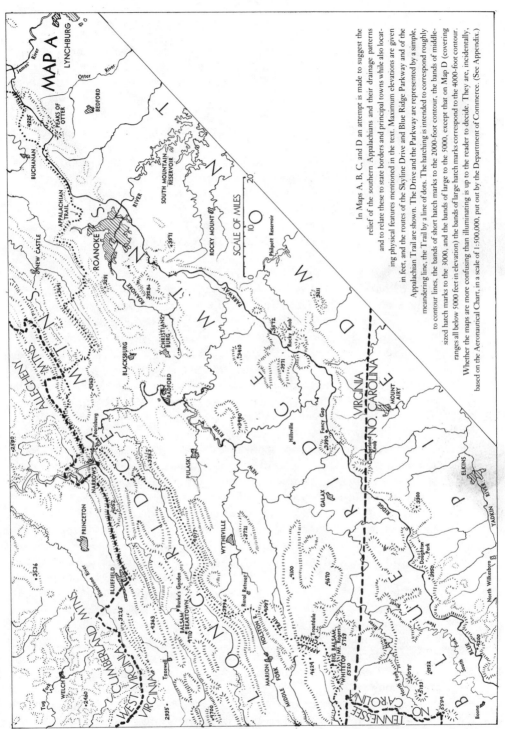

MAP A

In Maps A, B, C, and D an attempt is made to suggest the relief of the southern Appalachians and their drainage patterns and to relate these to state borders and principal towns while also locating physical features mentioned in the text. Maximum elevations are given in feet, and the routes of the Skyline Drive and Blue Ridge Parkway and of the Appalachian Trail are shown. The Drive and the Parkway are represented by a simple, meandering line, the Trail by a line of dots. The hatching is intended to correspond roughly to contour lines, the bands of short hatch marks to the 2000-foot contour, the bands of middle-sized hatch marks to the 3000, and the bands of large to the 5000, except that on Map D (covering ranges all below 5000 feet in elevation) the bands of large hatch marks correspond to the 4000-foot contour. Whether the maps are more confusing than illuminating is up to the reader to decide. They are, incidentally, based on the Aeronautical Chart, in a scale of 1:500,000, put out by the Department of Commerce. (See Appendix.)

SCALE OF MILES

in northern Virginia to the southern border of the Great Smoky Mountains National Park in western North Carolina.

The Drive, it is true, has been destructive. Mountainsides have been grievously sliced into, especially in the newer southern third where the slopes are highest and steepest. In the northernmost sector, the Skyline Drive for its full 105 miles has been put down the spine of the range and through the center of the narrow Shenandoah National Park, thus reducing the width of potential wild areas. I should hate to see the Blue Ridge Drive used to justify other mountain parkways. And of course others are being urged. An Allegheny Parkway would run from Harper's Ferry to Cumberland Gap and a Scenic Drive along the crest of Virginia's Iron Mountain Range, while if some interests have their way the Blue Ridge Parkway itself would be extended into Georgia. Perish the lot of them! The place for roads is down below.

The Blue Ridge Drive has, however, been built. Rejecting it will not restore the mountainsides; it may as well be enjoyed. And I have to acknowledge that the trips Vera and I have made on the Drive have been almost unalloyed joy. Few signboards have been so welcome to me as those announcing "BLUE RIDGE PARKWAY 1,000 FEET AHEAD"; what they have always spelled is *sanctuary*. (Construction of the Parkway has been spread over four decades. During that time there were gaps in it where one had to make do with ordinary and generally tawdry roads until it resumed. The last of these is now, in 1974, being closed with, alas, the blasting of a way across the lower face of Grandfather Mountain, south of Blowing Rock, North Carolina.) As nothing else could, moreover, the Drive has opened the eyes of a substantial part of our population to the wealth of still-splendid mountains remaining to us in the Southeast, and exposed the public to their charm and regality. The number visiting it and the two parks it connects is now reported to reach over 15 million a year.

Except for its final 45-mile approach to the Great Smokies, the Blue Ridge Drive follows the seaboard flank of the range. (This is the side we are apt to think of as the eastern, though with almost equal warrant we could call it the southern, since the Appalachians run pretty much southwest and northeast.) A trip down the Drive can hardly be offered as a wilderness experience. You do, however, look upon wilds from it, near and far, and much of the time; the Drive is in National Park or National Forest for half its length, even without counting the Blue Ridge Parkway itself as a National Park, which it is, albeit one of an average width of only 800 feet. There are long stretches of it where by withdrawing 50 or 100 feet from the right of way you might go a year or even much longer without seeing another human being. In the Shenandoah Blue Ridge the wreckage of a small airplane that disappeared while attempting to cross the range at Swift Run Gap on July 26, 1964, could not be found until November 12th, or until well after the leaves were off the trees. The Drive gives you, moreover, a picture of the physiography of the Blue Ridge—the oldest and, with the exception of the Smokies, greatest component of the Appalachians—that you would be a long time acquiring piecemeal from other roads. The trails leading off from it will, I believe, take you into almost every kind of country the Appalachians offer.

I never set off down the Blue Ridge Drive without feeling that I am being borne along on cumulus earth-clouds. Fretfulness and anxiety drain out of me. The trees in their boundless multitudes, covering the mountains in a living quilt, have a pleasantly benumbing effect, augmenting the serenity the mountains themselves tend to induce by their example and their connotations of timelessness and unconfinement. Seas of green is the metaphor that the wooded hills inevitably call forth.

For a few weeks twice a year they glow with brighter colors. Of the two seasons my favorite, I think, is spring (except in fall), if only because rejuvenation does more for the spirit than the most flamboyant expression of life's ebb. And, while autumn's reds and yellows against a sky of intensest blue can engulf the soul in radiance, spring's luminous spurts of new foliage are subtler and more pristine in color, pale shades of green and honey, rendered in the technique called *pointillisme* among French Impressionist painters. With the budding leaves, too, comes the transfiguration of the flowering trees, Serviceberry and Flowering Dogwood that stand out as trees foliated in white, and the famous southern Appalachian Magnolias studded with the forest's largest flowers, of creamy white or pale yellows.

The arboreal colors come and go in a month or so, but for at least half the year, even in the northern Blue Ridge, roadside flowers are in bloom—from April's first Spring-beauties on the south side of a rock to the last florets of goldenrod or lavender aster in October. Summers of bright sun, light air, moderate daytime temperatures, cool nights and generous rainfall produce gardens of wildflowers in the southern Appalachians wherever the ground is open to the sky. John Bartram, the self-taught, eighteenth century botanist of Philadelphia, spoke for many who came after him when on his return from a collecting expedition between South Carolina and the Shenandoah Valley—the first by any botanist in the Southern mountains—he pronounced the variety of plants and flowers to be "beyond expression." Carroll E. Wood, Jr., of Harvard's Arnold Arboretum, has found that of the 1,032 genera of seed-bearing plants indigenous to eastern North America, over half—557—occur in the southern Appalachians. As large a proportion of the 384 introduced genera must also do so. The National Park Service unfortunately keeps the sides of the Drive mowed generally back to the edge of the woods, which is to say from about ten to thirty feet or more. If the object is flower-eradication, it is achieved. Even so, thanks to the difficulty of mowing the steeper and rockier margins, one seems never to come to an end of the floral variety along the Drive.

There are differences between the Skyline Drive and Blue Ridge Parkway. The latter descends to lower and rises to higher elevations. It displays a much greater range of scenery, and exhibits along the way a number of old mountain cabins and a mountain farm, all respectfully preserved, as well as a grist mill restored to operation; relics of the historic past along the Skyline Drive were eliminated. Designers of the Parkway, to be sure, had the benefit of what could be learned from the Drive. I was astonished to read in Harley E. Jolley's *The Blue Ridge Parkway* that the idea of a Crest-of-the-Blue-Ridge Highway was conceived back in 1909 by Colonel Joseph Hyde Pratt, head of the North Carolina Geological and Economic Survey, and that construction was actually begun just south of Linville Falls. However, World War I put an end to the plan, which was not thereafter revived until 1930. By that time, according to Professor Jolley, many men in influential places were thinking of a scenic highway to connect the Shenandoah and Great Smoky Mountains National Parks and "the existing depression coupled with the reception accorded the Skyline Drive made the extension of that road a very logical project for serious consideration." Land for the Parkway was donated by Virginia and North Carolina, which had won a keen struggle with Tennessee over its location, and construction began in September 1935. The Skyline Drive, begun in 1931, had been conceived a decade earlier. It would run along the ridge line of the northern Virginia Blue Ridge when and if this had been incorporated in a National Park—which would be the first in the East of significant size.

In 1926, when the Shenandoah National Park was authorized, the mountains it was to bring under protection had been almost completely logged. Felling of new growth, grazing and fires, many purposely set, kept much of the range bare. This was in contrast to the Great Smoky Mountains, where a still-virgin forest had been designated for incorporation in another National Park under the same legislation. Narrow, stony roads led up the Blue Ridge to backwoods farms on which 465 families—more than half with no equity in their land—were waging a losing struggle to make a living from depleted soils, and earning an average cash income of $125 a year. (They were to be moved to better lands nearby.) The Park would have to be a restoring as well as a rescuing operation. And without the promise of the Drive, the necessary support might well have been lacking. As it was, almost everyone was for the Park. It could be taken for granted that conservationists would be, including proponents of Benton MacKaye's daring new conception of a 2,000-mile-long Appalachian Trail, which would utilize the Park. But so were civic boosters in nearby towns. Harry Flood Byrd, the leading political power in Virginia and later a prime instigator of the Blue Ridge Parkway, had blessed it as "the greatest opportunity for the material advancement of Virginia that has been suggested for generations."

For the Federal Government to purchase land for a National Park was at that time unthinkable. But the public responded to the appeal—"Buy an acre at $6"—by contributing nearly $1,250,000 and the Virginia legislature came up with essential appropriations. This, too, was in contrast with the Smokies, where proponents of the National Park had to wage a bitter and exhausting struggle.

Of the more than 800 square miles originally authorized, the Park as achieved, sad to say, comprises only 300. But there could well have been no park at all; and while it will take hundreds of years fully to make good man's depredations upon the hills it encompasses, there is the special gratification of seeing the aboriginal forest gradually re-establishing itself on the steep flanks and ridges of the range. Wilds can be not only preserved but recreated. The National Park Service has recommended that 120 square miles of the Park be brought under the provisions of the Wilderness Act of 1964, which will exclude any works of man from the area designated. This is far short of the nearly 200 square miles urged by many conservationists, but again it is better than nothing.

If you enter the Shenandoah National Park at its northern end—Mile 0 on the Skyline Drive—you come in on the beginning of the Blue Ridge as a significant range. To the north it is only a low escarpment—though one cut by the combined Shenandoah and Potomac Rivers at Harper's Ferry to afford the view Thomas Jefferson thought worth a crossing of the ocean. (Jefferson was not alone in being impressed. The rivers, "uniting, appear to burst their way thro' the Blue Ridge," the Yorkshire-born botanist Thomas Nuttall wrote after visiting the famous water-gap in 1815, in "a landscape of horrible grandeur and wild magnificence, of mingled rocks, roaring rivers, and gloomy forests.") The escarpment begins in Maryland as South Mountain, where Lee's desperate defense of the passes bought a day's time before the bloody trial of Sharpsburg-Antietam, on up the Potomac. Even to the south, however, you find that for the length of the Park the Blue Ridge remains little more than the name indicates: a ridge. But it is a humped and serpentine ridge that gains in elevation, with other short, humped ridges projecting from it, like ribs from a backbone. On the Skyline Drive you are seldom far from views of the lowlands on either side. The mountains that rise around you run out on the east to the Piedmont. On the west they break away more sharply to the Shenandoah Valley. This is the most renowned sector of the Great Valley of the Appalachians, which runs from Kingston, on the Hudson River, to near Birmingham, Alabama, and separates the Blue Ridge and Great Smokies from the less ancient Appalachians—the Long Ridge Mountains and, beyond them, the Plateaus. The most easterly of the Long Ridges, Massanutten, bifurcates the Shenandoah Valley for 50 miles to present the most conspicuous terrain feature from the Skyline Drive. Around its northern end you can see others of the chain, ridge on ridge in the distance, like corrugations.

Below you, the far-spread toylands of cultivated fields and buildings among scattered, rug-like patches of woods detract nothing from the sense you have of the wildness of the forested heights in full scale before you; rather they accentuate it. On Stonyman's saw-toothed, greenstone crags you feel yourself at a celestial altitude above the settled valley; and, indeed, as an early advocate of the National Park pointed out, you are as far above it as you are above the Merced River on Yosemite's El Capitan. At night the sense of removal is intensified. In the dark you are a Toomai of the Elephants—Kipling's boy mahout—a very small Toomai among very great Paleozoic mammoths whose broad backs, blotting out the lower stars, seem

The Priest, one of the highest of the Blue Ridge Mountains of Virginia seen from the Blue Ridge Parkway, over the top of a Table-mountain pine.

halfway to the higher constellations above the galaxies of pinpoint colored lights in the valley. These are rocky mountains. Rock strews wooded slopes in weathered fragments, forms cliffs and bulges out of the forest floor in huge, rounded boulders up to house-sized.

Black Bears, entirely on their own, have returned with the forest. They are now numerous enough to require the Park Service to encircle its informational board signs with barbed wire to prevent their being chewed up. However, the Park being narrow, they are well acquainted with man on the outside and are shy and seldom seen. Still, they turn up regularly to munch October apples, as do deer, on the old farm backing up to the Park that my writer-and-ecologist friend Darwin Lambert and his wife occupy. And in the course of the years Vera and I have encountered a few of the stocky beasts, like solid shadows, always with a sense of shock that such a formidable-looking denizen of an America largely long vanished could materialize out of ordinary Eastern woods only 60 miles from the nation's capital and disappear back into them. On our last trip to the Park we were walking along the stretch of the Appalachian Trail south of Powell Gap, at Mile 70, and had stopped to admire a Yellow Moccasin-flower, an orchid with an egg-shaped pod of captured sunbeams set upon a cross of twisted, narrow sepals, when a dark-skinned Japanese backpacker came up to report with some excitement having just surprised a bear. It had been only 50 feet away, breaking a rotting log apart, and had retreated to a rocky cliff behind us, where he thought he had detected a cub. All these surprising elements, the rare orchid so brilliant under the indeterminate masses of low, dark clouds moving in from the northeast, the swarthy, voluble Japanese with his vermillion pack and the Black Bear back among the rocks, formed a kind of unity in my mind, as of the foreordained unexpectedness of a dream.

Deer you may count on seeing. Surprised in their gingerly browsing, they face you and with large, black-edged ears fanned forward and beautiful dark eyes wide stare at you with intense absorption. They are almost as fearless as range cattle, and some will even take food from the hand. Delicate and lissome as they canter off with a rocking-horse motion or take a weightless bound, they enchant all beholders.

South of the Shenandoah National Park the Blue Ridge fans out. The mountains lead off on both sides, fold on fold, their contours softened in summer by the bluish film that gives the range its name and characterizes the southern Appalachians in general: some believe it to be from the transpiration of the oceanic forest. Beyond the scattered little Appalachian farms in valleys leading down from the Drive, there might be nothing but mountains in the world. Through gaps between the nearer you see the summits of others, somnolent and dreamy in the distance. For miles the view to the east is dominated by the bulk, backed like a bison, of the Priest,

Close-up of the Mountain laurel.

a favorite of mine by virtue in part of the dark power and slightly menacing overtones of its name.

What is the best time of year for the trip? Whenever you can get away—bearing in mind that the higher sections of the Drive are closed in winter and others may be after snowstorms. But the first three weeks of June have especially to recommend them that you will then be in the overlapping blooming seasons of three of the four shrubs that, of all floral displays in the mountains, lend most resplendence to the rugged heights and the face of the ever-present forest. All are stellar members of the *Ericaceae,* the great and wonderful family of Heaths. The most generally distributed is Mountain-laurel, of glossy foliage against which the large, tight clusters of pentagonal flowers, white or flushed, opening from pink buds like half-furled parasols, stand out radiantly the entire length of the Drive. In the Smokies, stands of it fifteen feet high can resemble snow-drifts. The second, beginning eleven miles from the start of the Blue Ridge

Parkway, at home equally beside little cataracts in the dim recesses or on shadeless ledges, the Catawba Rhododendrons burgeon luxuriantly where the sun is brightest in clouds of blossoms, their flower-heads opening like purplish-rose grapefruits, each of many sections. On the mile-high crests of the Craggies above the Drive northeast of Asheville, they create a prodigality of floral beauty against the sky one would have to go far to see equaled, except where Catawbas garland the even higher crest of the Roan, north of Asheville on the Tennessee line. But at close hand, I think both the Rhododendron and Mountain-laurel are at their pictorial best against the rock that breaks out so abundantly in the Virginia Blue Ridge, standing in overgrown walls or protuberances like emerging subterranean monsters.

The third of the triumvirate begins farther south, on the long climb up from Roanoke.

Before that, the Drive has dropped to Otter Creek and a southerly forest of lofty, columnar Tuliptrees, Hemlocks, Short-leafed Yellow Pines and Oaks, which extends to the James. The river-crossing at 900-feet elevation is the lowest point on the Drive. From here and the humid heat of the valley, the Drive climbs through bend after bend to the highest of its northern two-thirds, gaining 3,000 feet in altitude in twelve miles. The drop in temperature when I measured it on one trip was from 86 degrees to 72. The heights are those of Apple Orchard Mountain, so called from the resemblance to orchard trees of the winter-dwarfed, squat Oaks on its 4,000-foot summit—disfigured in recent years by the glaring turquoise buildings and two structures in the likeness of monumental golf balls of an Air Force radar station. On June 9th, when I am on my way to the Smokies to begin my sampling of southern Appalachian wilderness, the oak foliage is not yet fully out and the Pink Azalea, which two weeks earlier had brightened the Skyline Drive with its warm glow, is still in flower.

After skirting the outstanding conical forms of Flattop and Sharp-top—the Peaks of Otter—the Drive descends again, this time to Roanoke and the Roanoke River. Here for a few miles the Blue Ridge suffers its greatest reduction in stature from one end to the other. Oddly, the gap is matched on the other side of Roanoke by the only blockage of the Great Valley in all its 900 miles; the Long Ridge Mountains, rising in south-western Virginia to their supreme development, occupy the Valley and here make it the divide between the Atlantic and the Gulf. (And here the pioneers, pushing down the Great Valley from the Shenandoah, through the rising corridors of the Long Ridges, found themselves at the headwaters of the westward-trending Holston River, with the Tennessee Valley and the continental interior before them.) From Roanoke southward into North Carolina the eastern Blue Ridge is a high, steeply rolling tableland falling off to the Piedmont. The Drive follows the edge of the escarpment. Gone from this central hundred miles are the mountains billowing to the horizons. Instead are farms and pasture land, but woods still occupy most of the landscape, and rich woods, too, where the Drive skirts a swamp or stream. For miles the trees rise from a sort of second floor of the ground formed by the top of the dense understory of Rosebay Rhododendron, which walls in the Drive with crowded, eight- or ten-foot-high pillows of solid, dark foliage. Elsewhere along the way are shrubs equally high that are, to me, among those absolutes in nature before which one can only stand helpless.

Flame Azalea, where it blooms abundantly, could give an instantaneous first impression of a sunset sky at the moment of its greatest glory seen through the interstices of a woods. Flame it is. Its delicate, flaring trumpet flowers, from which the long stamens protrude gracefully as if to represent the annunciation sounding forth, are all the blueless shades of fire, ranging from the yellow of a cream-yellow rose and a pale salmon through peach and orange to vermillion and scarlet. The variability in color is ascribed by some to cross-fertilization with White Azaleas, but if that is the explanation it is difficult to see why in the course of time a uniformly colored hybrid would not have become established. A typical example at a distance resembles a small tree of tangerines. Flame Azaleas probably put on their greatest show on Gregory's Bald in the Smokies.

On southward come greater and more frequent eruptions of mountains. Forty miles inside North Carolina the Blue Ridge may be seen mustering its forces for the main upthrusts that lie ahead. Already, 30 miles to the southwest, on the other side of Blowing Rock, may be discerned the peak of the first big mountain on the Drive. This is Grandfather, which rises almost right up from the Piedmont to practically 6,000 feet. André Michaux, the indefatigable French botanical explorer of our wilderness, wrote of it in his diary for August 30, 1794: "Reached the summit of the highest mountain of all North America, and with my companion and guide, sang the *Marseillaise* and shouted 'Long live America and the Republic of France, long live Liberty, etc., etc.' " One who knew nothing of the Western cordillera could be forgiven Michaux's mistake. The great monadnock ought by appearance to be at least the highest of the Appalachians. No other has a front at once so high and so bold as that formed by those cliffs of age-smoothed, weather-greyed granitic rocks, 1,100 million years old, forming Grandfather's sheer eastern face, up which the forest wages a losing struggle, its ranks of conifers petering out where scattered individuals hold hard-won rootholds at the foot of unscalable rock.

When you pass beneath those cliffs you are 160 miles from the Drive's end, with its most dramatic parts before you. Twenty-five miles beyond Grandfather the ascent to the Great Craggy Mountains begins. At about 4,500 feet the first Red Spruces appear, dark, symmetrical and erect as flagstaffs. The event is exciting, for it means that you are entering the

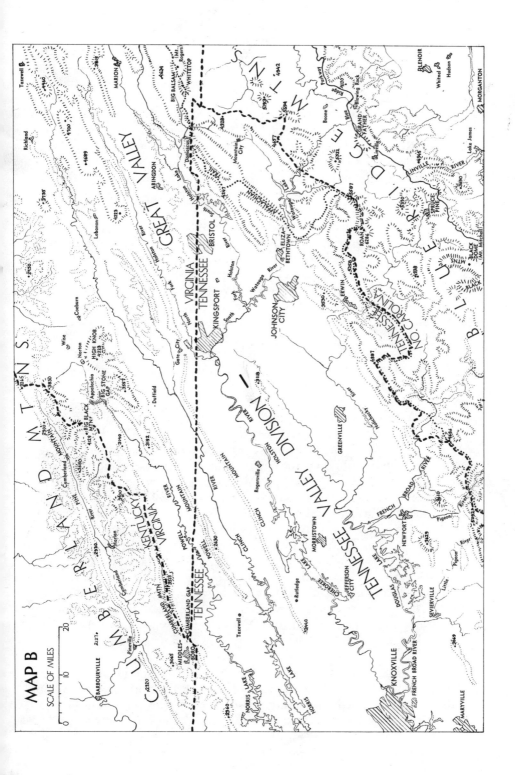

MAP B

SCALE OF MILES

0   10   20

Canadian Life Zone. It is a vivid reminder that in the Appalachians a salient of the North is thrust deep into the heartland of the South. Because of the drop in temperatures as you ascend the mountains, amounting to four or five degrees per thousand feet, a 1,000-foot climb is the equivalent in floral and faunal change to between 200 and 250 miles in northward travel across the country below. From Augusta, Georgia, to the nearest Spruce forest of the Blue Ridge is only 150 miles. But the trip takes you from the Lower Austral Zone of the Southern coastal plain through the Upper Austral Zone of the southern Piedmont and the Middle West, through the Transition Zone of New England, New York and Wisconsin to the Canadian of northern Maine and Ontario.

Among the irregularly-formed deciduous trees you would take the Spruces by their bearing for a kind of arboreal soldiery—house-guards, perhaps, of the great rulers to whose realm you are now ascending. And soon, where the road comes out into the open, snaking along the flank of a high mountain, there rise before you in a monster wall the greatest of all the eminences, the Black Mountains. There is something about superlatives; and even your knowledge of the paved road up it and the visitors' center and observation platform on its top do not deprive the Black Dome—Mount Mitchell—of the aura it possesses as the highest summit in the East, at 6,684 feet. The huge ridge may well disappear upward into a low cloud or be partially erased below by the gauzy vapors these mighty, green earth-welts attract or engender.

Black Mountains, Great Craggies and, beyond the gap at Asheville, Balsams and Plott Balsams: these are the master ranges of the Blue Ridge. And what mountains they are! Traveling down in the valleys your view is generally circumscribed by the lower neighboring slopes and your impression is of a country pre-empted by houses, towns and the manifold expressions of commerce. If you were looking for a great mountain range you would feel grievously let down. But from the Drive, up where Red Oaks, Beeches and Yellow Birches cower against the wind-blasted heights or yield to mats of Rhododendron and Huckleberry, or where the stalwart Spruces darken the huge summits, civilization has vanished with the valleys and you gaze across a wilderness of mountains, hardly able to believe yourself to be in the long-settled East. A range worn down and subdued by time, as the geologists tell us? You would not think it of the great finbacks rearing out of the chasm-like depths. You wonder if you could toil up them . . . and look forward to trying, to know them as they are and to pay them their due.

The road climbs long and hard. Up and up, and one great mountain coming into view around the shoulder of another, the Spruces standing up through the depressed but freshly green, broad-leafed vegetation like sachems with dark cloaks drawn around them. Where the forests are of deciduous trees the high mountainsides are russet from the oak foliage only just now (June 10th) coming out. These are the opposite of alpine summits, being capped not white with snow but black with coniferous forest. When the Drive, which has had a southwesterly trend from its start, turns northwest at Mile 424 of the Blue Ridge Parkway the forest alongside is almost solidly of Spruce. You are on top of the world. Gaining the shoulder of Richland Balsam you are in fact at 6,053 feet. One of the National Park Service's grey board signs with incised white lettering tells you that this is the highest point on the Parkway. Beyond the Plott Balsams on the west, the Great Smokies are now less than 20 miles distant as the crow flies. While their loftiest, Clingman's Dome, fails by 45 feet of equaling the Black Dome's height, the Smokies with 16 summits over 6,000 feet in height stand as the greatest uplift in the East.

The mountains around you seem not grim or hostile but, emphatically, commanding and imposing in their incorruptible and judicial mien. It would seem inevitable that their contemplation conduce to a sense of the inner self's enlargement—to a sense of assurance, even, of the reality of the infinite, and of the anxious, striving self's ultimate reconciliation with it.

IV *The Great Smokies*

The Blue Ridge Parkway, to one driving down from its upper end, moves to a climactic third and final act. From Mount Pisgah on, all is of heroic proportions, bold of contour, the sweep of storm-tossed earth illimitable, except as it may be veiled in clouds. The grades are steep and winding. Above the road the bare rock is craggy and dark, and usually dripping; Spruces cling to it where they can. After the ascent to Richland Balsam at over 6,000 feet it is down, and down, to 3,800 feet at Balsam Gap, and then up again into the Plott Balsams, to the shoulder of 6,292-foot Waterrock Knob. Here, looking back, you see the whole range of the Balsams, and ahead, beyond Soco—properly Sa-gwa-hi—Gap, the Smokies rising ridge on ridge to the long crest that gives them the name of Great. The denouement is a long descent that commences appropriately—for the last 11 miles is through the Qualla Reservation of the Cherokees—between banks stained a brilliant rust by a plant that looks as if it had been dipped, upside down, in essence of vermillion: Indian Paint-brush. Altogether you weave down about 3,500 feet in 18 miles to the Oconaluftee River and the entrance to the Great Smoky Mountains National Park.

It is never easy to say goodbye to the benevolently paternalistic Blue Ridge Drive, which insulates you from contemporary America for all its 575 miles, soliciting and informing your interest in natural and historical phenomena along the way. On the road in which it ends you are back in the world. This thoroughfare, which unfortunately bisects the National Park and crosses the divide of the range between its two highest summits, is a national highway, U.S. 441. Still, it offers an exciting enough passage when traffic is in abeyance, climbing from 2,000 feet on the Oconaluftee to over 5,000 at Newfound Gap, then winding down to below 1,500 at Gatlinburg through such bends that in one place it goes under itself. And it reveals the essential features of the range. The Smokies appear to me more crumpled than others of the Appalachians, steeper between the sharp crests that stand higher above the deeper valleys. The Geological Survey's contour maps seem to bear out this impression. The brown lines may be as crowded elsewhere, indicating slopes as precipitous, but nowhere else are there so many such large concentrations of them. You see the arching ridges not only steep in themselves but buttressed by lesser ridges close to the vertical in their crests and flanks. These are so sheer that little but Mountain-laurel can eke out a living in the pockets of soil with the rains that quickly run off; "slicks," the mountain people call such heights, from the gloss of the Mountain-laurel's leaves. The Chimneys, two arrowhead formations seen to good advantage from the highway—and to the profit of Eastman and Agfa—have slopes of this character.

It is from Gatlinburg that the trail starts on which it is possible to gain a mile in elevation in a day's hike up LeConte. (The border between the National Park and the town must be as striking a one as the country affords. On one side of an imaginary line is the edge of the deep forest wilds; on the other is a crowded resort of holiday bazaars and deluxe motels in astonishing array, occupied by vacationers in fashionable summer attire who spend their time on their balconies or strolling the streets and shopping.) I found it enough to ascend the mountain from Greenbrier Cove, seven miles east of Gatlinburg, from which the climb amounts to 4,800 feet in nine miles. ("Cove" is the mountain people's term for one of the shut-in valleys suitable for farming.) This is sufficient pull if you are carrying your own provisions. Doing so, by the way, is not essential. Since 1926 there has been a lodge with overnight accommodations for hikers just under the summit of the mountain. This, surely, is an anomaly in what should be wilderness. However, the log-built lodge and plank-sided cabins, all cut from the neighboring spruce and fir, and unpainted, are at minimum odds with their surroundings. There is little plumbing and no electricity and no access except by trail. The shortest, and the one by which most of the patrons come, is five and a half miles long and nearly 3,000 feet steep; it starts at Alum Cave Creek on U.S. 441.

The hike from Greenbrier Cove is to be recommended to anyone who seeks in the course of a day's effort to take the measure of the Smokies and absorb the quality of the southern Appalachians. If the absence of other human beings, together with a sense of Nature's primacy, be taken as the criterion, you are likely to have the feeling of wilderness from the start. Even in June I saw not another person from the cove to the summit.

The forest, the silence and the solitude that form the profoundest impression of the lone hiker in the Southern mountains enclose you within steps of your striking out. You are in the province of the trees, intensely aware of their presence through a swiftly sharpened alertness to externals. There are big ones—Tuliptrees, Yellow Buckeyes, White Oaks, Sugar Maples, Cucumber Magnolias—and their lofty, interwoven tops all but exclude the sunlight. But it is not the dimensions of the forest alone that connote wilderness. It is the fallen trunks of maximum size in various stages of mossy decay. Here trees live out their life spans and, toppled at last by the years, support a succession of lesser plants as they gradually return to the soil. It is the forest's realm, and the gushing of the Little Pigeon River, having the sound of distant thunder, is the voice of the god of waters. A Blue Jay, half wild, half curious, takes note of you and wings off soundlessly. You should feel an alien here, estranged by a lifetime, by generations, of civilization. Yet you do not. Countless preceding generations of forest-living have not been entirely obliterated. You are the prodigal son come briefly back, corrupted, it is true, by luxuries, exotic tastes and soft living on the ministrations of mechanical slaves. And yet the earth on which you set your feet, with instinctive conformity to the stillness, is native to them, and the undercurrent of communication just below the level of audibility is a language of inflections that are in your blood.

Aigrettes of the shrub-like Goat's-beard lean over the trail. And to let you know that you are in the heartland of the Southern mountains, there are beds of stiff, dark-green leaves, roundly heart-shaped and crinkly-edged, growing out of the root in a whorl on wiry stems. From many rise an eighteen-inch spoke of white florets. It is, of course, Galax, the source of bronzy-green foliage favored in Christmas decorations and of a bit of income for the mountain people who gather it. *Galax aphylla* is the sole member of its genus and a scion of a disappearing family, vigorously holding out, appropriately, in these ancient mountains. With it comes the first of the birds of the northern climes into which the southern Appalachians reach. Hopping, it comes closer, turning its head from side to side to see if you look the same way as the other: a male Canada Warbler, suede-grey above, brilliant yellow below with a necklace of dark slash marks. It sings every ten or fifteen seconds, in a clear, rich, hurried, cutting whistle: "Oh, see oh, see oh, see see me!"

At this altitude, the air is still warm and close, however. Climbing heavily, you conceive of yourself as a sponge being gradually squeezed.

The trail is incised in the precipitous mountainside up which it zigzags. Here you see exemplified a characteristic of the Southern mountains, not universal but common among them. However well-frequented a trail, you may expect wilderness to the sides of it. Where the slope is not so sheer that you risk your feet going out from under you on the dead leaves, it is likely to be so thickly grown up in brush and saplings—or blackberries where the fall of a forest patriarch has opened a gap in the canopy of foliage—as to make progress a battle. The going may be both steep and tangled. It is not that you cannot force your way along, it is that you have to be powerfully motivated to try. Also you have to get rid of your frame-pack, which will snag on a branch every few steps. And if you quit the trail you would do well to have a compass and have vowed not to disbelieve its report however

Galax, almost a floral synonym for the southern Appalachians.

crazy it may seem to be. You would not be the first wanderer in these hills to do so to his regret. It is possible but very unlikely that you will be disabled by a fall, swept away by a mountain river in flood, struck by lightning or, if it feels it has no choice, bitten by a rattlesnake or copperhead. Otherwise, you will not be in danger even if lost. This is a tractable wilderness. Should a cloud envelop the mountain, afflicting you with white blindness to everything more than four or five paces distant, you can still get out by walking downhill, though you may have a long way to go, much of it in streambeds, and come out far from where you would have chosen to be, with equipment jettisoned and clothes in tatters.

After an hour and a half on the trail up from Greenbrier you come to a southeast-facing slope which aridity has rendered comparatively open. From here, between trunks of scraggly Table-mountain Pines, you can see across the valley to a lofty ridge forming a skyline still high above you. Huge and many-humped, black where the Spruces march up its summits, it is flanked by buttress ridges like the vertical folds in a tented fabric, and these are stained faintly pink along their spines. The tint would be puzzling if you did not know the cause—the blossoms of massed Catawba Rhododendrons, which with the Mountain-laurel have replaced the forest on the ridgebacks. . . . Table-mountain Pines, like other short-needled, hardwood Pines, are trees of adversity. They cling to existence on desiccated heights of the southern Appalachians uncontested by other trees, twisted of both needles and limbs, their big cones, which may take many years to mature, held tight and defended by wicked hooks at the end of the scales; what is hard won is not readily yielded.

The more accentuated a topography, the greater the resulting climatic differences; and here the accentuation is sharp. Rounding a shoulder of the mountain, you enter a dark and damp realm of hemlocks and rhododendrons. The great, mast-like trunks of the conifers have but little taper and the delicate foliage seems almost extraneous to them, as filigrees of moss to rocks. Stems of Leucothoë, lined by glossy, pointed leaves, arch beside the trail, the new growth at the tips a lustrous reddish bronze. (This is also the source of Christmas foliage, but mountain men long have cursed it for the barriers to the hunt it forms. Dog-hobble is an English name for it, and dogs have broken their legs in tangles of Mountain-laurel and Leucothoë.) The vegetation not only shuts out most of the light but is dark in itself. So is the little Black-throated Blue Warbler, which with its brownish mate your presence is agitating. These are the depths of the forest indeed, their twilight never lifted winter or summer, seeming the more shadowy for the scattered beams of sunlight. Yet the ground-hugging Mountain Wood-sorrel blankets the forest floor with its bright green shamrock foliage starred with white buttercup-like flowers, delicately lined inside with pink, and there are beds of the little Foamflower, bearing white racemes of bloom like sparklers above hawthorn leaves—a highly-regarded medicine of the Cherokees.

These two plants are endemics of Canada. So is the author of the leisurely, discontinuous song of pure, sweet, rounded beguiling notes—a Solitary Vireo—and the minute Winter Wren which is pouring out a trilling, twittering, modulated, breathtakingly fast recitative. Does the recording of these facts convey any of the gratification of experiencing them? Or does the notation, after three and a half hours on the trail: "All of a sudden at 2:10 the Red Spruces appear, up to 70 feet tall, some of them two feet or more in diameter. Must be up around 4,500 feet. A Black-capped Chickadee singing." (Both Eastern Chickadees have a cheerfully plaintive, call-like song, but the northern Black-cap's is of two notes as opposed to the smaller Carolina's four.) Is the gratification perhaps peculiar to me, an echo of the excitement I felt at discovering for myself as a boy, in the sixth year of a dedication to birds, the Canadian character of the high North Carolina elevations? Or is it an emotion anyone would have on achieving the cooler, cleaner, sharper, more rarefied atmosphere of this northland of the clouds, of which he needs only to be reminded to have again the sense of achieving a higher, purer order of being and purpose?

However it may be, the Grey Squirrels of the lower elevations have been succeeded by the northern Reds. These seem fairly confident of the protection afforded by the National Park. One scolds at your intrusion with the sound and vigor of a wound-up, rusty clockwork mechanism come unhinged, its tail whipping and hind leg kicking in time with the raucous, syncopated invective.

Within an hour of the first Spruces comes the aroma that of all sylvan fragrances is to me the most delicious and stirring—the sweet scent of sun-warmed Balsam foliage. It is a little like that of raspberries simmering on the stove in the making of jam. Where the Red Spruce is a dark moss-green, the Southern Balsam (or Fraser's Fir) is a silvery blue-green, with wider, flatter and blunt rather than sharp needles. Growing not nearly as large as the Spruce, it appears to be even better adapted to the rigors of Appalachian summits. The two chiefly form the forest on up to the top. The higher and more exposed slopes of the mountain are, however, a battleground between the forest and the elements. On September 1, 1951, a storm dumped four inches of rain on LeConte in one hour. A resultant landslip at the crest, carrying the forest with it, left a scar visible from Newfound Gap, from which the huge bulk of LeConte dominates the outlook. (The flood waters also poured down Alum Cave Creek, knocking over the biggest trees in their path, and damaging bridges in Gatlinburg.) While the forest is reclaiming the swath, you see more recent blow-downs as you near the crest. The thin soil of the heights provides only poor anchorage and many trees go over, raising a disk of roots a man's height or more in which slabs of rock remain in their clutches.

To me the summit of LeConte is the most exciting, the most dramatic spot in all the southern Appalachians; and however grand the upper reaches of Mount Washington and Mount Katahdin in Maine may be, they can present nothing like the panorama of mountains LeConte commands. The ridge line is right-angled, like an L. The base of the arms is cloud-forest, a low, dense stand of spruce and fir, their trunks, mossy at the foot, rising from beds of deeper moss: a lofty forest chapel, hushed, cool, redolent of balsam incense. The ends of the two arms are open—heath balds they are called in reference to the kind of vegetation that cloaks them, mattress-like. Cliff Top, to the north, is rounded, with outcroppings of shingled sandstone falling off into the void. Myrtle Point, to the east, where the bare rock is shaly, is a narrow promontory, a mere catwalk in one place where a step or two to either side would plunge one to destruction—though even here the path is a bed of humus, like peat. But the view!

Directly before you, from north of east around to the southwest, runs the whole long backbone ridge of the Great Smokies. To the right it rises gradually from both directions to the gentle summit of the range's highest, Smoky Dome—Clingman's Dome—6,643 feet in elevation. Siler's Bald is down the ridge and, much farther, Thunderhead. Beyond that, faint beneath the afternoon sun, are the Unicois, rising to 5,580 feet. To the left the ridge rises to the conical crown of Guyot, second highest of the Smokies at 6,623 feet. To the right of Guyot, between 25 and 40 miles away, you can identify the Plott Balsams and Great Balsams, with a binocular, by the scratch the Parkway makes on Waterrock Knob and Richland Balsam. The pyramid of Mount Pisgah, farther still, is unmistakable from the faint, vertical line of the television antenna degrading its

The trail on White Rock looking south over the North Carolina and Tennessee state line. *United States Department of the Interior, National Park Service Photo.*

summit. Over Guyot's right shoulder, is not that smudge of a hump on the horizon the Black Mountains, 75 miles distant and the highest of all? And is not that similar smudge over its left shoulder the Roan, 80 miles to the northeast? I dare think so, in both cases!

The topography before you is odd in one respect. You would expect mountains of such steep sides to rise to sharp peaks, whereas a range of which the loftiest eminences are in general merely somewhat higher developments of the ridge they crown, you would not expect to drop so precipitously to the valleys as do these and their lateral ridges. This is characteristic of the southern Appalachians: the rounded summit above steep and broadly ribbed sides. You are especially aware of it in the Smokies, however, where the relief is so great; Clingman's Dome stands almost 5,800 feet above the lowest creek bottom. Incidentally, the configuration of these ranges makes it easy to understand why, until a century ago, it was believed that mountains were raised by the puckering of the earth's epidermis as the planet shrank with cooling. This, it seems, is the way they would look if they had been.

Only because trails have been cut through the shrub growth can you reach the ends of LeConte's ridge. The Mountain-laurel, Catawba Rhododendron and Sand-myrtle (from which Myrtle Point is named) cover all but bare rock in thicket so dense it would seem a rabbit could not get through it. You can understand how such cover would have protected T. J. Holt from the attack of a Golden Eagle on LeConte near the end of the past century, if not how he managed to crawl beneath it. The report, by the way, if true—and Holt, an engineer of Knoxville, is said to have known more about the Smokies in his day than anyone else—would be the best evidence I know of that the Golden Eagle has nested in the southern Appalachians, as has been often suspected; only in the vicinity of its nest would one have attacked a man. An eyrie of the imperial birds on those cliffs would be fitting.

The sheered surface of the brush, as smooth as any hedge, and the ragtag condition of the stunted Balsams thrust up through it, bespeak the lash of winter storms. They recall the experience of a party from a convention of the American Association for the Advancement of Science who on the last day of 1917 hiked up LeConte only to be caught by a 60-degree drop in temperature—to 20 below—and barely squeaked through. Yet I find the Rhododendron putting out its globes of luscious, lavender-pink blossoms and the Sand-myrtle its bunches of little white flowers, furry with pink-tipped stamens, as if they had never heard of winter; the gale-tormented heights are bowers. The cushiony little Sand-myrtle, a Heath like its partners, with narrow, stiff leaves only three-eighths of an inch long, grows even out of crevices in the rocks, a natural bonsai and, one is tempted to say, a lovable plant.

Below the lodge is a dump to which bears repair in the evening for the garbage while the guests watch from above. While I was there a mother bear with two cubs, maybe two such families, and one or two other adults appeared out of the forest. Through the evening they wandered about like Black Angus cattle, albeit with a difference, as they were to do again in the morning. It was not clear to me who was boss and I felt some qualms about laying out my sleeping-bag where the storm had leveled the forest two decades before. If nothing else, I thought I might be trod on by one of the beasts. I was the only camper apart from a dozen Boy Scouts with two leaders who occupied the open-faced cabin maintained by the National Park for backpackers. (Subsequently this was to be enclosed by heavy wire mesh across its front to keep the bears away from the campers' provisions.)

Directly after turning in I was visited by a young man and a girl from the lodge, one of the half-dozen youngsters who work there during the summer. Al Bedinger, as I learned the former's name was, had been hiking and otherwise wandering about the country in a free and footloose way, as a number of others I was to meet on the trail had been; he was even to spend the winter at the lodge, with a companion, for the experience. And I thought how admirable and enviable it was to take to the open road, embracing its chances, its adventures and its discomforts, before committing oneself to the treadmill. My generation had been mostly too cowed for that by the work ethic and the Great Depression. . . . I had no other visitors and suffered during the night from nothing but cold. But cold I was. I did not see how I could be so chilled on June 11th. In the morning it was explained: the ground was white with frost.

I had thrown a rope over the twelve-foot-high limb of a spruce and pulled a bag containing my edibles up to it in the prescribed method for outwitting bears. The Scouts had likewise strung up three big bags, but one of these was not high enough and in the morning the remains of its contents were scattered over the ground. A male bear returned to the spoils while I was making my breakfast and took an indifferent view of my somewhat restrained efforts to shoo him off. I am all for Black Bears. They are the only formidable animals left in the East, south of the moose. They mean wilderness as nothing else does. That anyone should find sport in killing bears—and killing them is permitted in National Forests, to which the remnants of the Eastern Black Bear population are largely confined—is to me incomprehensible. All the same, I shall be glad when everyone takes the measures necessary to break the association in bears' minds between human beings and largesse.

The views from LeConte led in August 1924 to an historic event. Two members of a committee formed by the Secretary of the Interior to make recommendations with respect to the location of a proposed National Park in the southern Appalachians, had hiked up the mountain in company with members of an organization formed in Knoxville to promote a Great Smokies park. At that time it seemed that the election must light on the northern Virginia Blue Ridge, which combined great natural beauty with accessibility to major population centers. But the awesome scenery of the Smokies and their floral richness convinced the committee members that two parks were called for, one in each range. Two years later, both were authorized by Congress.

It sounds simple, but it was not. Between 1923, when Mrs. Willis P. Davis raised with her husband the question why there could not be a National Park in the Smokies like those in the West, until the acquisition of land had been substantially completed by the end of 1940, an implacable opposition to the park had to be fought every foot of the way—and that says nothing of the efforts going back at least to 1899. In that year the Appalachian National Park Association was formed in Asheville to promote a National Park "in western North Carolina and eastern Tennessee (or, more definitely, in the heart of the Great Smoky Mountains, the Balsam Mountains, and the Black and Craggy Mountains) [where] is found not only the culmination of the Appalachian system, but the most beautiful as well as the highest mountains east of the lofty western ranges."

The exploitation of natural resources, for private gain, for economic growth, has always had an almost religious sanction among us, and the remaining virgin forests of the Smokies represented wealth. The lumbermen had already had their way with a large part of the range. As much as 200 miles of logging railroads were in use in it at one time, reaching up to 5,000-foot elevation, according to Robert S. Lambert. In his *Logging the Great Smokies* he points out that some tracks were laid straight up the slope with a yarding machine at the top to pull the cars up. Steam, he goes on to say, permitted the introduction of skidders that would drag logs out or swing them overhead on cables. It marked the end of selective cutting and the beginning of clear-cutting and, as well, a greatly increased hazard of fire, from sparks alighting on piles of slash.

Bringing trees to the mill was what lumbermen were in business for, and they were determined not to yield what remained. What their success would mean, Horace Kephart was there to testify. It had been more than twenty years since he had arrived in the Smokies to live an outdoor life, and his writings were known to many thousands. He spoke up:

When I first came to the Smokies the whole region was one of superb forest primeval. I lived for several years in the heart of it. My sylvan studio spread over mountain after mountain, seemingly without end, and it was always clean and fragrant, always vital, growing new shapes of beauty from day to day. The vast trees met overhead like cathedral roofs. I am not a very religious man; but often when standing alone before my Maker in this house not made with hands I bowed my head with reverence and thanked God for His gift of the great forest to one who loved it.

Not long ago I went to that same place again. It was wrecked, ruined, desecrated, turned into a thousand rubbish heaps, utterly vile and desecrated.

In the end the voices for the Park prevailed. Legislation authorizing it was signed into law by President Coolidge in May 1926. That was only the lesser part of it, however. As in the case of the proposed National Park in the Virginia Blue Ridge, authorized at the same time, there was the absence of any precedent for the public purchase of properties for a National Park. Heretofore the land had always been in Federal ownership to begin with, or, in the case of Acadia, in Maine, donated. The legislation creating the two new parks ruled out appropriations for land-acquisition.

Only with the greatest difficulty were the necessary funds obtained—$1,000,000 by popular subscription in North Carolina and Tennessee, including the nickels and quarters of countless school children, and $4,000,000 in appropriations by the legislatures of the two states, all of which would have been futile but for $5,000,000 in matching funds contributed by John D. Rockefeller, Jr. Even then, rising land costs required another $2,250,000, which the Federal Government under Franklin D. Roosevelt put up. And money was not all. Hotly contested condemnation suits had to be fought, against not just individual property-owners but powerful corporations, most of them lumber companies, which held 85 percent of the land required.

In the end, the nation acquired a park of nearly half a million acres and—accounting for two-fifths of the whole—the largest remainder by far of the magnificent forest the pioneers of the Eastern wilderness encountered. The cost was half that of one of today's advanced bombing planes, even allowing for inflation. Nevertheless, one cannot help reflecting, the incomparable treasure would have been left to the marketplace but for the indefatigable pertinacity of a small number of men like Willis P. Davis, Colonel David G. Chapman ("Father of the Park") of Knoxville and State Senator Mark Squires of North Carolina, and the generosity of a great private philanthropist.

Has it in fact been saved? You might doubt it when you see the packed campgrounds like country fairs and the lines of cars on park highways, adding a different kind of haze to that which gave the range its name. The figures take you aback: annual visits now topping seven million, hikers well over a quarter-million, with "back-country campers" in the neighborhood of 60,000.

Yet so far the congestion would appear to be local, confined to the reach of motorcars and the best-known trails. After setting out from Cosby campground, at the northern corner of the park, for Mount Sterling and a circuit via Tricorner Knob back to my starting place, I saw no one after

11:00 A.M. for over 26 hours, though this was still mid-June. The trail showed signs of heavy use, but by horsemen—whose numbers in the park have reached about 50,000 a year. (Bringing up stones with their hooves, breaking down the side of the trail on a steep slope and turning wet places into quagmires, horses each do more damage to a trail than a score of hikers.) My last human contact was with a young man with long blond hair wearing an Army fatigue jacket who was hiking alone. Like many of his generation—those with whom the adventure of rootlessness does not quite come off—he seemed to me a kind of waif. He said a Bear had ripped his sleeping bag the night before, with him in it, at Walnut Bottom, to which I was headed. It seemed that he had a chocolate-bar in his pocket. There had been a bad moment before the bear had betaken itself off.

Temperate Zone tropics: that is how I came to think of the well-watered reaches of the forest I walked through hour after hour, lush in its deep mosses and beds of fern. Its fecundity was almost palpable, in the clean, rich air itself. Rhododendron grew in jungles twenty feet high and its long, narrow leaves against the light overhead reminded me of looking up through bamboo. Lianas of grape vines hung from the treetops, the stocks as much as six inches in diameter. And there were plants of paired, deeply-cleft leaves, some two feet across, the largest I have seen in wild vegetation north of Florida: Umbrella-leafs they were, with clusters of cupped white flowers with yellow anthers on stalks above the leaf-juncture, very like the flower of the May-apple, to which the plant is related. As I marched steadily in a silence accented more than disspelled by the isolated songs of birds and the skippering of an occasional fleeing chipmunk, the sense I had of being in tropical woods may have been partly from a similarity in atmosphere to the trails I had plodded in Burma in a pack-outfit in World War II. The stillness, though not that behind which an armed enemy lurked, seemed the same expression of a diffuse but attentive and potent force. The barely audible clinkings of my pack-frame could have been those of a mule's harness-rings from down the line, and the sudden, irreverent loud yelpings of a Pileated Woodpecker the mirthless, whooping laughter of a band of monkeys, which used to catch us every time as unprepared as the first.

The tropical illusion was, however, limited. With altitude the trail was gaining the equivalent of latitude. The Wood Thrush of the sultry Upper Austral Zone had been succeeded by the Veery, that bird of the cool, Druidical Transition Zone forest. Several times one ran ahead of me up the path, head down as if charging, coming erect as it halted to become one of the brown leaves. Or I would hear the strong, descending whistle, "teeoo," then presently, as if in tremolos from Pan's pipe, the downward-spiraling song, vibrant with its own echo, that stirs the hair at its roots. I had left the world behind.

Like the Veery, the Yellow Birch begins in the Transition and extends up into the Canadian Zone. As I was to discover in the next few months, it is probably the outstanding tree of the higher Appalachian hardwood forests. It caught my attention from the start from the way its trunk would in some cases begin two or three feet from the ground, standing on bark-covered roots like legs. The explanation is that the Yellow Birch often gets its start as a seedling on a decaying log, which in time disappears, leaving it straddling empty space. Climbing to Pretty Hollow Gap, I came on four of the Birches growing from such a log, all connected by a single, massive root running along the top of it. The species is remarkable, too, in that, while growing to maturity as a typical Birch with papery, yellowish-platinum, satiny—and quite lovely—skin marked with horizontal lenticels, it begins to acquire rough, plated bark on its trunk and limbs as these exceed nine or ten inches in diameter, and goes on to become a virtual monarch oak with massive, irregular bole. At that stage, unless roots are exposed with the satiny, peeling bark of the young trunk, the only way you can be sure of its identity is by looking far up to the smaller limbs. I found in the Smokies that I was training my binocular less often on birds than into the tops of trees, to make out what they were.

Mount Sterling turned out to be marred by the presence of a lookout tower and cabin and, to bring electricity up to it, had been cleared of forest in a strip extending across the top and down the southern slope. I had it to myself, however, apart from a pair of Juncos; and after an 11-mile hike from 2,000 feet at the campground, up over a 4,242-foot saddle in the main ridge of the Smokies, then down to 2,800 at Walnut Bottom on Big Creek, finally up to Sterling's 5,842-foot summit, I was content to sit uncritically on the porch of the cabin and prepare supper. This amounted to adding Lipton's powdered tomato soup to a canteen cup of water heating on the little Optimus gasoline-burning stove, then dumping in the contents of a can of weiners and some granola. The meal was topped off by the richest cake I had been able to find. It had not taken me long to decide that while a somewhat Spartan regime was unavoidable on the trail, unnecessary Spartanism was not. Around the small grassy area I looked out on, the summit was densely forested in spruce. Some of the nearby trees were dead, but they were so foliated with lichens they appeared to be having a second life as ghost trees.

Nights on the ground are long for me. Despite my three-quarters-length air mattress, which I blow up before retiring, I am awake as much as asleep and am always glad to see the fading of the dark sky and the shrinking of

The Great Smoky Mountains—a summer squall coming up. *United States Department of the Interior, National Park Service Photo.*

the stars, if any. The question then is, will the little brass stove function? It had failed on LeConte (but only because I had neglected to bring the tool with a thin wire for cleaning the nozzle). After some sputtering it takes hold, however, and the collar of greenish blue, intense flame under a cup of water for coffee puts a different aspect on things.

From Mount Sterling it is 12 miles generally westward to Tricorner Knob on the Appalachian Trail, and I could believe it one of the most enjoyable mountain hikes in the East. Sterling Ridge passes you across Pretty Hollow Gap on to Cataloochee Mountain, Cataloochee on to Luftee Knob and Luftee on to Tricorner. You are up around 5,500 feet most of the way among Red Spruces and Yellow Birches that reach maximum stature. The former are as much as 80 or maybe even 100 feet tall and up to three feet through the trunk. And Harvey Broome, a founder of the Wilderness Society and veteran Smokies hiker, once counted 300 annular rings in an 18-inch section of a Spruce trunk. One of the ancient Birches has a trunk five feet through in one direction at head height, though more than half rotted away. Crowded plumes of fern give an effect of natural opulence —mostly one of the *Dryopteris,* probably Mountain Wood Fern *(D. spinulosa)*. The air is balmy and ethereal, cool in the shadows, the sun's warmth benign. After lunch, so readily did I dissolve into these surroundings, that, leaning back against the uphill side of the trail, I drifted off into a brief slumber, like an animal. . . . Another mile or two brought me to an open swath where I could look back and see whence I had come. Above a lower, compound ridge textured like a sponge with forest, and flesh-colored along its heights from the blossoming Catawbas, Sterling's broad cone could be seen a gratifyingly long way off. Rain was brewing in the steamy clouds above it. In the dry, clear air of the West, mountains look closer than they are. In the Southeast, their aspect softened by that summer-long bluish bloom, they recede into remoteness. The farther mountains of the range of shadow are themselves shadows cast against the sky.

A mile after I joined it at Tricorner Knob the Appalachian Trail rounded the summit of the Smokies' second highest. Great Guyot stands aloof from human society in its altitude and distance from any motor road, withdrawn in a Spruce forest confining the vision on all sides in a stockade of tall, slim trunks. All is still as if these were sacred precincts, and the fresh, vitally green ground-covering of blossoming Wood-sorrel a carpet laid down for the feet of reverential and garlanded pilgrims. Or so I could tell myself as I knelt for a ceremonial drink from a spring issuing from the mountainside, and pocketed for a talisman a chip of the half-billion-year-old, dark grey slate composing the mountain. Having to conserve my forces, I had to postpone to the next time a 200-foot climb to the very top. I had no permit to camp out that night, or on the Appalachian Trail at all, and to regain Cosby campground would mean altogether twenty-two miles that day, with a descent of 3,800 feet in the last five and a half.

The Maine-to-Georgia trail follows the backbone ridge of the Smokies—the boundary between North Carolina and Tennessee—for 68 miles, from one end of the park to the other. Among the other footpaths in the park, totaling 630 miles, some are certainly equally worthy. But this is one that primarily attracts the hikers, and when 130 congregate at night at a shelter built for fourteen, the rationing of overnight camping on the Appalachian Trail is clearly justified and necessary.

Rounding a bend in the trail shortly before Tricorner I had been startled by the apparition of what seemed to be three Indians, albeit one a suntanned blond, seated by the trail stripped to the waist, long hair caught up in the semblance of scalp locks. It turned out that they were young Floridians come up to see what mountains were like and eagerly voluble about a brush they had had with the Park Rangers for illegal camping at Newfound Gap; a fourth was back at the shelter with their packs. On the four and a half miles of the Appalachian Trail I met one other party of three, mother, father and adolescent daughter, out for their first overnight hike and rather anxious, I thought, to have their growing doubts about the enterprise allayed. Otherwise I saw no one all day until, done in, I hobbled into the campground at dusk. Previously, walking the Appalachian Trail westward for some miles from Davenport Gap, where it enters the park at its northeastern corner, I had encountered only two young men, together, and an unusual and appealing threesome, two boys and their sister, all nice-looking and clearly well bred, setting out for a week's hike the length of the park. Having shared the trails with so few, I brought back an impression perhaps above all of the solitudes of the Smokies.

That does not, of course, go for Clingman's Dome. When the park was created, a seven-mile spur road from U.S. 441 at Newfound Gap was constructed down the main ridge to the Smokies' supreme summit, or to within half a mile of it. Today the National Park Service would be highly unlikely to perpetrate such a violation of the integrity of a great work of nature's, which its mission is to preserve. The road is there now, however, doubtless for good, and the official leaflet says of it, "In summer you can expect extremely heavy traffic on this route." Still, the National Park Service is to be commended for having spared the mountain the indignity of a commissariat such as the state of North Carolina has imposed on the Black Dome, evidently on the theory that natural grandeur calls for soft drinks and candy. From the parking apron a paved walk ascends through close ranks of spruce and fir giving the great majority of the park's visitors their one view of the interior of such a forest, scented place of dark shadow and verdure, of silence and aeolian voices, of fitful sunshine and drifting cloud, of the calm of abstraction and of violence that topples trees or kills their tops. At the summit a flying spiral ramp leads up to an observation deck above the forest.

From Clingman's Dome a trail leads south along Forney Ridge to Andrews Bald, which was what I had come for. It was dark forest most of the way, though with Yellow Birch among the conifers; of the other hardwoods only Mountain-ash climbs as high. The gusts of wind had the sound of waves seething up a beach. After two miles the forest abruptly stopped and I came out on a broad, high, grassy ridge, under an open sky, and to almost as immense a vista of mountains as the 360-degree panorama from the tower on Clingman's Dome. A thick turf covered the ground, here and there a Balsam Fir or clump of rhododendron or huckleberry. How was the absence of forest to be explained?

Andrews is by no means the only "grass bald" in the Smokies. Gregory's and Spence Field Balds are crowned with more extensive meadows. The heath balds are easier to account for. They are features, usually, of high ridges with sharp crests and steep sides. As one observes on LeConte, trees can obtain only an insecure hold in the shallow soil of such places and may either be blown over or carried away in a land-slip. Or they may be burned off, along with the humus, by fires that race up steep slopes. And rhododendron and Mountain-laurel can subsist on these scarred ridges where trees cannot. Fire may well have given rise to the grass balds. But what has prevented the forest from reestablishing itself on the domes as well as the flanks of such mountains? The soil on top of them would appear to be at least as deep as on many forested slopes. The summer grazing of cattle and sheep on the grassy balds by farmers in the coves in the old days would have limited the growth of leafy shrubs and hardwoods on them, and if the herdsmen had fired them periodically, that would have made a clean sweep of them without killing the grass roots. In fact, it is said that forest plants have made substantial advances on Gregory's Bald since cattle were last pastured there in 1936. But in that span of years forest has reclaimed seemingly less hospitable tracts. Could the difficulty of growing up through the dense turf, combined with the ferocity of winter winds, be almost more than the seedlings of woody plants can contend with? The grass balds are puzzlers.

As well as by the solitudes of the Smokies I came away struck by the extent of modern man's reversion to the condition of an embryo. You cannot be in wilds without having it disturbingly borne in on you what a dependent you are in the womb of civilization. You are like a diver in an undersea world of coral and kelp, good only as long as his packaged air lasts. A consequence of the realization is that you look with a renewed and profound respect on the wild creatures you encounter. The little Chestnut-sided Warbler busy in a Pin Cherry on a shrubby ridge of Old Black,

Upper left, an Allegheny bellflower in the Cranberry Glades, W. Va. *Upper right,* Cardinal lobelia (America's favorite wildflower, according to Roger Tory Peterson) against gneiss exposed in a cut beside the Blue Ridge Parkway. *Lower left,* of the many flowers of the southern Appalachians no others have the glamor and enchantment of the orchids. Here, the Yellow Fringed orchis. *Above,* the flower of the Rosebay rhododendron.

Overleaf, oxalis and fern cover the floor of the forest of Southern balsam and Red spruce occupying the summit of Mt. Rogers, Virginia's highest.

and the Ruffed Grouse that with its fist-sized young roars off from the fine, bright green sedge carpeting an open woods on Cataloochee, lack your reasoning power, your far-ranging knowledge, your strength, your dextrous hands. Yet they are fully competent on their own in the wilderness, where you would prove more helpless than one of the little orange Efts scarcely able to inch along, toddling, that you occasionally meet on the trails.

Equally you think with deepened respect of the human beings who have survived on their own, or almost so, in the Appalachian wilds. Of them all, none had it harder than the Cherokees who fled to the fastnesses of these very Unegas from the implacable hostility of the white Americans. At the time of the outbreak of the French and Indian war in the mid-eighteenth century, the invasion of the Cherokees' homeland in the Southern highlands by whites from the North and East had not been long under way. However, the inevitable conflict had already established the savage pattern of reprisals and counter-reprisals. As the war between the two Old World powers intensified in the New, the Cherokees, thoroughly alienated by the American colonists, took up arms against their erstwhile British allies. Defeated, they fell back upon the most secure refuge they knew, the Atali Unega. Here, it is said, they lived like beasts. The Cherokees were not, it should be said, a tribe of primitive forest hunters. The first white explorers had found them dwelling in log huts in villages and growing maize, beans, sweet potatoes, squash and fruits. They were an advanced people, and their sufferings in the wild mountains were not much less than their dispossessors' would have been.

With the end of the war the security of the Cherokees' remaining lands was guaranteed both by a treaty of peace and friendship with their late foes, and by the Royal Proclamation of 1763 forbidding inroads by the colonists upon Indian lands across the Appalachians. But nothing could stem the tide of land-hungry Americans, which soon poured into the reservations. In 1776, rightly seeing no hope for themselves but in a British victory, the Cherokees again took sides against the colonists in the warfare. In retaliation, upwards of 6,000 well-armed Georgians and Carolinians razed their towns, killed all who could not escape, men and women alike, destroyed their crops and left their children to starve or sold them into slavery; it is said that children of the survivors twenty years later ran screaming at the sight of a white man. Again, those who escaped sought safety in the mountains. Here it was as before. Land too rugged for human acquisitiveness is unlikely to attract game animals either, and at the trails' ends in the Smokies the refugees barely staved off mass starvation on a diet of roots, frogs, snakes, berries and the inner bark of trees.

They came through, or most of them did; but even that was not to see an end of it, to be the last time. The Cherokees had come through the

Revolution still in possession of 43,000 square miles of territory. This the whites coveted. In 1828 the doom of the aborigines was sealed by two events. Gold was discovered at Dahlonega in north Georgia and the Indian-hating Andrew Jackson was elected President. It did not matter that the Cherokees had adapted themselves to white civilization, living on farms, governing themselves through an elected legislature and printing a newspaper in the 86-character alphabet devised by the illiterate genius Si-kwa'-ye—Sequoya—or that they had even been so elevated by our example as to have acquired Negro slaves. Georgia declared all their lands within the state appropriated, their legal rights abrogated, and was backed up by the Federal Government. General Winfield Scott rounded up 14,000 of them and in 1838 sent them off on the infamous Trail of Tears to Oklahoma, on which a quarter died. Of the expulsion a Georgian soldier, later a Confederate colonel, wrote: "I fought through the Civil War and have seen men shot to pieces and slaughtered by the thousands, but the Cherokee removal was the cruelest work I ever knew." Some one thousand of them, those of purest blood and most conservative outlook, according to Horace Kephart, eluded the troops and hid out in the Smokies, half of them—again according to Kephart—between Clingman's Dome and Mount Guyot. Here many died of starvation before General Scott was appeased and called off the hunt.

But there was blood to the end, which came with the death before a firing-squad of an aging Cherokee, Tsali, and his three sons. The four had been captured with their families by Scott's soldiers. However, when in the course of a forced march his wife had been prodded to keep up, Tsali gave the order to fall upon their captors, which they had done and killed them. The price of amnesty set by Scott was the surrender of the four. Tsali gave in to his chief, who had urged his compliance, and it was to the latter that his last words were addressed. He said, "And it is by your hands, Eutsala, that I am to die? We have been brothers together; but Eutsala has promised to be the white man's friend, and he must do his duty, and poor Tsali is to suffer because he loved his country. O, Eutsala! if the Cherokee people now beyond the Mississippi carried my heart in their bosoms, they never would have left their beautiful native land—their own mountain land. . . . It is sweet to die in one's own country, and to be buried by the margin of one's native stream."

Settlers had begun to penetrate the Smokies even before the turn of the century, beginning with the valley of the Oconaluftee, the main gateway to the present National Park from North Carolina. Almost as early, others on the far side of the range, moving down from the northeastern Tennessee settlements, began to push up the streams to fertile coves in the foothills of the Great Iron Mountains, as the Smokies were originally called. In 1818 John Oliver became the first settler in Cade's Cove, a valley bottomland looking southward up to the main ridge of the Smokies, dominated from here by Thunderhead. About five miles long by from one to one and a half wide, the cove was inhabited by a hundred families living much as their pioneer forebears had when it was marked for incorporation in the National Park. The cabin built by Oliver close to his original homestead has been preserved, as have a number of other houses and outbuildings of hand-shaped logs or locally-sawed boards and hand-rived shakes. Among them is an operating, water-powered gristmill. To prevent the reconquest of the cove by the forest and preserve its historic aspect, the Government leases the land for farming, under specified conditions. It is almost entirely in pasture for beef cattle; and if you take the 11-mile tour of the cove early in the morning you may well detect, along with the Herefords, a deer or two in the distance scrutinizing you.

So the Smokies were staked out by the whites for their livelihood. At the same time the white man's God was proclaimed among them. "In those days, as the saying went," Michael Frome recalls, "the first sound in the wilderness was the ring of the settler's axe and second the greeting of the traveling preacher, the circuit rider, at his front door." Baptists and Methodists, for the most part, these dedicated men rode the steepest and rockiest trails, through rain and swollen streams, to snatch souls from the evils of the frontier—drink, violence, profanity and estrangement from elevating influences. While adding another mouth to feed and body to bed down in the small cabin, they were generally welcome, at least as new faces and bearers of tidings from the larger world.

Disciples of that third preoccupation of white civilization, the quest for knowledge, came a little later to the Smokies, in the 1850's. The first of the explorers was Thomas Lanier Clingman, a man of energy and courage and also, it would seem, arrogance and ambition, a mining prospector who became a United States Senator and Confederate General. His natural curiosity and zeal to promote the North Carolina Mountains took him first to the Blacks and Balsams, then to the main ridge of the Smokies and to its supreme summit. In this expedition he was accompanied by two prominent scientists, Samuel B. Buckley, a naturalist, and Samuel L. Love, a physician. The most eminent scientist among the explorers, however, was Arnold Henry Guyot, a compatriot and lifelong friend of the great Swiss zoologist, Louis Agassiz. A professor of geography, Guyot became a luminary of the Princeton faculty as Agassiz had of the Harvard. After spending five years mapping the northern Appalachians and Adirondacks, he turned to the South. Working over the Black Mountains and finding eleven of their peaks higher than Mount Washington, he then, in 1859, came to the Smokies. Here, with Robert Collins, a local mountain man whom Clingman had engaged to act as his guide, and a horse, Guyot spent the summer "struggling up the steep, trackless, laurel-tangled slopes of

Smoky burdened with supplies for a week or more, and handicapped still further by a bulky, fragile barometer," a Tennessee historian of the Smokies, Paul M. Fink, writes. "But though laboring under such difficulties, so painstaking was Guyot with his observations and subsequent calculations that the figures he cites for the various points in the Smokies seldom vary as much as a score of feet from the latest altitudes announced by the United States Geological Survey." Guyot and Collins traveled the entire length of the crest of the Smokies, which the Appalachian Trail now follows, and must have been the first white men to do so.

All those explorers, together with Joseph LeConte (a chemist of Charleston) and those most responsible for the creation of the National Park, have had their names given to dominant mountains of the range. Most of the euphonious Cherokee names—names not easy for whites to remember, it may be admitted—have been supplanted. If mountains have to be named for human individuals at all, we may be grateful that the names of Clingman, Guyot and LeConte are distinctive and have a quality not unsuitable to the usage. But I could wish that I knew nothing of the finite human beings who bore them and could think them the names of mountains only.

As for the Cherokees, it is the descendants of the thousand who found refuge in the Smokies who today occupy the Qualla Reservation at the southeastern corner of the National Park. If, lacking sufficient agricultural land to support the 3,300 they now number, they are dependent on tourists for a living, half still normally speak their own language. Their traditional crafts have not been entirely forgotten, or their medicine, based on plants and practiced by conjurers. Restitution of what their people as a whole have lost is of course impossible. We can hardly hope that the slain Cherokees were warranted in believing, as they may have to the end, that their wounds would be assuaged in enchanted Lake Ataga'hi, beneath Kuwahi'—Clingman's Dome—invisible to mortal eyes. But perhaps the protection we have given the Atali Unega may be seen as a gesture of atonement to the spirit that they believed imbued the whole of Nature, animate and inanimate, and, all things considered, may be imagined to have made these mist-hung mountains its special abode.

V *The Progeny of Time*

On returning from the Smokies I obeyed an impulse to visit a range that was unknown to me and went off hiking in the West Virginia Alleghenies. These mountains I shall come to later in this account, however, in a more logical place. Recognizing, belatedly, that I ought to proceed systematically in exploring the mountains, I decided that the way to do it was to go down the ranges on the Atlantic side—the several components of the Blue Ridge —into Georgia, there turn westward and come back up those on the inland, or northwestern side. These latter, of a different age and structure from the Blue Ridge, reach their greatest development in the Long Ridge Mountains of central western Virginia and in the range from which I had just returned. The West Virginia Alleghenies are but little known beyond their immediate environs: how many persons have heard of Spruce Mountain? Yet they make up the second massif of the southern Appalachians—and Spruce is the highest mountain in a stretch of 640 miles.

The major massif, combining the higher Blue Ridge and Smokies, occupies western North Carolina and the adjacent margin of Tennessee and runs down into northeastern Georgia and up into southwestern Virginia. Its ramparts in Virginia were the first objective of my circuit tour, specifically the highest of them which is also the highest summit in the state. Mount Rogers, as it is officially called, rises on the far edge of the Blue Ridge—far, that is, to anyone coming from the east—just inside Virginia above the upper corners of North Carolina and Tennessee. That puts it pretty far west, as far west as Cincinnati, Ohio, and I had been driving in three of the five longitudinal strands that make up the Appalachians before I arrived at it. Of these it must be said, though, that two—one on either side of the Blue Ridge—would for the most part hardly seem to qualify as parts of any range. You have to look back a hundred million years or so to see them as such.

There are specialists who take close note of Appalachian geology. Mining prospectors, for example. Feldspar, kaolin, mica, granite, marble, co-

Gneiss, a metamorphic rock, in the capstone of mile-high Albert Mountain in the Nantahalas.

And in a rock ledge of Glen Falls, near Highlands, N.C.

rundum, gold, silver and iron have been or are being extracted from the Blue
Ridge. There is the wealth of coal in the West Virginia and Kentucky
ranges—to the land's sorrow. Gem-collectors forage through old mines for
garnets and rubies, beryl and emeralds. But to the traveler familiar with the
dramatic rock exposures of the West—the bowed and contorted strata
revealed in cliffs hundreds of feet high, the massive sandstones of varied
hues capping mesas and buttes and standing in huge, sculptured mon-
oliths—the Appalachians hardly suggest geology at all. What rocks jut from
their slopes are mostly so weathered as to appear drab and indistinguishable
one from another, and certainly, you would think, indecipherable. If,
however, you have an eye for the rock in the highway cuts, freshly laid
open, you will have a different impression. Then, as you see how this
changes as you cross the warp of the range, you readily deduce that this
must have something to do with the changing character of the land forms.
You understand how geologists might be able to find clues to the history of
the range in the rocks that compose it. That they have been able to work it
out in the detail they have, however, becomes the more amazing the more
you learn about it—almost as amazing as the story that has been unfolded. A
tremendous story it is—how tremendous has been discovered only in the

past dozen years. When you know its outlines you see the range with a much more perceptive eye and find that it means a great deal more to you.

In Virginia, both the Piedmont, which leads up to the Blue Ridge, and the Great Valley, on its other side, resemble the image we are apt to have in mind when we think of going back to the land to farm in an agreeable way in a moderate climate, living in a house seasoned with the memories of generations, under century-old shade trees giving on a prospect of orchards and stock on undulating pastures with flowing brooks in their folds. Many people who could live anywhere in the world do live in the Virginia Piedmont in such historic houses, joining in hunt meets and cantering on blooded horses over bold, grassy hills, past wooded slopes with the tranquil mass of the Blue Ridge on the horizon.

The Piedmont begins fairly level to the traveler from Washington and grows more rolling as it approaches the mountains. Here, where the old roads roll with it, the new highways are blasted through the hills out of the underlying rock. This is a grey, granulated, rather sparkly rock that the construction crews would tell you is excessively hard. It is granite, a rock formed only in the cores of great mountains. From the United States Geological Survey map of North America, which renders it in dark pink, you will find that it is very much the same granite as that on which the surf beats on the New England coast, and Arctic winds rage on the summits of Mount Washington and Mount Katahdin. The hills of the southeastern Piedmont and the White Mountains of New Hampshire would appear to be components of a single range. Why it should have worn so much lower in the former is not clear.

If, on reaching the Skyline Drive at Thornton Gap (through which probably the first road over the Blue Ridge crossed) you turn south onto the Drive you will find more granite in the tunnel through which it soon passes. Most of the rock of the northern Virginia Blue Ridge, however, shows in the road cuts a uniform consistency and a bluey-green tint. Fracturing, as you may notice, to a sharp edge, it is this rock that gives Stonyman Mountain its saw-toothed face and once gave the Manahoac Indians, who came up to collect it, many keen tools. It is such a feature of the scene that one of the turnoffs near the beginning of the Blue Ridge Parkway is named for it: Greenstone Overlook. Farther down the range you get back to the rock that is sparkly in the new cuts, making you think of grey loaf sugar. Often it is marbled with white, like two kinds of taffy pulled together. If you are the least bit of a geologist you will recognize all these as rocks that solidified of originally molten minerals or of pre-existing rock that was softened under pressure and high temperatures—igneous and metamorphic rocks. Of these the Blue Ridge is almost entirely composed.

You need give no thought at all to geology to have the main geological feature of the Great Valley come to your attention. It will do so through

Granite with phenocysts in a cut for the Blue Ridge Parkway in Roanoke Mountain.

The greenstone of the Virginia Blue Ridge derives from immense lava flows during the incubation of the range deep beneath the trough of the ancestral Atlantic. This is the peak stone of Stonyman Mountain.

the billboards advertising caverns. These can mean only one thing: limestone country. Limestone—calcium carbonate—is dissolved by acid. Where it forms the bedrock and is percolated by water of an acid tinge, sinks are leached out in which streams disappear (to gush forth somewhere else as springs) and caverns created. While limestone is being removed, however, some is being reconstituted—both by extremely slow processes, it should be said. Rain water, saturated with calcium carbonate after flowing through the overlying limestone, seeps into a cavern. Drops suspended from the ceiling evaporate, each leaving a microscopic film of calcium carbonate behind it; or, falling, they leave the deposit on the surface they strike. In the course of eons, icicles of stone creep down from the ceiling and, inverted, up from the floor beneath them. In time the pairs may join end to end, forming a pillar, or neighboring dripstones may coalesce side to side in draperies or the semblance of fused organ-pipes. Caves of such statuary, some with greenish, bluish or rufous tints from the chemicals the seep water has picked up, can be marvelous sights, almost beyond being ruined even by commercial exploitation. One can only imagine the sensations of the first person to push aside the vegetation from the entrance to such a cave and, by the flickering flame of a torch, to have beheld the pale ranks of eerie sculptured configurations against the darkness that would have swallowed the light within a score of paces.

In its northern part the Shenandoah Valley is so broad and flat that in crossing it you are likely to think of anything but mountains. But as you go south through and beyond it, down the Great Valley, the land progressively picks up relief. The underlying limestone soon begins to crop up in the fields like rows of bone-white teeth or boulders resembling the sheep sometimes grazing among them. In the cuts made for the new valley highway, Interstate 81, it is an attractive soft grey, pale or medium, as even in texture as butter, sometimes stained buff. You pass through beautiful country of low but abrupt hills, almost all fields and woods, with here and there a flock of sheep or a herd of black and white Holsteins, the farmhouses big and white, the barns grey or weathered red, always with the wild-looking Blue Ridge crouched in the east. Some of the pastures are as rocky as New England's. Beginning in the vicinity of Roanoke, the cuts in the limestone are 40 or 50 feet high, while the hills, rising to 2,000, then 2,500 feet, obstruct the valley for 40 miles. Geologists tell us that a layer of limestone 9,000 feet thick went into the making of the southern Appalachians. When we reflect that it was formed of the calcareous shells of mostly minute sea-organisms settling on the ocean floor, we have an intimation of the vastness of geological time.

The Great Valley divides the forged-rock Appalachians—the Blue Ridge —from the less ancient sedimentary-rock Appalachians. The stratified shales and sandstones of which these latter are composed are exhibited

Limestone outcropping in Great Valley of Virginia.

The tilted, sedimentary rock of the Longridge Mountains here seen exposed in Cumberland Gap.

better than anywhere else I know in the cuts through which U. S. Highway 50 passes west of Winchester, Virginia. In these cross-sections the layers, fine or thick, stand at angles varying from the horizontal to the vertical and come in a variety of colors from nearly white to nearly black, with greys, buffs, golden tawny and maroon in between—the colors of the muds and sands that formed them. Unlike the rocks on the other side of the Valley, these contain fossils. The fossils are relics of early Paleozoic seas, commonly of trilobites and brachiopods, in the Long Ridge Mountains and of much later, Coal Age plants and animals in the Cumberlands and Alleghenies, farther inland.

Eight or nine years ago I had occasion to learn all I could take in of the formation of the Appalachians. Since then, however, the science of geology has undergone a revolution. It has been discovered that the earth's crust, far from being solid and fixed, is made up of mobile plates. Of heavy basaltic rock, these plates, numbering between eight and a dozen, float on a hot slush of even heavier minerals. Some underlie the oceans, others bear the continents, as on rafts. And, albeit fully contiguous, they are in constant movement with respect to one another at a rate of an inch or two, more or less, a year. A theory of "continental drift" was proposed over half a century ago by the German geologist Alfred Wegener, who argued that the continents had at one time all been joined together. Wegener's theory accounted for the intercontinental distribution of plants and animals and the apparent continuity of mountain ranges separated by oceans. It was the only theory offered that did. Nevertheless it was generally dismissed, even derided. What it lacked was proof that the continents moved and an explanation of the power that could move them. The proof has now been supplied in the form of evidence that the ocean floors are in movement away from the mid-oceanic ridges, and the cause of the movement persuasively been conjectured.

The power is that of radioactivity within the earth. This heats the rock of the planet's interior, rendering it plastic and setting it in circulation, terribly slowly but irresistibly. The analogy is drawn to a saucepan of thick cream soup on a burner in which similar currents produce upwellings at the surface separated by down-folds. Hot, softened, basaltic rock is forced up between the plates underlying the oceans, creating the mid-oceanic ridges. The plates, with the new rock annealing to their edges, are forced apart. On their opposite sides they are thrust under the continental plates and back into the earth's interior. Their down-turning causes deep oceanic trenches along the continental borders, such as are found today along the coasts of Japan, the Philippines, Chile and the Antilles. Plate movement may close oceans altogether, as the Mediterranean is slowly being closed today, and bring continents into juxtaposition, as all were brought together about 250 million years ago. Then again it may create a widening gulf between them, as the Red Sea is widening today.

I first encountered the application of the new geology to the Appalachians in an article in *Scientific American* by the marine geologist Robert S. Dietz. The drama it unfolded, carrying not only far back into the past but far ahead into the future, was to me utterly gripping. The British physicist Nigel Calder's book, *This Restless Earth,* completed my enthrallment to the dynamic new conception of earth processes. Among other enigmas that were cleared up were two besetting mysteries about the creation of the Appalachians, one of them shared by other folded-mountain belts, as they are called—the Northern Rockies, Andes, Alps and Himalayas. Among these great ranges, by the way, it seems that the Appalachians are a model for their clarity of pattern. It is not to be wondered at that it was by studying them that an American geologist, James Hill, a century ago laid bare the origins of all.

The Appalachians are not the oldest of mountains, even of North American mountains; the hills terminating on the northern shore of Lake Superior are the latter, according to the geologist Philip B. King. But no mountains of their height anywhere in the world are of their antiquity. If we are to understand what we are seeing when we look at them we have to go very far back in time. To visualize how the stage was set for them, Dietz suggests that we regard our eastern seaboard today. This seaboard is geologically quiescent because it is the trailing edge of a westward-moving continent. Gravel, sand and silt from the eroding Appalachian highlands carried southeastward by the rivers have for 150 million years been settling on the margin of the continental basement, beyond the Piedmont. (The continental basement is the bedrock of the continent, formed of the planed-down remains of inconceivably ancient mountains and of lavas that came to the surface during their birth.) The coastal plain is formed of these sediments, which deepen toward the sea; they are two miles thick at Cape Hatteras. The edge of the continental basement and the adjacent sea-floor, it is certain, are sagging beneath their weight. What we have is a trough that deepens as it fills. It seems likely that this was the situation in early Paleozoic times, 450-600 million years ago.

The analogue of the Appalachians of that time, the source of the sediments that were washing down onto the continental shelf, was a range called the Grenville. This had come into being half a billion years before in the same way that the Appalachians were to come into being several hundred million years in the future. It stood about where the Appalachians (not counting the Piedmont) do now. By about 450 million years ago, however, it had worn so low that no further sediments came from it. This was not surprising. Those it had produced had accumulated in the trough to thicknesses of up to eight miles. The sea advanced over the vanished range's roots and for tens of millions of years at a time held sway over much of the continent. This was when that 9,000-foot layer of limestone was laid down.

At the same time, however, other sediments derived from the erosion of rock were washing in to add to the deposits. Products of volcanic action accompanied them. On the principle that the finest sediment travels the farthest, geologists long ago determined that the source was this time in the opposite direction. It was from offshore—where the ocean floor is entirely of basalt and has never supported any land. Where the devil, then, did all that material come from? That was puzzler number one.

Geology now has the answer.

Back even before the period we have been talking about, a movement of crustal plates portentous for our continent was taking place. The plate underlying the ocean off its east coast (what is now its east coast, that is) was being rammed into the plate on which it rode and thrust under it, back into the earth's molten depths. Heat from the zone of conjuncture of the two plates was melting the rock in the zone and forcing it up as lava. Some of it, consisting of the scrapings of the oceanic plate and continental sediments carried down by that plate, was made up of the lighter-weight minerals that derive from and go into granite—chief component of the continents—and contained much water. That made it explosive. It burst forth in jets to create, and augment, an arc of fuming, erupting volcanoes, to which the Aleutians, Antilles, Kuriles and Indonesian archipelago of today are analogous. Other lava melted out of the basalt of the plates was heavier and relatively waterless. Forced upward into the outer part of the trough, it spread out in huge sheets beneath the sedimentary deposits, which had now become rock. In time it was to turn up, altered by later events, as the greenstone along the Blue Ridge Drive.

While this was going on, another movement of plates was closing the distance between North America and northwestern Europe, then evidently a continent unto itself. Perhaps as early as 450 million years ago the two collided. A combined continent was formed with a coastline stretching along the present line of the Appalachians and across the southern British Isles, northern France and Germany. The trough filling and deepening with sediments along the eastern coast of North America was evidently continuous with one developing similarly and for similar reasons along the southern coast of northwestern Europe—or what would now be eastern and southern. The mountain range destined to emerge from the combined trough was going to be a long one.

With the continued underthrusting of the Eur-American plates by the oceanic, the heat from the impact spread. The adjacent sedimentary rocks in the trough were softened or melted outright. So was the rock of the continental basement beneath them. Thus, as they resolidified, there came into being the metamorphic rock and granite bodies of the Piedmont and adjoining portion of the Blue Ridge. These, moreover, were invaded by masses of magma—hot, liquid rock—from below the basement. And now, as we look back on the course of events, we find the answer to the second mystery: what force could have raised mountains? It was the opposing movement of crustal plates. Enormous pressures were put on the newly forged rocks, and these were pushed up out of the trough in huge folds, beginning with the rocks of today's Piedmont. The Appalachians were being born.

The gestation period was, however, far from over. As the new mountains emerged, sediments from their erosion spread out over the accumulation in the landward side of the trough, which had remained undisturbed. This must have gone on for nearly a hundred million years. However, there impended a compressional event far greater than that which had given the rocks of the Piedmont and Blue Ridge their initial elevation. From across the narrowing ocean, imperceptibly but inexorably, Africa was approaching. The force that could raise mountains was about to display its full might.

Probably between 250 and 300 million years ago, when fishes had made good their claim to the sea and given rise to land-dwelling amphibians, Africa and Eur-America nosed together. The volcanic archipelago, or what remained of it, must have been rammed slowly into the mountainous coast of the Piedmont. Over a period of another hundred million years, until the end of the Paleozoic Era and the dawn of the Age of Reptiles—the Mesozoic—the two continents were progressively crushed together, the sea between them being squeezed out. Squashed, the rocks of the Piedmont and Blue Ridge were pushed upward and downward. More, an immense slice of the foundations of the range that had preceded the Appalachians was forced up to form the major part of today's Blue Ridge. The pressure also accordioned the sedimentary rocks of an ancient sea-bottom on the other side, from which the Great Smokies were to take shape. These rocks all came up in inland-listing folds which, as they grew more acute, tended to snap, undoubtedly to the accompaniment of shattering earthquakes, with the forward "limb" of the fold sliding forward many miles. It was a little like waves breaking, but over a period of millions of years. How older rock thus overrode younger may be seen at Cade's Cove in the Smokies. There the ancient rock of the range has worn through to expose limestone two-thirds its age. (Before being raised in mountains, the sedimentary rock of the Smokies was partially metamorphosed, the alteration being greatest where closest to the Blue Ridge.) To the east, along the Piedmont edge of the Blue Ridge, another "window" opened up, but one in which the order is reversed. There the overthrust rock parted as the 1,100-million-year-old rock of the continental basement was thrust up to form Grandfather Mountain.

The compression this time was farther reaching. The sedimentary rock-strata in the inland side of the trough were raised in great folds, like a carpet being pushed from the edge, also to snap in overthrust faults. While compression became less severe northward into Pennsylvania, southward of Roanoke the displacement inland of the rock-masses reached a total of a hundred miles. Where a particularly thick belt of limestone was turned up, its erosion was to leave the Great Valley. Beyond the Valley, the Long Ridge Mountains were to appear. Their ridges today do not, however, correspond to those of the original folds. They stand where they do because that is where the edge of an upturned layer of hard, resistant sandstone gives protection to weaker shales. (Continuing on U. S. 50 west of Winchester, you can see up on the ridges it crosses the massive, tough sandstone, very different in appearance from the easily fractured, crumbly shales in the highway cuts in the valleys.) We have to remember that superincumbent sedimentary rocks miles deep were to be worn away before the rocks we see in the Appalachians appeared.

What the range looked like at its highest we have, of course, no way of knowing. We may assume, however, that it conceded nothing to the Alps in stature. In length it was enormously their superior. "The dinosaurs," says Nigel Calder, "could have marched along that chain of mountains from Poland to Alabama, by way of Ireland and New York." The evidence of the rocks indicates that they could have marched all the way to western Texas. The conjunction of the continents did not, however, long survive its full consummation. Thereafter North America and its Old World partners began to pull apart and the gap to be filled by a sea destined to widen into the Atlantic Ocean.

The events of eternities ago may seem to have little bearing on the present-day Southern mountains. Yet you miss much about them, much that is momentous, if you are unaware of their great antecedents, from which their unbroken descent spans 250 million years. And you feel yourself enlarged, too, by the vistas of time they open up. These lead before us no less far than behind. Sediments shed by the Appalachians continue to accumulate on the continental shelf and slope. Eventually, if the past is a guide, our Atlantic coast must again become a zone of plate convergence. "There will be a new ocean trench in the east," Nigel Calder says, "with a 50 per cent chance of volcanoes in Charleston and New York City." Robert S. Dietz foresees a recurrence of the processes that created the Appalachians. Whatever the model, it seems predictable that the miles-deep sedimentary rocks along the coast, formed of Appalachian clays and sands, will be tempered under the high temperatures and pressures of the earth's depths, invaded by molten rock and raised in new mountains. With them, if Dietz is right, slices of the continental basement beneath them, created as the foundations of the Appalachians, will be thrust on high. There will be an Appalachian resurrection. Once more, many millions of years hence, when even the ravages of man's heavy hand on the earth will have been made good—though not perhaps altogether his eradication of many forms of life—rocks of the ancient range will pierce the realm of the year-around snow-clouds and, as D. H. Lawrence says of the Alps, stand white-fanged and tiger-like.

VI *Virginia's Greatest and the Complete Mountain*

"Big Balsam," the old man called it when I stopped to ask directions to Virginia's highest mountain. It was a dripping April evening, and in the end I contented myself with spending the night well up on the state's second highest, Whitetop, which has a road to its bare, 5,344-foot summit. That was some years ago, but the name the old mountaineer brought up from the past has stayed with me as far more appropriate to the 5,729-foot dome than that of the New Englander geologist William Barton Rogers, after whom it is officially called. Big Balsam and its neighbors not only mark the beginning, just inside Virginia, of the great North Carolina massif, they are also the chief features of the recently designated Mount Rogers National Recreation Area. Fifty-five miles long, half in the Jefferson National Forest, it is one of two such areas in the southern Appalachians. (The other, also incorporating the highest mountain in the state, is in the West Virginia Alleghenies.) Plans for the 240-square-mile area call for "recreational complexes" to handle 5,000,000 annual visitors within the next 25 years. Accordingly one is thankful indeed for the provision that the less accessible heights are to remain roadless. The plans also include a Scenic Highway to run the entire length of the narrow reservation from Damascus in the west along the crest of the Iron Range (north of Big Balsam) to its eastern border on the New River. But Congress has yet to appropriate funds for this uncalled-for work of destruction—enough mountain scenery is already visible from scenic highways in the East to sate the appetite of anyone content to see it from a motorcar—and the Iron Range may yet be saved. So, one hopes, may .the New River, threatened with drowning along with 43,000 acres of valuable and picturesque valley for a hydroelectric project of very doubtful defensibility.

The Forest Service maintains an exceptionally attractive campground in a woods predominantly of Beech at 3,700 feet on Big Balsam's northern slope. To cap its sylvan atmosphere when I arrived late in the afternoon, a trim, woodsy little girl in a short-skirted version of a Ranger's uniform was in charge of the information booth. She came, I learned, from a local mountain farm and was only seventeen. I questioned her about trails but was so taken by her pretty face with its large, wide-set eyes, her natural manner and her quaintly flat, rural-Virginia speech that I hardly took in what she said—to my later regret.

Big Balsam. . . . There is nothing like setting off up a mountain in the freshness of the new day and of one's morning vigor, full of curiosity about the personality of the great earth-being that is about to unfold before one. Leaning into the shoulder straps of one's pack like a rested horse against the traces, one even looks forward to being taxed: a good fatigue brings out the satisfactions one earns with it, as shading brings out highlights.

The trail to the summit from Grindstone Campground proved to afford as pleasant an ascent of 2,000 feet as I have met with. Commencing along a stream it plunges one immediately into a submarine half-light. Rosebay Rhododendron has an affinity for darkness. Even when growing in sunlight it suggests shadows and in the open, as along the Blue Ridge Parkway, seems to contract upon itself. It is never the profuse or colorful bloomer that its smaller cousin, Catawba, is. Its flowers are white or pink-tinged, though on inspection the throat of the uppermost petal may be seen to be spotted with chartreuse. Yet, taking light with luminous translucence from a beam of the sun against the dark and mossy background, it has a virginal glow that seems a specific against all darkness. It is a Persephone in the underworld, that Persephone at whose "footfall" Sappho heard "the flower spring." On July 21st it was just coming into bloom.

Where Rosebay is plentiful, look for Hemlocks. You find them here, and with them their other frequent companion, Mountain—otherwise Fraser—Magnolia. This is a tree with foot-long leaves growing in whorls and with "crooked wreathing branches arising and subdividing from the main stem without order or uniformity," as it was described by its discoverer, William Bartram, who named a summit in the Blue Ridge after it: Magnolia Mountain. The Magnolias are among the oldest flowering plants we know of; and, as if they still feel that flowers are an exciting novelty to be sported as prize accomplishments, they put out blooms up to eight or ten inches in diameter in the mountain species—twelve in one of them—far and away the largest of the forests'.

As the going steepened came tall, ample Basswoods of large, heart-shaped leaves, the American counterpart of the tree that is a Lime to the English, a Linden to the Germans. The fibers of the inner bark, called bast (hence basswood) supplied the Indians with rope, while the small but abundant blossoms of the genus are a source of a highly-regarded, light-colored honey. Bigger than the Basswoods and more copious producers of a fluid second to none in sweetness and flavor were the Sugar Maples. These are tapped for their sap by the hill people of Virginia and Maryland no less assiduously than by Vermonters, if less celebratedly. (The South has never enjoyed the North's public relations. Maple sugar from its mountain groves, to command premium prices, must be shipped to New England and retailed under Vermont labels.) Sugar, or Hard, Maple is one of the three trees that have most attracted furniture-makers to the Southern mountains. The other two are Black Walnut and Black Cherry. The former, always rather thinly distributed, has become so scarce that walnut-rustlers have appeared. Their forays are not confined to the back-country, either. A few years ago they made off with a prize specimen from a city park in Washington, D. C. The Black Cherry, although it grows throughout the East and down through the mountains of western Texas and southern Mexico to Peru, reaches its supreme development in the southern Appalachians. The magnificent stands that met the first settlers there have long since disappeared, of course, much of the reddish-brown, lustrous wood having gone into the paneling of Pullmans and trolley-cars.

With the Sugar Maples, largest of the tribe, was one of the smallest, albeit the one with the largest leaves of all. Striped Maple is a little tree with cool, lime-green, palely-lined branches relished by beavers and hoofed animals; hence the name Moosewood in the North. While Beeches held their own, a northern tree supreme in another tribe was becoming increasingly prevalent: Yellow Birch, of wood that has held strong in many a wheel-hub, sat light on many a yoked ox, and given much cabinetry the look of satin. . . . I had read enough of the literature now to know that I had been seeing Cove Forest grading into Northern Deciduous.

Overall was the ancient Appalachian silence. The only sounds were the absent-minded singing of a Red-eyed Vireo and from afar the clamorous, raucous calls of young crows which rose to turkey gobbling when food was administered. As long as I live, I suppose I shall exclaim over the rapidity with which one leaves the world behind in the range of shadow. In a telephone conversation with my wilting wife, I had learned that the lowlands were sweltering in the worst heat wave in several years; but the cloisters of the high woods were cool and grey. One was almost surprised to see a bumblebee lurching about on its rounds.

Black and yellow, fat and hairy, bumblebees are found pursuing their independent ways all through the mountains once summer has come. Though they are said to form colonies of up to two hundred, they must scatter widely, one so often sees them singly. Honeybee colonies may be a hundred times the size, or more. It is odd about the smaller, tawny honeybees. They are part of traditional America. The drone of the swarms in the Tupelos, Hollies, Sourwoods and Basswoods, always mysterious and seemingly distant in origin for the first moment, is a sound of school's end and of timeless early summer for that fortunate number with whom it is a childhood association. Bruin up a tree raiding a beehive and licking the

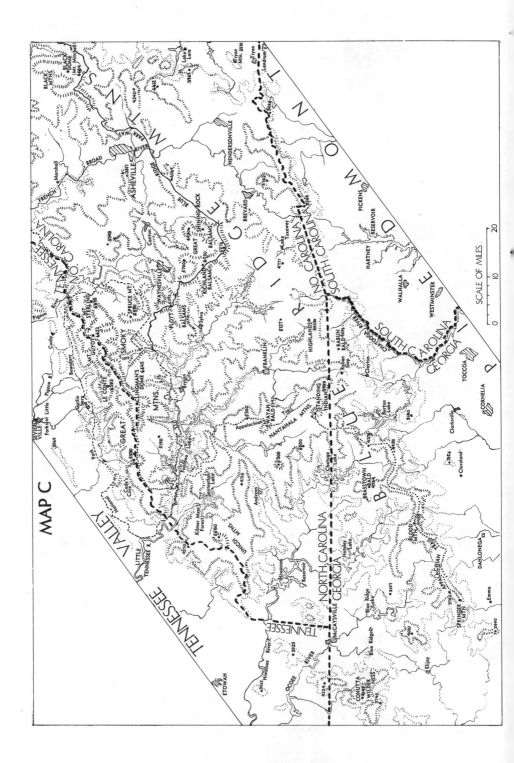

MAP C

SCALE OF MILES

0   10   20

honey from its paw is a staple of the popular lore of wild country. Other than molasses, honey was the only sweetener known to many a Southern mountain family of the past, and the discovery of a bee-tree an important part of the round of events. Two or three bee-gums were the rule in the yards of mountain cabins. (The Black Tupelo, or Black or Sour Gum, is subject to heart rot in maturity, and hollow sections of the trunks of gums made natural hives.) Yet honeybees are aliens. It is true, though—we have Thomas Jefferson's word for it—that they "generally extended themselves into the country, a little in advance of the white settlers." The native collector of nectar and pollen, the bumblebee, makes its obscure nest in burrows, where apparently too little honey is accumulated to excite men or bears. I must say I find its industry puzzling and disturbing, coming as it always does to naught. Every autumn workers and drones die off and the abandoned nest is scavenged by moths and beetles. Only the mated queens survive by hibernating. Rearing eight or ten new workers in May, they start the whole doomed process over again.

The bumblebee that set off this train of thought was collecting from a plant with an umbel of white florets borne on a foot-high stalk. Wild leeks were then in bloom in sprinklings throughout the mountains. They will grow under the heaviest deciduous cover, for they get their work done before it closes over in spring. Their long, lanceolate leaves emerge from the bulb with the first warm sun and start to brown off when the stalk bearing the flower bud reaches its full height, standing like a slim maroon spear. To the mountain people the crisp, fresh vegetable tissues of the bulb, coming after a winter-long starchy diet, were part of returning life, like the freshets from melting snow. I find a leek quite good eating. Vera says that the flavor is like that of a shallot but, as she points out, the aftertaste is more like garlic. Even today in some localities an event is made of spring forays for "ramps," as they are called, and festivals are held at which quantities are consumed raw and cooked. Maurice Brooks is authority for the story that a mountain weekly, to evoke nostalgia among its errant subscribers, had ramp oil mixed with the printer's ink before a run—effectively, but without arousing demands for a repetition. The leek flower, standing all by itself, is refined and chaste, a diadem in ivory, a tiny inverted chandelier in the shadows.

After an hour and forty minutes I reached the top of the ridge, though I was still less than half way to the summit. The woods here were park-like, with big trees, many of them oaks, and more than a few blown down. A deer a hundred feet away, which turned and fled on finding its stare returned, was much in keeping.

Nothing impressed me more up here than the tenacious hold on life of the Yellow Birches. The quality is the more surprising in a tree that, in its youth when its bark is like silver leaf tinted with gold, is something of a

A Yellow birch—which grew over a boulder—which subsequently slid down hill.

dandy. It has the singular capacity to begin life on top of a boulder, extending its roots under the mosses, which store moisture, or down fissures, which do likewise, and so finally making contact with the earth. Up on damp mountains like Big Balsam it is possible to find Yellow Birch saplings several feet high still growing clear of the ground. Under one mature tree up here the boulder on which it had grown had slipped a few feet down hill, leaving its tenant high up on spread legs. The remains of another, a giant, encompassed a boulder with an almost solid spread of roots 12 feet wide. Only hammer blows of fate could have done it in, I am convinced, for the species is unyielding to ordinary adversity. One patriarch just below the ridge crest had a largely rotted trunk, its bark like old shingles, ten feet eight inches in girth and broken off 30 feet up. It ought to have been dead, but it was beginning life anew with a trunk-like limb from near the top of the stub, shiny as platinum.

Beyond the park-like shoulder of the mountain, the trail followed the ridge at some distance below the crest. From here on rocks broke massively through the soil, one outcropping standing 40 feet high above trail. All bore spongy green mats of vegetation. Where, in the arid desert, it is moisture plants struggle for, having all the space they want, here where moisture was plentiful it was space that was at a premium. The woods were a greenhouse, especially after the spruce forest had begun, two hours from the campground. Decaying logs were living bolsters and the most exposed rocks were colonized by mosses and lichens. One of the most conspicuous of the latter is Rock-tripe, which freckles big boulders in leathery flakes up to three or four inches long. A dull green after a rain, they appear dead when dry, curling away from their anchorage to display a charred-looking undersurface. (All the same, *tripe de roche,* boiled, has seen many a trapper and Indian through lean times in the Far North.) The generous rainfall favored more luxuriant vegetation, however. Deep-pile mosses covered most of the rocks and with them what a crop of other plants!—Clintonia Lilies; tough little evergreen Rockcap, or Polypody, Fern; Shining Club-moss like forests of three-inch-high Suguaros bristling with tiny pointed green leaves; Skunk Currant, which sends up foot-high branchlets from recumbent stems and when crushed (any part will do) smells identically, uncannily like its namesake.

The shadows were brightened by that ground-cover so much at home on Appalachian heights, even in the acid soil under conifers that few other flowering plants can tolerate: creeping Mountain Wood-sorrel. Still bearing a few delicately-complexioned blooms, it carpeted the earth for the last half mile and on over the top of the mountain. This, apart from a few Mountain-ashes, was forested in Southern Balsams with a sprinkling of Red Spruce. I did not know it at the time, but this is the last sizable island of Southern Balsam not yet infected by the Woolly Aphid. An almost microscopic but prolific parasite—one pair can produce three million offspring in a single season—*Adelges piceae* entered New England from Europe, apparently on nursery stock, around the turn of the century. First discovered in the southern Appalachians on the Black Dome in 1957, it had killed 275,000 Balsams in the Black Mountains within eight years. Balsam Fir forests in New England and Canada have been hard hit and hundreds of thousands of acres of fir forests in the Pacific Northwest ravaged. The aphid has natural enemies—mites and a fungus—but so far nothing has checked its depredations. While the Southern Balsam can be preserved from extinction with seed from a few expensively-sprayed groves, the natural stands of the species throughout the southern Appalachians are threatened with destruction. So we are seeing the fruits of another of our bungling interventions, comparable to our introduction of the Chestnut blight.

Unaware then of the magnitude of the disaster that impends, I drank in the sweet fragrance of the Balsams where the sun struck them beside a clearing where I had lunch. At my elbow was a Southern Mountain Cranberry, a shrub several feet high but with the same flowers as the little creeping Cranberry of Northern bogs and turkey dinners, the petals curving back from the cone of anthers to form a half-inch, down-dropping pink rocket-head. A tiny Winter Wren paid me a visit, as near a little round puffball of a bird as there is. It could not remain still and, when not hopping or flitting about, bobbed up and down in a calisthenic way peculiar to it. After the four-hour climb, my pack off, I let my shoulders sag and savored the sense of my fatigue seeping out of me into the ground. I was very much at peace. The mind is too much of a goad, I thought, a fomenter of unrest and anxiety. Yet it can be appeased and quieted. It can be separated from the clamor of human excitations and taken tramping where the only communications are from nature, in the accents of an illimitable vision and patience. Physical exertion is good; a million years of human evolution in wilderness attuned our constitutions to taxing demands on them, and no reign of machinery a few generations in duration is going to transform the body's needs. But what also makes for the stabilizing and tranquilizing influence of the wilds, I reflected, is the dignity of nature. A quality easier to recognize than to define, it gives wilderness part of the attraction it has for us, I think. Those who live close to nature, while lacking so much else, tend to share it. The rest of us regain a sense of dignity in ourselves as we return to nature; five minutes in the woods in solitude will make a difference. Nature, though it abounds in beauty, is not invariably beautiful; and God knows it holds the lives of its progeny cheap. But mean, squalid, meretricious, unworthy in motive—those things it is not. It seemed to me in those mountains that dignity was epitomized in its remote but pervasive presence.

The Appalachian Trail, having been dispossessed of its route along the crest of the Iron Mountains by the projected Scenic Highway, had just been relocated over Whitetop and Big Balsam. About two miles back it had joined the trail up from the campground. I meant to follow it northeastward for the rest of the day. It appeared, however, to go no farther than the rounded outcropping of rock constituting the mountain's absolute top. A covered coffee-can here contained messages written by members of the local Appalachian Trail Club relating to the clearing and blazing of the new trail. But of the trail beyond the summit I could find no sign. Since I saw nothing to be gained by proceeding over a trackless and unknown terrain without a compass, I turned back down the mountain, very much put out.

And lo! On my reaching the junction with the Appalachian Trail there suddenly appeared coming up it the pretty Rangerette from the information booth guiding a party of four adults. They had driven to the pass between Whitetop and Big Balsam and were hiking to the campground. It is surprising how odd the unexpected appearance of human beings is after only five hours alone in the woods—a little like coming on a bear. But if odd, the encounter was the saving of my expedition. The Appalachian Trail at the top of the mountain, said the little girl, curled around the outcropping, out of sight, and dropped directly downhill.

So back I went, and it was as she had said.

Swinging off down the gradual decline, I found myself for the next four miles in a totally different, largely open landscape. Spruce, Balsam and Mountain-ash formed scattered groves and blackberry extensive stands along with other brush-growth, including Southern Mountain Cranberries, but much of the mountain was in rank grasses, among which Bluets of an intense shade were still in bloom beside large-flowered Star Chickweed. Most strikingly, off to the south, were mountains unlike any I had ever seen in the East. Treeless, their broad heights dominated by huge outcroppings of worn rock, they called pictures of Wyoming to mind. Rawboned and formidable they looked. A scattering of bleached, fallen tree-trunks told their story of logging and fire. In addition to these gaunt highlands, much of the adjacent heights in the Recreation Area, including the slope of Big Balsam I was on, had been deforested, too, and are now in pasture for the benefit of private herds of cattle and sheep.

This brought to my mind a question I was unprepared to answer and decided I must leave to the Party theoreticians of conservation: to what extent is man to be considered a legitimate part of nature, like, say, the beaver, whose industry deforests valleys but also creates ponds eagerly adopted by other aquatic life? Should we wish to see all North America east of the prairies restored, insofar as possible, to the forest? My fellow hikers in the mountains, I have found, especially esteem those stretches that are open where the vision, unconfined, can sweep the dome of the sky and the far ranges. In my own case, I have analyzed the urge I habitually feel on the trail, even when tired out, to keep going—to round the next bend or top the next rise—and have detected behind it an instinct to reach an opening, where I can see around me. Yet a deforested Appalachia would be a bleak horror. As for the mountains on my right as I tramped the long eastward-, then northward-leading spur of Big Balsam, they were grand and exhilarating in their lofty spaciousness and suitability for Golden Eagles. They were also more than a little appalling in their unnatural, brutal nakedness.

In time I had ahead of me similar enormous warts of rock forming the bare backbone of the ridge I was following. Parts of the slopes below were occupied by sheered, shoulder-high thickets of Catawba Rhododendron I could hardly have forced a way through to save my life. This was a point that occurred to me because the trail disappeared again—really disappeared this time. It had been scarcely a trail in any case—there had been no time for a path to be beaten—only a succession of white blazes on rocks. These having ceased, I was left wandering about among the thickets trying to find a way through in the direction in which I had been going. At length I came to a stile over a barbed-wire fence I had been following, and there was a little white blaze again, and very welcome.

For some time I had been progressing toward an emanation of sullen clouds from which ruminative mumblings sounded. As the vaporous greyness spread, these protestations grew louder and more insistent. Soon the heavens were reverberating to detonations that seemed to ricochet from one horizon to the other. Odin was venting his mighty anger and the troop of his Valkyries careening across the sky. With the ridge like a stage mounting to the grey, rocky parapets ahead, lightning flickering in the congested heavens and the kettledrums rolling in stupendous peals, one was, at least, put powerfully in mind of Wagnerian opera. More germane, however, was the narrowing of the interval between the flash and detonation to eight seconds: the lightning was already striking only about a mile and a half away. These electrical discharges, which shiver tree-trunks by exploding the sap in them, converting it instantly to steam, have my respect. They disincline me, anyhow, to make myself the most prominent object on a ridge line while they are going on. So, overtaken by the rain where the trail traversed a birch woods, I took off my pack, donned my waterproof suit and sat down in the shelter of the trees—as I trusted it was—to let the shower pelt down and the salvos resound overhead.

The rain slowly petered out and the sky cleared.

With forethought, I could have strung out my nylon tarpaulin and have collected rain enough to fill my canteen. That would have enabled me to spend the night on the prairie-like summit of Pine Mountain, at just under 5,000 feet, as I should have liked to. But, despairing of water at that elevation, I set off for the Appalachian Trail shelter 2,000 feet below and several miles farther on. This I reached just before six after a light-hearted descent through a forest sparkling in its wetness from the rays of the sinking sun. The joyful refulgence of a countryside on which the sun shines after a rain is like the unexpected receipt of good news.

Old Orchard Shelter, an openfaced cabin set beside a meadow, already had a tenant, a bearded young medical student whose gear included two tomes he was lugging into the mountains to study. Later a young couple appeared, devotees of the outdoors from farther up the state who had been backpacking in Yellowstone Park the year before but somewhat put off by dysentery and Grizzly Bears.... The longer one goes without seeing others of one's species, the more congenial a meeting is apt to be. Or is if there is as much to talk about as backpackers habitually have.

What makes backpackers, and increasing numbers of them? The cause should reveal something about wilderness, that it should have such an attraction for so many of us, whose customary lives have become so estranged from it. Of course many answers can be and have been given. For one, as many of the children of the generation now in power have, I think, come to recognize, technological civilization, with all it has done to enrich our lives materially and make them healthier and longer, is in the end death-dealing. This is not so much a matter of its depleting and poisoning the earth and the waters and threatening its own extinction by its improved instruments of massacre. That is the Mr. Hyde of technology, whose horrid works we have the possibility of ameliorating; but it is the Dr. Jekyll, of which Mr. Hyde is symbolic, who is extinguishing life for us at its source, by kindness and beneficence. The pulse of life is the response within us to challenge. The life force we contain gains in strength as it rises in us to meet cold and rain and all inclemency, miles to be covered, burdens to be shouldered and the myriad natural demands on our energies and endurance to be proved equal to. We live to the extent that life is adventure, which is to say as it is unrehearsed, unexpected and chancey and requires of us the full range of our powers.

From all that, good, solicitous Dr. Jekyll is saving us. If technology has its way, what lies ahead for us is return to the womb. Perfect security, an insulated and regulated environment of optimum conditions, the anticipation and satisfaction of all our physical wants without bodily exertion on our part: that is the goal. All that will be demanded of us is the intense employment of our wits and brains in highly specialized capacities, if we are to get ahead individually and civilization's ever more complicated instrumentalities are to function. The danger is not that the machine will come to do our thinking for us. It is that it will do everything else—that it will do our living for us.

With sunset, seduced by the softness of the meadow grass, I laid my sleeping-bag out under the sky instead of under trees. The results were predictable. Where the air is moist and the nightly drop in temperature one of 20 or 25 degrees, condensation is terrific: I was soaked with dew.

It was a misty morning. When, having walked the three or four miles back to the campground by road, I set off by car to the southwest, the mountain I had climbed the day before and its imposing neighbor stood as enormous tarnished-silver silhouettes against the brighter silver of the southern sky. The route to Roan Mountain, for which I was headed, lay first to Damascus on U. S. Highway 58 down the twisting, richly forested gorge of Laurel Creek, which no one traveling in the vicinity should miss; "laurel" is the mountain term for rhododendron, and rhododendron darkened the banks of the stream for miles. ("Ivy" is the mountain term for laurel.) From Damascus the route followed a valley of mostly open fields with the long range of the Iron Mountains on the west, Forge Mountain and the Doe Mountains on the east—territorial sovereigns of unknown purport for which I felt lacking in respect to pass unvisited, a truant

On the northern side of Roan Mountain, the coniferous forest is compressed against the slope of the summit.

pilgrim. Beyond the end of Watauga Lake it turned east for the town of Roan Mountain.

I had made the Roan my next objective for two reasons. The cluster of mountains it tops is the highest formation between Big Balsam and the Black Mountains and Smokies, more than halfway to Georgia. (It is also the only one in all that distance higher than Big Balsam except Grandfather, which rises due east of Roan.) Further, of all the Southern mountains, Roan is probably held in the highest regard by the greatest number. The most famous of American botanists, Asa Gray, returning in 1884, 43 years after his first visit, called it "our favorite Roan Mountain, on the borders of North Carolina and Tennessee, one of the highest in the Atlantic United States, and the finest, the base and sides richly wooded with large deciduous forest trees in unusual variety even for this country, the ample grassy top (of several square miles) fringed with dark firs and spruces." Gray also wrote of the "thousands of clumps of Rhododendron

Catawbiense" that "adorned" the "open part"; and it was probably the mottled pink effect of these at a distance in early summer that suggested the mountain's name. Subsequently uprooted wholesale for nursery stock, the Rhododendron has recovered as has the forest, of which the mountain was also stripped. The 1920's were the last decade of the Cloudland Hotel's existence, for reasons I have been unable to ascertain, and upon its failure scavengers removed it fixture by fixture and plank by plank; four or five houses down the mountain are said to be built of it. Roan is probably less marred by civilization today than at any time since the 1870's. Cars may be driven up it, however, and a great many are.

The road up from the town of Roan Mountain, Tennessee, climbs 3,300 feet in the last 10 miles and must be one of the East's major motor grades. In my little camping bus I was in second speed most of the way, through curve after curve. In the still murky atmosphere, the temperature dropping steadily, the mountains of the group were little more than spectral bodies appearing through breaks in the forest, but with each shoulder surmounted they seemed to gain in altitude. At Carver's Gap the road passes over a mile-high saddle of the main ridge to descend to Bakersville, North Carolina, through a grade equaling that on the Tennessee side. From the gap a spur leads nearly to the Roan High Knob, which, at 6,286 feet, is virtually identical in elevation to Mount Washington.

What is special about the Roan is that its heights have everything a southern Appalachian summit very well could have. Verdant forests, deciduous and coniferous; bits of meadow; the famous stands of Rhododendron; a nearly sheer face topped by bare rocks—it is all there and, augmenting the sense of having left the earth below, and its claims on one, as at a way-station to immortality, the sweep of the giant balds sharing the ridge on the east and included by Gray in the "several square miles" of "grassy top."

The Catawba's flowering in June brings visitors to the mountain by the hundreds. On July 22nd, however, only a few browning clusters were still hanging on, marking the absolute end of the species' blooming season, which had begun on Lookout Mountain in Alabama three months before. The day being Saturday, there were still plenty of people; but Americans in the mass do not stray far from their motorcars. The Appalachian Trail, following the crest at a little distance from the road and picnic areas, could have been an aisle in the remote North Woods. I thought as I walked it and continued on up to the High Knob that these summits—summits that reach up into the zone of continual cool summer rains and cloud spume that go with the sub-zero winters—convey an impression that an inversion had taken place and what had been green-shadowy gorge, ferny in the spray of cascading waters, had become lofty peak. The closed-in forest of Spruce and Balsam clothing the High Knob, above, in places a veritable turf of

Balsam seedlings, looked as if it had been steeped two feet deep in a soup of algae and mosses which, in draining away, had left tree-trunks, rocks and earth stained or furred in brilliant green. On the precipitous northwestern side, however, the forest was diminished to a pelage of stunted conifers with tattered and abbreviated branches extended behind them, like feathers on a war-bonnet, and almost touching the nearly vertical mountainside. After my visit—my first visit, I should say—the United States Forest Service built a big, circular, railed wooden platform on the rock ledge from which one looked upon this mountain wall, on which winter's fierce assaults are pitted against the dogged trees' will to live. Thus for no other reason than to satisfy a bureaucracy's hankering to improve on nature, a battleground of primal forces, stirring to the imagination, has been subordinated to a meaningless convenience and reduced to the level of an officially approved view.

I was to be back on the Roan early in March, and, apart from the intrusion of that platform (which perhaps something will destroy in time) found the mountain more in character, entirely deserted. It had been an eerie drive up with the forest in cold shadow, the clouds down low and white statuary of ice affixed to the black rocks by the road. Though the High Knob was almost as green as in summer, apart from remnants of snow-drifts, cloud vapors like cold steam drifted up the northwestern face and through the Balsam forest, expunging it in the space of a hundred feet. I recalled how Edward B. Garvey, who in 1970 became the thirty-second person to hike the full length of the Appalachian Trail in a single season and the first of them to write a book about it, found a patch of snow on the way down from the crest of Roan on May 1st.

In July, flowers everywhere caught one's attention, even where none might be expected. The deep woods produced a dark-pink sport of the Mountain Wood-sorrel. Abounding on the rocks, springing from cracks even on the steepest, was a plant of delicate stems and foliage and tiny white flowers of five petals that made me think of little figures of Dutchmen. A plant I was to find growing where nothing else could down into Georgia, it was Michaux's Saxifrage, an endemic of the southern Appalachians. This I learned from a tall, grey-haired, studious-looking man I saw bent over a plant with buttercup-like flowers on tall stems above crinkly leaves which had especially puzzled me. Since he was examining it with a hand lens, I made bold to ask him if he knew what it was. "A *Geum*, clearly," he replied. "Let's go back to the car and look it up." On the way I sought to exchange views of various popular flower-guides, forcing him finally to confess that he operated "on a somewhat different level"—at which I thought his wife smiled a little. I could see he did from the volume he consulted—*Manual of the Vascular Plants of the Northeastern United States and Canada*. Gradually, somewhat red-faced, I came to comprehend

Part of the 700,000-acre Chattahoochee National Forest of northern Georgia.

The widely-distributed forest onion, the Wild leek or Ramp, was eagerly consumed by mountaineers long ago when the leaves first appeared in the spring and is still celebrated in festivals. The leaves disappear before the flower stalk grows. *Below,* a Mountain-ash on the summit of Stonyman in the Virginia Blue Ridge.

that my acquaintance, Arthur Cronquist, was co-author of the *Manual,* Director of Botany at the New York Botanical Garden and one of the world's foremost plant taxonomists.

The *Geum* was *G. radiatum,* a southern Appalachians version of the Mountain Avens of alpine summits in New Hampshire and Maine. Dr. Cronquist, taking a busman's holiday with his wife in a well-traveled station-wagon, had been looking forward to an exploration of the Roan, which, among its other distinctions, has had a special prominence in botany ever since Gray's first visit in 1841. He said that *Senecio robbinsii,* for instance, grew on Roan and was not known to do so elsewhere within 500 miles, being at home in New England and the Adirondacks; "Robbins's Butterwort, or Ragwort, you could call it." But there was some doubt, he went on, as to whether Roan was uncommonly favored botanically or just by botanists.

The grassy, shrubby balds to the east of Roan proper raised the question of why there should be these treeless heights in the southern Appalachians, which fail by thousands of feet to reach a climatic timberline. The factors of fire and grazing are conventionally cited. Dr. Cronquist speculated on the possibility of another. It had to do with post-glacial warming periods, when mean temperatures were higher than today. At such times the base-level of the spruce-balsam forest—the minimum elevation at which it could hold its own—would have risen. On mountains below a certain height, it would have risen right off the top of them. With the return of a colder climate, this northern forest, where it had been able to hold out on the high summits, would have descended to recoup its losses. But where it had been lifted altogether off the mountain it could not. At the same time the deciduous forest found those heights insalubrious, and that permitted a tough shrubby or grassy growth resistant to invasion by the conifers to establish itself on them. The principle quite evidently operated in the case of northern mammals on the same mountains, for example the Water Shrew, Northern Flying Squirrel and Rock Vole; these, says Charles O. Handley, Jr., of the Smithsonian Institution, are found today as low as 4,000 feet on the very high mountains, but not in similar habitats of the same elevation on lower mountains. It has this also in its support, that the grass balds are all high but not the highest of the southern Appalachians.

I set out in the morning and hiked over the balds we had been discussing. The sky was blue overhead but the surrounding mountains faded into haze, the more distant little more than planes of mist. The northeast wind was live and free, the air pure and fresh as only the mariner and mountaineer know it. Tremendously exhilarated, I followed the Appalachian Trail over the humps of the great ridge, rounded as a big beast's back and with a close and shaggy coat like a beast's. Round Bald, the first, was mostly in grass and herbaceous plants. Bluets held their faces up to the sky they emulated—

Houstonia serpyllofolia, according to Dr. Cronquist, a little larger and darker than the common species—and with them was an appealing little plant with flat, round flowers of five white petals on wiry stems trembling in the breeze. This was Three-toothed Cinquefoil. Its appeal is perhaps chiefly in the idea of it—a little rock-lover that spreads its three glossy leaves in a double V-sign from Labrador down the rocky coast of New England and southward in the Appalachians from one wind-swept summit to the next. But that is not all. A local bird-watcher, Fred W. Behrend, discovered, astonishingly, that Snow Buntings, those sturdy, white-and-sandy-colored Finches that winter brings to our northern frontier and down the northeast coast, are regular winter visitors to the Roan ridge balds. And Maurice Brooks, obtaining from Behrend specimens of plants the Buntings depended on for food, was able to write that "I had one of the high moments of my nature experience. The first plant I looked at was a three-toothed cinquefoil"—the Snow Buntings' associate of rocky headlands in the northern seas. I nursed a faint hope of seeing one on my March visit, but though I walked over the balds I met with no birds but two Song Sparrows and a few pairs of Juncos. These latter—little grey and white sparrows that might be called *the* birds of the southern Appalachians—are not to be deprecated, however. Though the side of my face was numbed by the spicules of a drizzle, and the cloud battened down on the sere and lonely summits, I was cheered on my way in several places by the jingling of a Junco singing from the top of a low, bare tree.

From Jane Bald the ridge rose to Grassy Ridge Bald—"my last 6,000-footer," Garvey wrote, "until Mount Washington in New Hampshire." With them came acres-wide hammocks of Alder of purple or magenta twigs and leaves incised by veins and of a vigorous green: Mountain Alder. It seemed to grow by putting out one stem after another from the crown, each appearing to reach an invisible barrier at about shoulder-height, whereupon the plant would try again with another stem. On Round Bald, a few Serviceberries, ordinarily a small tree, grew in the same way, trying with one little trunk, then another, to break through that ceiling. Spruces, especially on Big Yellow Mountain, stood in mature ranks down the slope, as if seeking to gain the top, but they hardly appeared to be making rapid progress, if any. They did have a few outposts in the van of the main body, and so did the deciduous forest, but some of these had been stricken and died. One would almost have thought some supernatural barriers were in effect. Yet grass thrived, and so did Blackberries—the thornless Mountain or Canada Blackberry (as I believe it is) that grows all through the southern Appalachians, up to their highest tops where there is a break in the forest. Its canes, forming thickets, stood erect or gently arched, the deep red of a Winesap apple. And certainly the Alder luxuriated—up to that mysterious point.

The Alder had almost closed in on a side trail to Big Yellow, the highest of all the balds at nearly 6,200 feet. I had to fight a way through it and, worse still, through long stretches of Catawba Rhododendron, which reached out with its stiff, scraggly branches, as with so many grasping hands, to yank me back by my pack-frame. For the rest it was a morning of sheer glory up on those mountains, which, soaring in their expansive amplitude, made one think of them as mirror images of clouds. I made myself some coffee among the rocks breaking through on a grassy height and watched a fellow backpacker on the Appalachian Trail, with whom I had been talking a quarter of an hour before, reduced to a fleck of vermillion in a deep saddle between the balds; like others among the few solitary hikers I met he said he was walking alone for a chance to think. His pack was the only spark of vivid color in that misty morning panorama of pale blue space and softened greens of the billowing earth-waves, apart from specks of a subdued and darker red nearer by where a stalk of Bell Lilies grew.

From Grassy Ridge Bald the trail swung around to the side of the northward trending ridge. After a number of extremely boggy parts it reached one of the shelters, this one uninviting on a dank, bare slope with much half-burned trash in an open firepit. A party of twenty-(more or less)-year-olds was in occupation. I could have envied them their youth but was reminded of what the actuality was like by the sad sight of one of their number: a girl, sitting oblivious by the trail with her head in her arms, evidently in difficulties with a young man—an unshaved ballet dancer in appearance—reposing coolly nearby. Then shortly I came to a nook in the woods in which a most agreeably civilized-looking middle-aged couple was enjoying a refreshment break on a Sunday hike; and their air of relaxed and interested accommodation to life made me think that there is much to be said for the finished product as against the raw material, and I might better aspire to the condition of the one than regret that of the latter.

There was no one else all that day until, on my return, I was to meet the group from the shelter, on the way, they said, to U.S. 19—the girl with the ballet dancer, at the end of the line, still looking unhappy. The trail went down, down, down—all, I reflected, to seem three times as far up later—through Yellow Birch woods liberally grown up in Wood Nettles two to five feet high varied with patches of Jewelweed hung with orange cornucopias. Shortly after it had turned up again through a partly over-grown cow pasture which I took to be Yellow Mountain Gap, I made an end. For lunch I picked a big rock on which I could put my wet shoes and socks in the sun while I aired my feet. Not to my surprise, blisters were revealed on each. However, I had gauze and adhesive tape. And with my back to the rock, consuming my sandwich (cheese in English muffin) and Fig Newtons with a cup of milk (water from a spring by the shelter and

An Appalachian Trail marker on Round Top, Roan Mountain, in cold cloud.

skimmed-milk powder), I savored the pure pleasure of it. Deep yellow Cone-flowers and crimson Oswego Tea bloomed along the fence line and a Junco, a Towhee and an Indigo Bunting sang. With a day of exertion under the sky, away from the obligations of civilized man, you make yourself accessible to nature's gift of the completeness and sufficiency of the present.

It was indeed a long climb back up. And coming out of the woods into the open even at 5,500 feet the still air was sultry and heavy with the scent of blackberry canes. Thunder was sounding as it had ever since Yellow Mountain Gap, as if portions of the distant heavens were crumbling. The sky was steamy. . . . But then there came a current of air, as there will in the mountains, as cool as spring water.

On Grassy Ridge Bald, the sight of the Appalachian Trail ascending the other two balds on the way to Roan made me think that nowhere else in the southern Appalachians could so much of it be seen at once—in few other places more than two or three hundred feet of it. The vista, coming near the end of a day on the great footpath, made me stop and think what an amazing thing it is that such a trail could have come into being, that Benton MacKaye could ever have thought it might.

"It was a clear day, with a brisk breeze blowing," MacKaye recalls. "North and south, sharp peaks etched the horizon. I felt as if atop the world, with a sort of planetary feeling. I seemed to perceive peaks far southward, hidden by old Earth's curvature. Would a footpath some day reach them from where I was then perched?"

A landscape architect and forester now 95 years old, MacKaye says it was on that day on Mount Stratton in Vermont or even earlier that the idea of the Appalachian Trail first came to him. "But," he adds, "it wasn't until 1921 that the idea had crystallized. On Sunday, July 10, at Hudson Guild Farm in New Jersey, I sat down with Charles H. Whitaker, editor of the *Journal* of the American Institute of Architects, and Clarence S. Stein, chairman of the AIA's Committee on Community Planning. I explained my idea for a trail that would run in a wilderness belt from one of the highest mountains in New England to one of the highest in the South. Both friends encouraged me to write an article setting forth the idea. I did, and in October 1921 the *Journal* of the AIA published 'An Appalachian Trail, A Project in Regional Planning.' "

The proposal met with immediate and wide interest. Far-reaching cooperation was required to carry it out and was forthcoming, from private individuals and organizations and from federal and state agencies. Within two years the first section, through Palisades State Park in New York, was completed. By 1926 other sections had been put through in Massachusetts, Pennsylvania and northern Virginia. The most difficult proved to be the final 280 miles through the Maine woods to Mount Katahdin, but with the help of the Civilian Conservation Corps this was completed in 1937. The Georgia-to-Maine "Footpath for those who seek Fellowship with the Wilderness," as the bronze plaque at the trail's start on Springer Mountain has it, was a reality. The trail today is 2,031 miles long, going through parts of 14 states, two National Parks, and eight National Forests. Thirty-four local clubs maintain the trail and the 238 overnight shelters for hikers. These clubs are banded together in the Appalachian Trail Conference, which met first in 1925. Benton MacKaye states that "The creation of the ATC was one of two pivotal events in the history of the trail; the other was the signing of the National Trails System Act in 1968." Under this act, federal protection for the trail was provided. It came none too soon, for house-builders were impinging on the trail—600 miles of which is still on privately-owned land—and in places forcing its relocation. It can only be hoped that the legislation is sufficient safeguard.

That evening on the Roan I met two boys—brothers—who had started hiking the trail at Springer 32 days before. Their intention was to go on to

Damascus at the Virginia line and there take the bus back to their home in Cambridge, Massachusetts. They had already in previous summers, it seemed, covered most of the trail in the North. Having a quiet supper at a picnic table, they were matter-of-fact and unassuming about their undertaking. That of course only increased the admiration with which I regarded their having chosen an arduous 420-mile march through mountain solitudes—brothers who were also companions—among all the effortless diversions that pull their contemporaries in by the herds. I trusted that the gods, in the stern balance-sheets they maintain for the world's peoples, would take note of such as they—to whom the next day I added a band of eight shaggy, mostly bare-chested young men I met on the Roan's northern slope.

In contrast to the evening before, there were few others on the mountain by then. I was parked for the night near the little lavatory building by a small meadow. Here, twenty-fours hours earlier I had somehow fallen into conversation with a large-bellied man in a T-shirt, having supper at a picnic table with his wife and children. He had rather surprised me by expatiating on the beauties of a waterfall at the foot of the mountain and urging that I stop at the nearby gas-station he operated and let him direct me to it. But what most took my interest was the information that his grandfather had worked on the building of the Cloudland Hotel. In a recital buttressed by details of construction practices beyond my grasp he told me how his forebear had been careful in carrying on his job never to have his back to a fellow worker who had threatened to kill him. It was less of a threat, however, than a simple statement of fact. Inasmuch as this menacing figure had already done in seven or eight others it was to be taken seriously, too. As I recall, the grandfather had finally felt it necessary to leave the area. I know that—the straight man—I asked if he could not have got the police onto the killer. Replied the narrator, "There wasn't enough law around here in those days to do any good."

I had not known it, but the hotel had stood not thirty feet from my bus. All that marked its foundations were two lines of irregularly-shaped rocks standing no higher than the grass, at right angles to each other. In the woods below, however, was a chimney of rocks with a fireplace marking the remains of a house, perhaps one where the teamsters had put up. It seemed extraordinary that so capacious a theatre of so much volatile, complicated and intense human life and interrelationships over half a century could disappear with so little trace remaining. No wonder mankind has so generally convinced itself of the existence of ghosts. To a reasonable mind they are virtually a necessity. But ghosts or no ghosts, while my taste for nature finds much greater satisfaction in a wild mountain than in one appropriated for present human activity, I am most stirred of all by one with the remains of man's erstwhile tenancy crumbling upon it.

I was curious to see the Appalachian Trail up the Roan faced by hikers from the south (who actually approach the mountain from the north), for from Hughes's Gap the ascent is one of 2,250 feet in a mere 2.4 miles. That must make it one of the most taxing stretches from Springer to Katahdin. After having gone most of the way down and climbed back up, I was ready to believe it *the* most. The ridge it follows, as it mounts toward the top through a forest of Yellow Birch, Beech and scattered big Sugar Maples, is of knife-edged outcroppings of rock. Higher, just under the summit in the damp, soundless twilight of the mountain's Spruce-Balsam mantle, it approaches the angle of a ladder in spots and you clutch whatever you can to help yourself up. I was plodding up the trail, thinking with respect of the party at Grassy Ridge Bald shelter, who had hiked up from Hughes's Gap the day before, when the group of eight in garments stained from the elements appeared, going down. I stood aside to let them pass. Buccaneers, to look at, they were descending at a half lope, preoccupied and rather fierce in expression, oddly almost without encumbrances. I was still puzzling over them when I learned from a pair of hikers farther up that they were completing the graduation exercise of an outdoor-survival course and had been living off the woods for a few days.

I thought it great that young men would willingly undergo the trials that kind of course entailed; an idea of the sort of protein the forest afforded had been conveyed to me by a tannish, emaciated little toad I had just photographed down around 5,200 feet. And in view of the vulnerabilities of the world we are constructing, it seemed to me possibly a good idea for our race to keep its hand in with respect to the crafts required to make do without the appurtenances of the machine age. It will be ironical if technological civilization reaches the critical point—in the sense in which fissionable uranium is said to reach a critical mass—at the very time the last people on earth to have retained their primitive skills will have abandoned them to become its dependents.

From the high summits I visited I carried away a vivid impression of the vitality and ubiquity of the mosses and also some specimens of the commonest types. These on my return (looking ahead now) I took to the resident bryologist of the National Museum of Natural History. Harold E. Robinson was a tall, slim scientist with boyish features and eyes that suggested habituation to microscopes. Two of these were before him, magnificent binocular instruments finished in black enamel and chromium (or nickel), both soft-polished. (No wonder we are all sycophants at technology's court!) Most of my specimens required the use not only of the low-powered microscope but also of the 40- and 100-power magnifications of the other, this in some cases after a minute leaflet from the moss had been sliced for a cross section. Here was a relief. I need not reproach myself for being a bryological illiterate; the mosses were no field for a dilettante.

To begin with, two of my plants were not mosses at all but liverworts. These, I had read, required in general a wetter environment than the mosses and they seemed to be more flattened, but Dr. Robinson dismissed these alleged differences. The actual differences turned out to be so recondite that I decided to be content with his initial formulation: "The liverworts are a distinct group related to the mosses." My two were both scaly. *Scapania nemorosa* from LeConte resembled matted chains of tiny, opening leaf-buds, *Bazzania trilobata,* which I found on Big Balsam and is generally distributed in eastern North America and Europe, a Medusa-like mass of little blunt green worms of a double row of scales in herringbone pattern.

Of the mosses, two *Hypnums—H. imponens* from Big Balsam and *H. pallescens* from the Roan—resembled tiny prostrate ferns, the one, a coarser, having fronds like braided upholstery binding, the other a finer, also having braided-looking fronds, fringed with almost microscopic sickle-shaped leaves. Another, very small moss from the Roan and also from Big Balsam, had rather scale-like leaves but with curved, hair-like tips: *Brotherella recurvens.* The third from the Roan was like a fine, yellow-green pelage: *Paraleucobryum longifolium.* A Haircap from LeConte with upright stems bristling with tapering, spiny leaves, superficially like a seedling conifer, was *Polytrichum ohioense.* One, resembling a tiny feather boa, from Big Balsam, *Dicranum scoparium,* grew in vast mats in Appalachian Oak Woods, according to Dr. Robinson. The last and largest, with two- or three-inch-long strands like feathers with barbs perpendicular to the shaft, or fishes' backbones and ribs, brassy-green and spongy-looking, like Sphagnum, I had found abundant between Clingman's Dome and Andrews Bald as well as on LeConte. It was *Ptilium crista-castensis,* well named Knight's Plume.

How could mosses thrive where they did, in situations of light and soil that would starve any seed-bearing plant?

Dr. Robinson replied that fundamentally it was a matter of their structure, or near lack of it, a simplicity adequate for their small size. They did not need to build vascular tissue. They did not need to budget for flowers or fruit. Their requirements of sunlight and nutrients were minimal. They were specialized for prosperity on leached soil and could quickly move in on the alkalized soil left by fires. Wetness they did demand: the sperm required a film of water in order to reach the female organs. However, a mere splashing of rain was adequate in some cases, while mosses that grew in situations so dry as to render them brittle could reproduce vegetatively from pieces that broke off and were carried elsewhere. About all they needed in the way of a substrate, as Dr. Robinson termed it, was fixity; a sand-dune had to be stabilized for a couple of years before mosses could colonize it. A *Grimmia* had been grown on the interior surface of a block of

Blue Ridge granite split for the experiment. The mosses were soil-builders, pioneers of the flowering plants, and their economy of needs gave them wide distribution. "A fern-like species called Stairstep Moss—*Hylocomium splendens*—covers much of Canada, in the North Woods," said Dr. Robinson, "and extends down the Appalachians beneath the spruce-fir forests. A little greyish moss you can find growing in cracks in sidewalks—*Bryum argenteum*—occurs on all seven continents."

The Roan was one of the parts of the southern Appalachians where I said to myself that if a stranger were allowed to visit but one other after LeConte this would have to be it. However, if I were absolutely pinned down to two, I think the other would be the next great feature of the range I came to in my progress down it. It was one that revealed another aspect of the range's character, for it was not a mountain at all but what in the West would be called a canyon.

VII *Depth and Heights of the Blue Ridge*

The Linville River was named for an explorer who in 1766 was killed beside it by the Indians, as was his son. It rises on the other side of the Blue Ridge from the Roan, high on Grandfather Mountain, and flows beneath the Blue Ridge Parkway about 15 road-miles to the southwest. A mile south of the Parkway it pours through a series of cataracts and a serpentine bend among leviathans of rocks. You view it from high above the gorge it has cut, the sides of which are in part too steep even for the rhododendron, and there stand as walls of layered rock that must be the oldest-looking I have ever met with. As I have seen it in the off-season, framed in a damp forest rendered Gothic by pines and hemlocks, detached mists drifting up from the woods down the gorge, it is a place to involve the imagination —one to have given rise to myths of gnomes, giants and beasts in half-human roles. In a way to being hypnotized by it, I gazed so long at the falling water of the bottom cataract, which resembled a mane of wavy white hair, that on looking away from it finally I plainly saw the solid rock of the cliff in an area the size of the cascade flow upward past the neighboring rock, soft as taffy.

From the falls—purchased with their environs and given to the nation by John D. Rockefeller, Jr.—the Linville River flows to the Piedmont through the deep ravine it has cut, tumbling 2,000 feet in 12 miles. A little below the falls it enters the 7,600-acre Linville Gorge Wild Area of Pisgah National Forest. "This area is a challenge to the most experienced hiker," the National Forest Service folder warns, and urges anyone planning to hike in the gorge to notify a Ranger: "This is important!"

My feeling tends to be that invaders of wild areas should have to take their chances, that being what wild means, and not become public charges. Accordingly I am always of two minds about Ranger-notification. In this case, seeing no one to notify anyway, I merely filled out one of the cards provided at the trail-head at Pine Gap, near the upper end of the Wild Area. However, I do think the cautionary tone of the folder justified. I

96

Ancient rock and ancient tree, Linville Gorge.

spent ten hours in the gorge, covering about half its length, at one point
crossing the river with the aid of a cable slung between boulders to hike
part way up Spence Ridge on the eastern side and back. (There is no trail
in the downstream half of the chasm.) At the end of the day, regaining the
Forest Service road that skirts the gorge on its western rim, I was so
exhausted and footsore that after another mile or two I was glad to accept a

ride back to the campground. What made the walk hard with a pack, even without a bedroll, was the steepness of the trail, which would zigzag down to the river and then shinny up again, and the trees that had fallen across it and would have to be awkwardly clambered over. Where it edged an especially steep drop my discomfort would have been considerable, for I have little stomach for heights, had not the blessed vegetation of the Southern mountains masked its sheerness.

But it was thrilling. A largeness and grandeur, even recklessness of conception, was exemplified in the profundity of the gorge, which falls away as much as 1,800 feet from the 3,400-foot summits on its rim—2,800 feet between two 4,000-footers downstream of the Wild Area. And the trees were in keeping, the obstacles to their removal having discouraged the lumbermen and preserved the virgin stands. From the downward-dipping trail, which passed beneath protrusions of jagged, stratified rock, pictur-esque if stern, the big hemlocks were sheer boles without crowns or bottoms in sight, though a gentle, light rain of needles descended from them. One looked through and over a luxuriance of Rosebay Rhododendron across a subsidiary ravine to a slope sheathed in the somber foliage and set with the clusters of pale blossoms like spectral lamps in the green gloaming. Far below, the swirling river where it could be glimpsed, white in its rapids, was shot with light. So idealized did it all seem as a fastness of a dramatic and verdant, brooding and romantic Nature, lanced by the sun's rays to its hidden depths, that one felt that to be in character with it one ought to be freed of human limitations—be tireless, anyway. The voice of the river was that of the surf. Above it could be heard once or twice the intricately modulated, stuttering, fairy minstrelsy of a Winter Wren and its antithe-sis, the unhurried, sweet, cajoling notes of a Solitary Vireo. The latter's song, almost coquettish, came in phrases with pauses between, as if the singer were gauging the effect. One could imagine oneself being enticed on by a lovely, invisible forest girl.

High time I got out into the open, I thought, and this I did on reaching the bottom. The river and its rocky banks created a break in the forest into which the sun flooded. Everywhere huge boulders blocked the course of the stream, which poured, churning, around them and over the ledges forming its bed. On one of these, which sloped down to the river from the bank, I set up the little brass Swedish stove for the mid-morning cup of coffee. While I was enjoying this, a creature I first took to be a swimming frog, though its progress was too slow for one, went gallumphing across a large pool of rainwater on the ledge. It turned out to be one of the mottled brown Fishing Spiders, of the genus *Dolomedes,* about an inch in body length and three in span. Though not fast, it was quite at home on the water, resting on the surface film, which sagged beneath its feet like a trampoline but did not break. Water-striders sharing the pool approached its arrested figure, but not too closely. While they do catch minnows and tadpoles, Fishing Spiders are mainly insect-eaters.

There were also the usual bits of paper and a can or two for me to bury; I carry out my own refuse, of course, but not others', as Garvey admirably did. No part of the Appalachians is too remote for the louts to mark with their enduring spoor. It is a constant mystery how people can be attracted sufficiently to the wilds to pay the admission price in exertion and yet care so little as to leave their trash behind them. Beside fishing water—and anglers and gunners, to give them their due, will go almost anywhere in pursuit of their booty—the litter is likely to be particularly bad; fishermen are great for leaving a can perched on a rock. Down river at Sand Flat, accessible by an easier trail than the one I had taken, was a pile of refuse too big for me to deal with. It was particularly exasperating because some of the grandest trees I had seen in the East were here, Hemlocks, Tuliptrees and a White Pine of bole so great and tall I had difficulty making out its foliage to identify it. It must have risen seven floors without a twig, and so must some of the magnificent Tuliptrees and Chestnut Oaks past which I labored on the climb on Spence Ridge.

The specialty of the gorge is Carolina Hemlock. This does not grow as large as the Eastern species, is bristlier—furrier and firrier—has larger but

Carolina Hemlock.

still small cones and is said to be more akin to the Western Hemlock. Found only in the core of the southern Appalachians and not commonly even there, it stands characteristically, sturdy of trunk, a cliff-dweller among trees, above the gorge where the sides are steepest and one step off the trail would be one too many. Here you might expect to find Table Mountain Pine nearby, and so you do; also Red Maple and Black Tupelo. Sharing the sun-soaked heights are tangles of Mountain-laurel and Catawba Rhododendron, the lesser Carolina Rhododendron with reddish stems and smaller leaves, these here rolled up to reduce transpiration, little Wintergreen (or Teaberry) and Trailing Arbutus of coarsish, rather wavy leaves. All these, and the Azaleas, Blueberries, Huckleberries, Cranberries, Leucothoë, Pipsissewa and the waxy Indian-pipe or Ghost-flower, are members of the family I cannot stop exclaiming over. Though no heather—*Erica*—is native to the New World, the Ericaceae, or Heaths, are almost the floral emblems of the Southern mountains. And it is here in the Southeast that the family produces one of its only two real trees in North America, the Sourwood. (The other is the great orange-limbed Madrone of the Pacific coast.) In bloom, the Sourwood is arrayed in hands of white fingers sloping down and out from the ends of the branchlets, handsomely set off by the lustrous long leaves and giving somewhat of a pagoda effect. Each finger is a row of little white puffed-out pantaloons of flowers, a third of an inch long, for which Sourwood is sometimes called Lily-of-the-valley tree.

One stood, looking bridal, against a rugged chimney of rock where I had lunch, high above the river, gazing across to cliffs on the other side. These were formed of dark rock hundreds of feet from top to bottom, incised vertically as well as layered and having the appearance of ancient, inchoate visages. Beside me was a thick carpet of Reindeer Lichen. Actually not unlike the horns of reindeer in miniature, but multi-branched, bone-pale when dry, pea-soup green after a soaking, this staple of caribou diet occurs all down the Appalachian heights where infertile soil is exposed to climatic extremes—which means usually in company with Heaths. Here with the rhododendrons were beds of Galax and a pungent odor I have found only where one of or perhaps both these plants grow and have been puzzled by since boyhood. Suggestive, but not unpleasantly, of human perspiration or skunk, it is to be met with frequently in the mountains of North Carolina and northern Georgia but nowhere else I have been. Mrs. Cronquist, the only other I had known to remark it, described it as "musky, faintly skunk-like, but perhaps not unlike what we might imagine finding in a bear's den." Later, she and her husband satisfied themselves that it came from Galax, having found that even "without first noticing the odor, we could smell it by burying our faces among those low, glossy leaves." Yet for me this deepens the mystery. I have put my nose to much Galax and have detected the odor less often than not.

At lunch my appetite was sharper and sense of well-being more pervasive even than usual at refreshment time. Separation from the human race as a steady thing would probably lead to dementia, but as the exception the sense of it is sweet, certainly when it is earth and forest that stand between you and mankind. But beyond that I had had a bath, my first since leaving home. The trail on its last upswing had come to a pool fed by a softly tinkling stream and just large enough to take a prone body. In water shaded by the forest and probably but newly emerged from underground, the dip was brief and more stimulating than hygienic; my breath caught in my lungs as I lowered myself into the liquid. Drying off with a washcloth afterward, I had the sensation—an interesting one—that comes to you when naked in the woods or countryside of being embryonic Man. The washcloth lent itself to be carried hung on the back of my pack, for it was green like the latter; I had been lucky enough to find one that color simply by picking it up, still in its original wrapping, on a street corner. In hiking you have to decide whether to carry a brilliant red or orange pack to show up at a distance if need be, or a green one to help keep you inconspicuous to wildlife.

While I was working on my sandwich an answer came to me to my question of man's legitimacy as an ecological force, one satisfactory to me, anyhow.

Insofar as our circumscribed apprehension permits us to adduce a purpose in Creation, the aim is enrichment. That is the direction in which life has moved since its beginning. It has evolved from the simple and uniform to the more and more complex, manifold and varied. A wealth of plants and animals staggering to the imagination in their diversity, as in the artistry of their patterns, has been brought into being. To the extent that man has promoted the variety and richness of the living world, he has been a partner of Creation. This role he has filled most dramatically in the multiplicity of cultures he has generated, essentially dividing his species into many. At their finest the many offshoots of the human stock have rivaled nature in the beauty of their artifacts, building with a splendor worthy of the noblest natural setting and in their poetry and music lifting the expressiveness of life to exalted heights. Man has done the work of Creation, too, in varying and enriching the environments available to other forms of life. Opening windows of meadow, pasture, brushland and farmstead in the forest that once shrouded the eastern half of our country and giving opportunities to many species ill-adapted to sylvan shadows may, up to a point, be accounted such a contribution. But more and more man has been proving himself an agent of an altogether different kind. As his own cultures become increasingly uniform around the world—and some would say more sterile—he is progressively despoiling the earth for other living beings. More and more he is the impoverisher of life.

That the present belongs to man can hardly be doubted. His hegemony over the planet is complete; he has nothing to fear but the consequences of his own actions. If all living beings do not cower before him it is only because they are unwitting of his full powers of destruction. Man holds all the cards—and, it is a fair guess, may for that very reason be expected to overplay his hand. The wilderness is waiting for him to do so—and, it may be, if he has not meanwhile done it too much damage, to give him a new chance when he has come a cropper. Creation, in any case, has time on its side, time beyond conception.

Anyone to whom that consideration lacks reality would have it brought home to him, I should think, by what lay ahead of me as, late that afternoon, I persevered up the side of the abyss to its top. This was the spectacle of Linville Gorge from a promontory of the rim at about the midpoint of the Wild Area, named for an early landowner—and since a spur of the Forest Service road takes the public to it I suppose it had to be called something—Wiseman's View. From the abutment of rock falling away into the gulf, the full height of the gorge's mountain walls and the topping summits are in sight—the precipitous, seamed and chiseled rock, the miles of forest. Of no great dimensions by the scale of Grand Canyon, it provides its own, and by that standard it is awesome. And it comes nearer to Grand Canyon than anything I know in the East to conveying equally an impression of a reservoir of time. Similarly it instils a feeling as of the confines of your little temporal cell falling away to expose you to the immensity of the earth's endurance. The present is engulfed and, reduced to your place in the vast perspective, you feel you might be gazing into the pantheon of the ageless deities.

The steep ups and downs of the gorge had left me done in; as I said, when a car came up from behind me on the gravelly, hilly Forest Service road and the young couple in it offered to take me in, pack and all, I did not hesitate and rode with them to the start of the road, where I had left my bus. From there it was less than two miles back to the pleasant National Park campground at Linville Falls.

Among rivers and streams below the Roanoke gap in the Blue Ridge, the Linville River is almost unique in crossing the Blue Ridge Parkway from northwest to southeast. More: among water courses between the Roanoke and Ashville gaps it is unusual in crossing the Parkway at all, for in all this distance—260 road miles—the Parkway is almost always on the divide between the Atlantic and Mississippi watersheds. That this is so is surely remarkable, for the whole way the Parkway follows the outermost escarpment of the Blue Ridge, that nearest the Atlantic. I mention this because I feel I can no longer put off taking note of the odd behavior of southern Appalachian rivers. They have a propensity for crossing mountain ridges. North of Roanoke the rivers originate well over on the inland side of the range and, collecting tributaries in the long valleys, break through the mountains on their way to the Atlantic in often striking "water gaps." The Delaware Water Gap and the Potomac water gap at Harper's Ferry are well known. Goshen Pass, cut by a major branch of the James through Virginia's Long Ridge Mountains between Warm Springs and Lexington, is so beautiful, especially when the Rhododendron is in bloom on the steep, forested sides of the rocky defile, that Matthew Fontaine Maury, the father of oceanography, asked that his body be carried through it on its way to burial. Goshen Pass sounds most un-Appalachian—even the original Dunlap Pass does; it is the only use of the term "pass" in the whole range that I can think of, "gap" being the conventional expression. Conceivably it comes down to us from John Lederer, Governor Berkeley's German explorer, who is supposed to have made his way through it in the 1670's.

Below Roanoke the perverse rivers generally originate on the easternmost escarpment of the Blue Ridge and cross the whole remainder of the Appalachians to send their waters finally to the Mississippi and the Gulf. Among them, too, the water gaps can be notable. One is the Narrows, a gorge in which the New River pours through the last barrier of the Long Ridges, on the West Virginia border, offering a challenge to white-water paddlers. (According to the geologist Raymond E. Janssen, the New is well over 100 million years old, which some say makes it, after the Nile, the oldest river in existence.) Another is the Pigeon River gorge at the eastern end of the Great Smokies. Alas for their character, both have been converted to corridors of motorized traffic. This has been the fate, too, of a more famous pass, also through the last barrier of the Virginia Long Ridges but far to the southwest of the Narrows: Cumberland Gap, which, having been cut by a stream, was deserted by it.

The question has always been, how did the rivers force a passage through high ridges of solid rock? The theory is that in the long courses of time the Appalachian range at least once and probably several times was worn down to a peneplain; that over this "almost-plain" the rivers flowed gently; and that as the range slowly rose again they ground a way through the ridges as fast as these emerged with the lowering of the softer rock between them by erosion.

Well, I can understand how the range kept rising as it wore down, for its constituents went deep into heavier rocks and would have been buoyed up as the overload diminished, just as an iceberg floats higher as its top melts; the principle is called istostasy. Only somehow the idea that these great mountains would wear flat, more or less, on the way to rising thousands of feet more—and not just once but two or three times—has never rung true to me. I can remember when the Colorado River was believed to have cut the Grand Canyon through the Kaibab Plateau in accordance with the same scenario, to use the current metaphor: it sawed its way down as the Plateau rose beneath it. Now the accepted explanation is that, flowing to begin with down the western side of the Plateau, it ate its way back through to the other by the process called "headwaters erosion," there "capturing" the waters of a river which, having previously flowed into the Gulf of Mexico, now joined the Colorado on its way to the Gulf of California. If the Colorado could back its way through the mile-high Kaibab, the Appalachian rivers should have been able to back theirs through the ridges they now sever. Be that as it may, I am glad to see that a new school of geologists is prepared to dispense with the peneplain idea on other grounds. John T. Hack of the United States Geological Survey suggests that "the present landforms . . . developed by the continuous downwasting of the topographic surface for many thousands of feet": a mountainous terrain was lowered without ceasing to be mountainous. And he adds, "The broad outlines of the present range developed by the beginning of the Tertiary [60 million years ago]." Since then there has been "continuous downwasting" but with "isostatic uplift probably maintaining the elevation of the range."

Especially am I drawn to that conception and away from the peneplain theory when I look upon the grandest of all spectacles from the Blue Ridge Parkway, which from Linville campground stood only twenty-five miles farther on my way to the southwest. This was the enormous ridge of the Black Mountains. While still a little footsore and stiff the morning after my day in Linville Gorge, I was impatient to make a start up it. Not only was I eager for the feel of climbing it and the gratification of having done so, but I had amends to make for the several times I had taken the road up it by car.

The formation is a projection of the Blue Ridge escarpment bordering the Piedmont (to which many persons confine the name Blue Ridge) extending almost due north. Black it looks, too, when nimbus clouds overspread it. If other North Carolinian ranges are mantled at comparable elevations by forest equally dark-hued, it was the Blacks, rising 5,000 feet above the Piedmont within eight miles or so, that were the first so attired to meet the awed and intimidated gaze of early settlers pushing westward into the mountains, and later of aristocratic summer refugees from the malarial lowlands of South Carolina; hence it was they that received the name. How the range's—and the East's—highest summit received the name affixed to it goes back to 1835. In that year Elisha Mitchell, a native of Connecticut and professor of science at the University of North Carolina, climbed the ridge of the Blacks, which by means of barometric readings he found to top Mount Washington, then thought to be supreme in the East. But had he

Amianthium lily—Fly-poison—high on a slope of Mt. Mitchell.

taken the elevation of the Black Dome itself, the highest of them? Thomas Clingman, who climbed and measured it in 1844, claimed to have been the first to do so. Mitchell, who again climbed the ridge that same year to refine his measurements, maintained that he had been. The dispute became acrimonious between the two explorers and their respective supporters. It was rendered moot in 1857 when Mitchell fell to his death in a pool at the foot of a waterfall on the western slope of the range. His body was discovered only after a week's search, and by his friend "Big Tom" Wilson, a local guide and character. Clingman and his faction graciously gave way. Elisha Mitchell, who must rank several hundred thousand down on any list of Americans deserving of special honor, had the Black Dome renamed after him and his body vaingloriously buried on its very peak.

As for the ridge of the Black Mountains itself—No, I thought as I made my way along it, nothing could surpass it as an expression of the Appalachians, and the supreme.

I started hiking from the Forest Service campground on the South Toe (properly Estatoe) River. The climb was from about 3,500 to 6,684 feet in eight miles; under a pack you knew you had had a walk. Interestingly, I met several pairs of other hikers on the trail. Whatever one's regret at finding the wilds less than wild, it is counterbalanced by encouragement at the discovery of how many others respond to their appeal. In this case two of the others, a mother and young daughter, were turning back. There were no animals, the former said, explaining with a smile at her own credulity that she supposed they had expected to see rabbits looking at them from the bushes. And it must be true that nature films on television, in their very excellence, lead to unrealizable anticipations of a walk in wild country. . . . After having started at one o'clock, I came to the first grove of Spruces at 2:45 and the first Balsams half an hour later. At 3:30 the trail reached true Spruce forest, of old and mighty trees. But from then on, with Balsams increasingly predominating, its stature diminished. Near the top, trees stood stark and dead on every side. Shocked, I wondered if this were the handiwork of the Woolly Aphid. And in part it was, I was to learn: the Aphid has claimed a horrifying million victims among the Balsams here.

The Black Dome had changed greatly since I had first seen it, in 1929. Then, cars went most of the distance up on a barely-improved old logging railroad roadbed. The way was rough and narrow from start to finish and nothing marred the summit but a watchtower of logs. We were in a Model A Ford touring-car. Having driven up in the morning, the car's owner decided we should drive down in the morning, too, though the forenoon was reserved for up traffic. Raburn Monroe, a dark, intense young scion of several prominent New Orleans families, then about to enter law school, was driven by some kind of demon which, while it gave him no rest until his untimely death, did not affect his good nature. It affected mine on the way down, however, when we came to passing several cars on the way up, on the outside, once with our right-hand wheels having little under them but some clumps of rhododendron overhanging the abyss. (Clingman's Dome has changed, too, since we hiked to it that same summer after taking a Model A pickup truck as far as we could get it to Newfound Gap, up the wagon-track from the village of Smokemont, hauling it by rope toward the end—Ra's idea. At that time only a semblance of a trail reached the great Smokies summit, on which we spent the night up in the chill, dark sky warmed by the embers of a fire, the sense of adventure, youth.) Of the paved road now taking traffic up the Black Dome, the power-lines and the swaths cut for them, the parking plazas, the motorcars, the shop and snack-bar, the less said the better. Time, however many millennia of it may be required, will efface these profanations of a noble mountain along with Mitchell's paling-enclosed grave. And as it is, they are diminished by the view from the observation tower of the range extending north and south like the back of some half-breached sea monster ridden by ants, separated by aching gulfs from only somewhat lesser monsters. Moreover, the developed area is quickly left behind on the trail northward along the crest of the range.

Crest of the Black Mountains looking north toward Hair Bear.

Seen broadside, the Southern mountains are gently rounded and re-poseful. End on, it can be a very different matter. The Blacks in this view looked as steep to me as the letter A. Walking the crest I felt in places that I could well go head over heels down either side. The next morning, several summits farther on, trying to locate a spring I had heard of from a Ranger, I picked my way some two hundred feet by mistake down the side of Cattail Peak and found it a tricky business, even without my pack and despite all the trees and Rhododendron to hold onto. Where the range rose to one of its razorbacks, it reminded me of a wave peaking to a breaker. And like a frothing wave much of it had a pale crusting. That was where the forest had been reduced to whitened skeletons. In part the aphids were to blame. According to the Forest Service, however, the great majority of these trees—Spruces and Balsams alike—were stripped and killed by winter gales, which have reached 125 miles an hour on the Dome. Beneath the relics a vigorous crop of their bright green progeny had sprung up and flowering plants crowded in the sun, among them beds of Turtle-head, a Snapdragon of warm, pure pink.

I camped just under the summit of Hairy Bear. North Carolina would like us to call this peak Big Tom, but since Big Tom Wilson's claim to fame rests chiefly on the number of bears he slaughtered—something like 650, I seem to recall—we can forget that. North Carolina is as liberal in awarding its mountains as it is niggardly in protecting them. A state park of a miserly 1,200 acres takes in little more than the crest of the Black Mountains, and that for less than half its length. While most of the eastern side is in the Pisgah National Forest, the western and the northern end are entirely in private hands.

Hairy Bear is the lesser of the two peaks of the mountain called the Black Brothers, of which the greater rises to 6,645 feet; it was gratifying to know that I had the second highest mountain in the eastern three-fifths of the nation to myself. The evening was still and mild and quite bright yet when I strung up my nylon tarpaulin across the trail, not to be caught unprepared by a shower. With darkness, however, a wind came up and whenever I lay awake during the night I could hear it. The first light discovered the top of the mountain in a cloud. Heavy mists were blowing across it, through the forest. The wind still sounded like the sea.

And so it continued all that morning, which was as dramatic and stirring in its quality, in the mood it evoked, as any I have known in the mountains: the cloud streaming by; the trees ahead, living and dead, erect or toppled with their disk of roots on edge, taking form and solidity out of the mist; the trail skirting the jutting rocks that gave the range a knobby spine, here and there dropping five or ten feet down a shelf, in one place squeezing through a deep cleft in the rock; the drifting, eddying fogs parting to disclose blue sky, a sweep of wooded valley below, some wild, unknown, sunlit mountainside or the acute, high summit of Balsam Cone, Cattail Peak, Potato Hill or Deer Mountain ahead. Along with the winter-ravaged promontories were dark, damp glens along the crest and frequent beds of paired, Lily-like leaves. Most of these were probably of Clintonias, but I felt sure some were of orchids—and it was strange to think that plants one associates with the lushest tropics should make out quite well where winds rampaging from the Arctic have taken heavy toll of boreal forest. A few times, grey as the rocks, the stripped tree-trunks and the fog, a Junco flitted off ahead of me, flirting its white-edged tail; or, unseen, one replied to the chill drafts with its literally chipper song, a chipping or tinkling. However rugged and comfortless the high Appalachian mountain-back, if there is no other bird there are likely to be Juncos, and if the fog is too thick to make out anything else of one, you can see its white outer tail feathers when it flies off. They are given to placing their nests in the low bank of vegetation likely to border a trail, and I had flushed the owner from one high on the Black Dome, still with eggs in it, though the date was July 26th. . . . Wonderful, I thought, that Creation, which worked on the heroic scale of cloud-essaying mountains, turned its attention as painstakingly to the lively minutiae of birds and the jewel artistry of plants. This was here displayed in the stalks of Turk's-cap Lilies over four feet tall at Deep Gap, and in the clusters of small scarlet berries of the Red Elders occasional among the stunted Pin Cherries and stubby Yellow Birches. The Red Elder, Pin Cherry and Canada Blackberry are outstanding plants of opportunity in the high southern Appalachians. Their seeds must be sowed everywhere in the droppings of birds, for let there but be a clearing made in the highest forest and up they spring. . . . Alone on that paramountain, if I may call it that, lost in the heavens where the spectral mists that nourished the lichens opened and closed unpredictable vistas around one, I felt raised to a bridgeless remoteness from the human world.

On the Blue Ridge Parkway from where the Black Mountains first come into view—if you are driving down from the north—until the long, steep descent to Asheville, you are above 4,000 feet for 35 miles. Wild-looking mountains you pass, too, with spruce rising slim and tall from nearly vertical slopes. As you get into the Great Craggy Mountains on a windswept ridge at about 5,500 feet, the spruces give way to low-branching hardwoods like witches' trees and rhododendron clings to black, dripping rocks from which sphagnum burgeons. The Parkway passes between Craggy Dome and Craggy Pinnacle at 5,640 feet. On the broad, high summit on either side only shrubby vegetation grows, the soil apparently too shallow to support anything greater. June and the flowering of the Catawba Rhododendron turns them into Elysian Fields; yet even at that season their spareness and the inclination of the scrubby trees below calls up a picture of scourging winter westerlies. The trail up Craggy Pinnacle rewards you with the phenomenon, unusual in the southern Appalachians, of a natural summit commanding a 360-degree panorama. To begin with, the Rhododendron, along with contorted Yellow Birches gripping the rocks with writhing roots, forms a jungle well over head height, its limbs coppery brown like those of its Western relative, Manzanita, and running to more than two feet in circumference. But it shrinks as the trail climbs and at the summit is barely waist high.

That is one footpath the motorist on the Parkway has little excuse not to take; it offers so much for the effort. Another is up Richland Balsam, 60 miles farther on, after the climb back up from Asheville and the French Broad River. At 6,430 feet, Richland Balsam is the highest of the Great Balsam Mountains; and these, on my relief map, which shows increasing elevation by darkening shades of buff, claim the largest area of the darkest shade after the Smokies. The trail, which begins at 6,050 feet, mounts through a shadowy forest of Spruce and Balsam standing, as on other high peaks, as close as the bristles of a brush with little growing in the damp, black, buttery soil beneath but some moss and ferns and the little light-thrifty Mountain Wood-sorrel. As I know the peak, it is chill, and cloud vapor is filtering by, the sun occasionally breaking through to glisten on the wet trunks and foliage; and it is in my mind that this is the last aerial island of boreal woods southward. In the hush I could well believe that the Appalachians preserve the silence that reigned upon earth when their rocks were being formed. The forest opens sufficiently at the top to permit High-bush Cranberry to grow and reveal a sweep of the Balsam Range to the east, which you had passed on the Parkway. You can see the cone of Cold Mountain eight miles away and, almost as far, the white quartz outcropping of Shining Rock Mountain. The former is near the northern end of a Wilderness Area (one of the two in the Pisgah National Forest) to which the latter, toward the center, gives its name. Shining Rock Wilderness, the Forest Service explains, is a "13,600-acre tract . . . set aside to provide a primitive, natural environment; a retreat from civilization; a treasure of native flora and fauna; a place for inspiration and scientific study."

The invaluable *100 Favorite Trails of the Great Smokies and Carolina Blue Ridge,* put out jointly by two local clubs of the Appalachian Trail Conference, showed the Art Loeb Trail going due north through the Wilderness Area after coming east from near Brevard. The 28-mile-long trail is exceptional for the southern Appalachians, where, apart from the Appalachian Trail, long trails are, regrettably, lacking. I set forth on it from its crossing of the Parkway. The yellow-blazed trail, I found to my surprise, wonderment and very lively interest, led over a succession of great, high, grassy domes. Probably because I had never been there, I could almost imagine myself in the Scottish Highlands; there was even, to suggest blooming heather, a mauve grass on one of the crests. The landscape was a grand and spacious and moody one as I saw it, heavy, moist, grey clouds passing over, the sun breaking through to light up one or another of the surrounding mountains while a wind came in gusts that made me roll down my sleeves. In all that wide vista no sign of man's occupancy was to be seen. I felt like a discoverer.

The wind strengthened as I walked, flattening the grass and bringing fine, stinging showers. With the concealment of the wooded mountains the sun had picked out, it was more than ever like my idea of the highlands of Scotland or Wales. Only the elevations above sea-level were greater than any in the British Isles. One of the arching summits over which the trail passed was 6,040 feet high.

Perhaps the most singular aspect of the scene, in view of its derivation, was its seeming naturalness. But for a scattering of melancholy tree-stumps, part charred, mostly bleached, which testified that these uplands had once been forested, one would have thought they had always been like this. Doubtless one would suppose the same of the Scottish Highlands, which also were once in forest, for the most part. Here, in the mid 1920's, a spark from a logging locomotive ignited the underbrush and 25,000 acres were burned off. Then in 1942 fire swept 5,000 more. The intensity of

Bush honeysuckle, abounding in the Shining Rock Wild Area.

these fires, the Forest Service says, left the soil incapable of supporting further tree-growth, though presumably the forest will eventually reclaim the area. This may have a bearing on the origin of the grass-balds, which the forest may also eventually reclaim.

Despite the destruction of humus the big domes were entirely vegetated, supporting a turf of grasses and other low growth and unparalleled quantities of Hairy Angelica three feet high with flower heads just emerging from pods like small ears of corn. The flowers would resemble those of that other Parsley, Queen-Anne's-lace. Nature, if deprived of its first choice in landscaping, will settle for a second: if not forest, then grassland and a wholly different flora. Except where conditions for life are already marginal, as where drought or cold prevails, there is always another cast waiting in the wings. The understudies, though, may be only ragamuffins like Plantain, Dock and Ragweed, which will crop up wherever soil is exposed, or Galinsoga, the weed with tiny Daisy-like flowers that Londoners dubbed Gallant Soldier when it overspread the rubble of their bombed city.

Other parts of the 45 square miles burned over had grown up in scrub vegetation—Pin Cherry, blackberry, rhododendron, Mountain-laurel *and* Bush-honeysuckle. There must have been the world's largest concentration of this last, lurching bumblebees avidly probing its funnel-shaped, greenish-yellow flowers; horticulturalists would recognize it as a Weigelia. I had come up through this part the day before, starting at Graveyard Ridge on the Parkway and entering the Wilderness Area from the east. The trail followed the roadbed of a logging railroad, very likely the one from which the fire started, to Ivestor Gap, where it joined the Art Loeb Trail. From the juncture it was only two miles to Shining Rock Mountain.

By the time I reached the mountain a fog had drifted in. The wildflowers on the brushy slope—pink-lavender Phlox, Wild Sunflower and the Lily Amianthum, bearing foot-long truncheons of white florets on two-foot stalks—had the soft, muted quality of plants (and of the lovely ethereal maidens who disport among them) in Arthur Rackham's paintings, which in my childhood gave me the impression, as they still do, that our everyday world is but a crude, overdrawn approximation of a more delicate reality that eludes our gross apprehension. The extraordinary outcroppings of white quartz at the mountain's brow, like snow banks through the mist, contributed a somewhat ghostly presence to the effect. But unless you accepted them simply as components of an artistic vision, you could not but speculate on their origin. How did quartz bodies plainly visible at seven miles distance come into being? Of all the common constituents of rocks, quartz—silica—has the lowest melting point. When molten rock cools slowly, as it does deep beneath the earth's surface, quartz is the last to solidify of the minerals plentifully represented in it. In metamorphic rock,

Shining Rock summit in the cloud, showing part of the huge quartz outcropping that gave the mountain its name.

partially liquid quartz may be free to collect in interstices of rocks of other composition or invade cracks in them. In this case a combination of unusual circumstances, long before the Blue Ridge rose, must have filled a great cavity with quartz.

The end of July is a time when birds, perhaps weary from raising young and beginning to moult, are likely to be inconspicuous. Apart from insects I saw little animal life on the hike, though a Turkey Vulture rose a long way ahead of me from the logging roadbed and proved to have been feeding on the well-aged corpse of a small Wildcat—cause of death unascertainable. Several other parties of backpackers were on the trail, however. Always curious about these present-day pilgrims, I had a talk with a particularly attractive set—six or seven young men and women who turned out to come from Atlanta, my natal city. When I asked how things were there a chorus of condemnation answered me. Said one of them, a slim, very pretty girl, "More polluted all the time—water polluted, air polluted, and pollution by people." They were full of the hiking they had done, very eager about it, and full, too, of the beauties of the mountains. They were also very concerned about the country. I was greatly taken by them. The exceptionally pretty girl and her husband—Elaine and Ted Turner, they said—had been backpacking in the West and were enthusiastic. "Animals are much more cherished in the West," Elaine declared, "and consequently the deer are much tamer. We saw thirty-eight deer in a couple of hours one day in Utah, and they were so tame they almost came up to you to be fed." She and her husband, a rather Botticelli-like young man with long, blond ringlets albeit with a rather unsuccessful beard, were looking for somewhere to settle. They very much liked Colorado, having just come back from a hiking trip there, but found it filling up rapidly and growing more polluted. Ted had had two years of architectural school but appeared to be dismayed at the thought of destroying more natural areas for buildings. I ventured to suggest that buildings were going to be put up anyway and that what was needed was designers to see that as little violation as possible was done to the natural landscape, in part by good architecture, in part by concentrating the population. Another young man from Atlanta, introduced as an urbanologist, appeared to agree, as did Elaine, who was keen to have her husband go ahead and get his degree.

The sun broke through the overcast briefly while we were talking and they welcomed it vocally. However, they seemed not put off by the prospect of rain; they were used to it from Colorado and had black polyethylene sheets for their protection.

I had been returning when I had met them and after I left them thought of them with commiseration, for it started to rain, and it rained without letup all during my walk back. And there can be no denying that rain, even with polyethylene, takes away the pleasure of camping. From Graveyard Ridge to the Parkway there was no recognizable trail, and pushing through the tall grass and brush growth and ducking under trees, I gave great praise to the inventor of the rain-suit, one of whose creations I was wearing; nothing is wetter than dripping vegetation brushing against you.

The next day, coming down from the grassy domes at Ivestor Gap, I met the Turners and two of the others returning to their car. Having camped at Shining Mountain Gap, they had been somewhat discouraged by the rain, which had been plentiful during the night, but more so by a visitation of skunks. They had had to look on helplessly while the untouchables invaded their tent and gorged on their provisions. Another party I met later, who had camped at the same place, had had the same experience. For the Striped Skunks of Shining Mountain Gap it had evidently been a night to remember.

There are often days at a time of sublime weather in the Southern mountains, especially in autumn, but the possibility of rain at any time and in any amount has to be accepted. Winds from the east bring clouds distilled from the Atlantic Ocean, those from the south come similarly laden from the Gulf of Mexico. Striking the cooler temperatures that prevail over wooded mountains, and at the heights to which the winds deflected upward by the ranges carry them, the clouds are condensed and their burden streams earthward. It can be copious. When Hurricane Camille settled over the Virginia Blue Ridge on August 19, 1969, and kept pulling in clouds from over the Atlantic, it dumped 27 inches of rain on the watershed of the James River in four and a half hours. Unofficial reports of 32 inches in the same period would make it the heaviest rain ever known, anywhere. The floods and avalanches it caused killed 152 persons, 126 of them in Nelson County. That was the worst natural disaster in Virginia's recorded history. Even downpours that are regular in the southern Appalachians exceed any I have known on the Amazon River or under the wet-monsoon skies of Assam. At Highlands I have been totally soaked within 15 seconds of the first drops.

Deluges so swamping, accompanied by electrical discharges, are generally short-lived, and such torrents as I once ran into in a car on the Blue Ridge Parkway above Roanoke, so blinding as to make driving impossible, are exceptional. Still, rain is the contingency to be prepared for in this range. Hiking in it, I should never be without that rain-suit if I could help it. It is true that you perspire in one, but I prefer to be wet with perspiration, and warm, than to have cold runnels down my back or my trousers clinging flowingly to my legs when walking through soaked vegetation. Equipped with a rain-suit, and with a waterproof tarpaulin for a canopy and another for the ground, one need not be intimidated. On a day of bright, warm sunshine it seems that rain is only a remote contingency and will be a mere trivial inconvenience if it comes, while on a dark day of steady rain you lose faith in the sun's ever coming out again. You are as far off the mark in the first instance as in the second. Yet, as I learned in war, there are worse fates than looking out on the rain from a shelter and feeding a cheerily flaming fire. To have a fire it is worth carrying tinder and kindling. However, one can make do with a little gasoline- or gas-burning stove; that suffices for the hot food and drink that make all the difference in chill and rain. On the Appalachian Trail there is a three-sided lean-to every eight and a half miles, on the average, each theoretically containing a supply of dry wood which the user is honor-bound to replace. But an outpost of civilization, possibly crowded, is not quite the same as a camp of your own with no other sign of man around.

Half the preparation is mental—accepting the rain as the animals do. In the high forest, grey with cloud, when to shiver in the cold wet might seem to be all one is good for, the Winter Wrens and Juncos carry on as animatedly as ever, and apparently in as good spirits. A little pale moth flies off among the drops, unfazed, and as soon as the shower lets up the bees are back as industrious as ever. Rain is an essential part of the Southern mountains. It feeds the brooks that tumble chortling down from them. It supplies the panoply of plants that enchants us and protects the slopes from erosion; and it enables the mountain wilderness to recover as quickly and well as it does from man's ravages.

At its worst the rain brings out the inhumanness of the mountains, and in this they are as they should be. Probably thousands upon thousands of persons profess to love the southern Appalachians and no doubt do when the spring sun brings out the flowers, the summer's day is bright and benign, the autumn brilliant. Only they are not thinking of being up on that ridge in the black of night or when the hiss of rain is buried beneath the volleys of thunder. Yet that dark wildness is at the mountains' heart and in their ultimate inaccessibility—for which one gives thanks in an East cloyed with humanity.

Of this I was particularly aware in the high Balsam range south of Mount Pisgah. I wrote: "My mind is filled with these great humped shapes, and with their unapproachability: there is no getting close to them. You see them with their tops dissolving into the grey vapors, the pointed conifers in their black cloaks dominating the fresh green of the leafy vegetation and seeming—I don't know how—to be pressing forward up the slope, and you feel at the northern end of everything. Morning and evening, white mists lie in the valleys—is it because the cooler air, settling in them, condenses the moisture?—sometimes silhouetting each ridge like an aureole, and streamers of mist flow up the ravines to be drawn through the gaps. Or, enormous, they may obliterate a range, and trail pendant wraiths through the woods, then thin out to disclose a mountain rising immense, bathed in humid sunshine, unmoved, withdrawn and superior, untouched by the passage of clouds and of millennia."

Knowing the geological origin of mountains, one should see them as the simple products of physical, even merely mechanical, forces. Yet they stand as assertions, unique and commanding, of the planet's inner life and of the energy that is the motive power of the universe. Powerful in their forms, they are equally so as symbols of the steadfast and enduring, of what is lofty, grand and inscrutable in Creation. I must confess that one can come to feel a subservience toward them, as to the unknowable, the unrealizable, which makes hiking their trails a willing duty to their greatness and a satisfaction of an inner need.

As I prepared to move on from the Great Balsams, the overcast had receded from the west. Driving along the crest of the range I could see beneath the radiant-edged clouds far mountains that seemed to go on forever, sheet after sheet of them, those beneath the sun appearing to be composed of luminous dust. Somewhat south of west were those I was to come to next, the Nantahalas, of lovely name. A raven was circling over the chasm-like depth the road overlooked. As well imagine witches without their black cats as the southern Appalachians without their ravens—except

Raven, *Luther Goldman.*

that ravens have no quality of sorcery about them. Far from being birds of a kind to make somber visitations on midnights dreary, they have great gusto and love of aerial acrobatics. Size being deceptive, they may best be told from crows in flight by their proportionately greater development forward of the wings, their shaggy throats and the wedge-shaped end of the long tails. They are also much more prone to sail out over drops of a thousand or more feet, soon to be reduced to a black, winged flake in several cubic miles of empty space. As I drove three more came over the road, one making a feint at the other two; they are great at that. . . . Mountains in shadow, mountains in sunshine; mountains all around. . . .

After the descent from Richland Balsam to Balsam Gap came the turnoff onto U.S. 23 to Sylva and across the Cowee Mountains (the farthest point William Bartram reached, arriving from the opposite direction and here turning west to the Nantahalas) to Franklin. Came also the traumatic return to the rushing, roaring motorcars and trucks and the myriad boastful commercial solicitations and impositions of an arterial highway and ad-jacent urban districts. One positive result it had for me anyhow. It resolved for me, finally, a question I had been puzzling over: what is vulgarity that it should be absent in nature and inescapable in contemporary human soci-ety? I had thought about it recurrently on many a mile of trail.

Vulgarity was abuse of one's setting. It sprang from insensitivity to one's surroundings combined with self-assertion at their expense. The vulgarian imposed himself on the scene heedlessly, loudly, jarringly. Nothing in nature could afford insensitivity like his or the luxury of a cult of the self. For both predator and prey, a self-denying, unflagging attention to the environment and an acute, respectful responsiveness to its every nuance were the keys to survival. So long as mankind continued to better its advantages over nature faster than education and cultivation of mind could be imparted to it and impose their own restraints, vulgarity would burgeon; and the need to get away from its sway to preserves of nature—and, I mentally added, to the cultural monuments of the more balanced societies of the past—would continue to grow apace.

VIII *The Last Ramparts Southward*

In its map of the Nantahala National Forest, which occupies the south-western corner of North Carolina, the Forest Service translates the Indian name as "Land of the Midday Sun." My impression from other sources, however, is that this is a free rendition of words that more nearly mean "a cleft between ridges." This could be taken to signify a valley that the sun reaches only when it stands at its zenith. It would also justify the rendering given by Charles Lanman, a New Yorker who traveled in the southern Appalachians in 1848 and wrote of what he saw in *Letters from the Alleghany Mountains:* "Woman's Bosom." Taking "bosomy" to mean, as the Oxford Universal Dictionary says it does, "full of sheltered hollows," the two translations are not far apart. By that definition, bosomy is aptly descriptive of the Nantahalas. They are indeed full of sheltered hollows, with streams trickling or pouring through them. And after the somewhat savage attributes of the higher peaks to the north and east, bristling with dark conifers, the Nantahalas seem touched with softness—femininity.

Like the Great and Plott Balsams, the Nantahalas make up a transverse range connecting the flanks of the great massif of Blue Ridge and Great Smokies. It is rather as if an acutely tilted H had two crossbars. The Appalachian Trail follows the crest of the Nantahalas from the Piedmont-facing southern Blue Ridge to the Tennessee-Valley-facing Smokies. From a Forest Service campground at White Oak Bottom on the Nantahala River, seven or eight miles below its source, I had a long climb to meet the Trail at Deep Gap and another following it up Standing Indian, the highest mountain of the range. It came to 2,000 feet altogether and carried me from lush, tropical-looking verdure through progressively more open forest, which declined to the squatty, lichen-grown oaks of an extreme Appalachian elevation. Only three miles north of the Georgia border, Standing Indian is the last of the 5,000-footers southward, and with 500 feet to spare. The last few paces of climb delivered me to the narrow, grassy tonsure of the absolute peak, where, though already August,

Three-toothed Cinquefoil was still in bloom. From here the view was open to the southwest and to the broken, sharply-formed highlands of northern Georgia topped by Brasstown Bald, the state's highest at 4,748 feet. As I looked around, a Broad-winged Hawk, which had been sparring with two others in a display of dives and recoveries, made a pass within 20 feet of me to look me over. I whipped out the camera, but too late; and nature, as they say of Shakespeare, never repeats.

The Appalachian Trail, after crossing from Georgia into North Carolina, turns back on itself to pass over Standing Indian before turning north again almost back at the Georgia border. So, following it northward, you descend the mountain by its southern ridge. This proved to be quite open in places, with only a thicket-growth of rhododendron, Mountain-laurel and Wild-raisin Viburnum, and hence many flowers—Black-eyed Susans, Fire Pinks and Phlox—and Reindeer Lichen. But the rest of the day I walked through forest. When six o'clock came I was on a high ridge among big northern hardwoods in a park-like setting.

Two hours of daylight still remained, but rain threatened and I had found a level enough spot to sleep on, with anchorages for the tarpaulin cords, and decided to camp there. Having an hour left after supper before I could very well turn in, and nothing else to do, I went for a walk. Freed of my pack and with my stick I felt like a boulevardier. Almost everywhere the earth spouted sprays of fern; one thought of green geysers from an underground irrigation system. They were of a lacy, delicate-green kind—Marsh Fern evidently; there were miles of it in the Nantahalas. The air was light and refreshing. But the few sounds of animal life in the forest had subsided: the occasional singing of a bird, the more frequent chippering of a fleeing chipmunk, twice the muffled thunder of a Ruffed Grouse bursting off. Though there were two young men—Georgians, by their speech—in a red nylon tent a few miles behind me at Beech Gap, I thought it must be as lonely a spot as any in the East. It certainly seemed so later while I lay awake listening to drops of drizzle or condensation falling from branches onto the tarpaulin. My watch said 2:45. Shortly before dawn it began to rain in earnest. Then about six, while it continued, a Veery sounded its confident, descending *queeu* note, several times. Fortified by its companionability, I hitched myself out of the sleeping-bag and, awkwardly under the tarpaulin, got my clothes on. The little brass primus stove and coffee were made for such a morning.

Congenial company would have added pleasure to my journeyings in the mountains, without a doubt. However, with Vera unable to accompany me, I was as glad to be alone. There is much to be said for being able to set your own pace, to hike as far as but no farther than you feel like. And if your aim is to expose yourself to the quality of the wilds you do so more thoroughly if by yourself. That quality becomes particularly real to you when you reflect on how it would be if you turned an ankle some miles from the nearest chance of a human encounter. Wilderness that requires no vigilance is hardly wilderness.

That day I walked by the hour the trail that had been the longest continuous marked footpath in the world until the Pacific Crest Trail, which it inspired, was put through. I followed it through tunnels in the Rhododendron and out under the open sky along mountain spines thick in Heaths and flowers, like the south ridge of Standing Indian. I struggled with it up the side of 5,250-foot Albert Mountain, the steepest section of its length I have seen, under the novel necessity of stopping continually to let my wind catch up with me. (If my heart can stand this, I thought as it pounded between my heaving lungs, it must be sound.) And that afternoon, suddenly, I found myself exceedingly moved by that trail. I was walking through woods in which the rank growth of nettles, grass and fern nearly closed over it. How inconsequential it seemed!—and generally does seem, as if it would soon end in a road or simply peter out. And yet it does not. On it goes, the white blaze on tree or rock to tell you that this slight path can be relied on for tens and hundreds of miles—and you must hike tens of miles to know what they are—to a total of two thousand, for the little path is the A.T., as its devotees tend to call it: the great A.T.! "Yet I doubt not thro' the ages one increasing purpose runs," I remembered—in this case not an increasing but a steady purpose.

The Appalachian Trail! It is a symbol of dependability and loyalty to an elevated ideal on the part of those all along the way who built it and maintain it, and to me, like the two young brothers on the Roan, it speaks appealingly for our people, more appealingly than all the Interstates laid end to end. Is it any wonder that I cannot pass its marker at a highway crossing without pangs of conscience that I am not afoot upon it, pack on back? The evidence is plain that it exercises a growing hold on the American imagination. Colonel Lester Holmes, director of the Appalachian Trail Conference, told me that in 1970 nine persons completed hiking the entire trail; in 1971, 21; in 1972, 34; in 1973, 88 (accredited; the total that year was probably 98). Colonel Holmes would not give me separate figures on through-hikers. He did declare enthusiastically that the 1973 figure included nine-year-old Robin Pearson; the Pearson family, of Ohio, had spent weekends and vacations on the trail for three summers. Professor Frederick W. Luehring completed the trail in 1963 at the age of 82—"and is still going strong," said Colonel Holmes. Another professor, George F. Miller, of Washington, D. C., was the fifth through-hiker. He started at Mount Oglethorpe (the original Georgia end of the trail) on April 18, 1952, weighing 140 pounds, and reached Mount Katahdin on September 3rd, 139 days later and 22 pounds lighter—at the age of 72. Perhaps I shall manage the whole trail yet. Emma, "Grandma," Gatewood became the

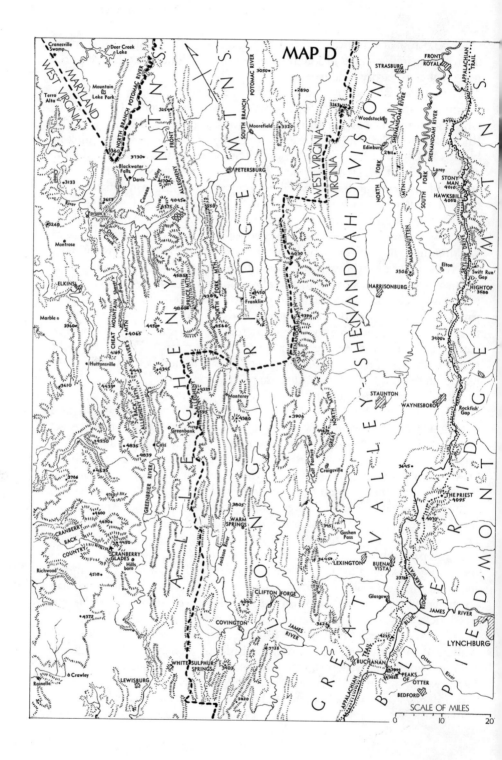

first woman through-hiker when she completed the trip in 146 days in 1955 at 68 and the first and so far only person to have hiked it twice when she did it in 142 days after turning 70.

Almost all through-hikers begin at the Georgia end, usually early in April when the danger of serious snows ahead will have passed. They follow the spring, then, lagging the season, the summer northward, pressing forward in the knowledge that, unless they are exceedingly fleet and have caches of food at highway crossings along the way, they are going to meet autumn coming southward before they finish, maybe even running into the onset of winter at the far end. To reverse the course means starting later but still probably catching late snow on Katahdin if you are to make it through the North Carolina mountains in time to escape the danger of blizzards there, and even then quite likely being snowed on before the finish. Peggy Thomson, a writer in Washington, D. C., who interviewed a number of the through-hikers, wrote that the only question they dodged was: Why attempt the trail at all? "But," she added, "most seem to agree with the through-hiker who paraphrases, 'For those who understand, no explanation is necessary; for those who do not, none is possible.' "

Earlier that morning in the Nantahalas, coming out on a high, brush ridge I had been delighted to find a small bed of Yellow Fringed Orchis. No other flowers have for me the style, the quality of the highly-evolved order of *Ochidales,* which, with "their many beautiful contrivances," as Charles Darwin said, "exalt the whole vegetable kingdom." One associates the orchids with the tropics, where, indeed, most of their 15,000 species live. However, six grow in Arctic tundra and perhaps three dozen in the southern Appalachians. Some are as small as, or even smaller than, the retiring Little Green Wood Orchis I had found growing in shadows among club-mosses near Shining Rock Gap. The largest are the bold, familiar Lady's-slippers, or Moccasin-flowers, Pink and Yellow, which bear single blossoms consisting of a cleft oval pouch and long, narrow petals pointing downward from its top, like long, thin ears or twisted horns. Kneeling to examine one of the Yellow Fringed Orchis (which are not yellow at all), I had seen the little apricot-colored flowers as tiny, gnome-like gargoyles with plumes for cravats facing out in all directions from the top of a pole. They had reminded me of the animal-behaviorist Demorest Davenport's observation that "more often than not orchid flowers are zoömorphic—they may resemble spiders or insects, even tiny birds or other animals." Orchid seeds are minute and light and travel easily, with the result that orchids are widely distributed, but certain fungi are essential to the growth of the seedlings, which means that their distribution is likely to be very local.

It was from that same ridge, the time being about eight o'clock in the morning, that I looked eastward upon a scene that remains as my most striking memory of the Nantahalas. Below me clouds extended over the horizon to merge with the far sky; I was on a lofty island above a white sea. These clouds could have been the primordial mists from which the earth would be born. Ectoplasmal or protoplasmal vapors, they slowly rose, slowly flowed, slowly parted, fitfully disclosing a dark mountain-top below or a higher in the distance. It was as if the Creator were moodily materializing them only to eradicate them—trying his hand and still uncertain of his ultimate intention, maybe even of the worth of it all. I must have stood nearly a quarter-hour in a gap in the Catawba Rhododendron at the edge of the ridge's steep flank, watching. Without pause or change of pace the mists proceeded in their deliberate and solemn flux. Gossamer waves, elongating and contracting, they thinned above a flange of the ridge on which I stood, as the shoulder or summit of another mountain emerged from them only to be stealthily engulfed and effaced again. I thought that now and again I could identify the peaked-loaf form of Satulah, rising above Highlands, and the cone of Rabun Bald, Georgia's second highest, with which my youthful associations were, in the time-scheme of the spectacle, matters of a distant future.

I left the Appalachian Trail to return to the campground at White Oak Bottom on a blue-blazed trail—laterals of the Appalachian Trail are so marked—that utilized one of the narrow-gauge railway roadbeds. None I had been on had nearly so many ties so well preserved as this one. Clearly the Nantahalas were one of the last ranges the logging railroads penetrated. The lumbermen must have found rich pickings from what Charles Lanman wrote of the Nantahalas in 1848, that "among the forest trees were many chestnut and poplar [Tuliptree] specimens, which were at least seven or eight feet in diameter." Washington Irving called Lanman—a painter, editor and writer—"the Picturesque explorer of our country."

Trees such as Lanman saw are still to be found on the watershed of Little Santeetlah Creek near the northwest corner of the Nantahala National Forest. That 3,000 acres of virgin forest have survived there, mostly of Hemlocks, is owing to the power of inferior art. We have seen this illustrated many times. All Hermann Goering's *Luftwaffe* could not have done what Sigmund Romberg's commonplace operetta did, and have saved Heidelberg from Allied bombing in World War II. An embarrassingly poor poem by Joyce Kilmer entitled *Trees* led to the preservation of the noble forest on the Little Santeetlah when in 1935, at the behest of the Veterans of Foreign Wars, the United States Government set aside the creek's entire 3,800-acre watershed as a memorial to the journalist-poet, who had been killed in World War I. I have yet to see the Joyce Kilmer Memorial Forest, but Elaine and Ted Turner, whom I had met on the Shining Rock trail, had spoken of it with the same enthusiasm I have heard others voice: they said it had taken five of them to encircle a Tuliptree there with arms outstretched. And a young man with a stubble of whiskers I was to meet on Blood Mountain said that it was the only forest in the East to have given him the same feeling he had had among the giant trees of the West.

Neither in that forest nor in any other, of course, will Chestnuts like those Lanman exclaimed over be found. The American Chestnut was, *par excellence,* the tree of the Appalachians, which formed the core of its range. Quite apart from the beauty of its abundant, rich foliage billowing superbly in mighty spread around a trunk that could reach ten or 12 feet in diameter at shoulder height, it was with little doubt the single most valuable tree of the Eastern deciduous forest. No food the forest produced, other than game, had such importance to the first settlers and those who followed them as its bounty of nuts. These "wild fruict," William Strachey wrote after visiting Virginia in 1610, "I maie well saie, equallize the best in France, Spaine, Germany, Italy or those so commended by the Black Sea, by Constantinople, of all which I have eaten." Paul Tilden, a conservationist with a special interest in *Castanea dentata,* observes that "The American Indian living within the natural range of the tree depended heavily on the wild chestnut crop to feed his family in autumn and winter; the sweet nuts were eaten roasted, boiled to a broth, or ground into paste from which bread was made." To the Appalachian hill-folk who came after him "the chestnut was ready money . . . where money has never been easily acquired. There was a steady market for nuts in the big city, while the gathering and sale of chestnut bark for the extraction of its profuse tannin occupied the slack days of the winter months. The cabin of the mountain farm might be framed with locust and logged in with chestnut, its roof covered by shakes of the same wood rived out of specially selected trees." Chestnut was the source of the best rails for the mountaineer's snake fences as it was for telephone poles, while the rich, reddish wood made interior wall paneling not out of place in the grandest mansion. Exposed to the weather, chestnut was almost impervious to decay, and this very resistance was to add a grim aspect to the tragedy to come.

Unsuspected at the time, the doom of the species was already sealed when in 1904 a few Chestnuts in the New York Zoological Park were found dying. Within a few years the lethal agent was identified as *Endothia parasitica,* a fungus afflicting chestnuts in the Orient, though not mortally. Both American and European Chestnuts succumbed when the fungus's mycelia, invading the tree's living tissue, ultimately cut off the flow of sap. No treatment availed, no measures of quarantine stayed the advance of the fungus's spores. Within forty years the Chestnut's entire range had been blanketed and every tree of the species killed to the ground—killed but not felled. In death the tree was as invulnerable to fungus as it had been vulnerable in life. For year after year the bleached skeletons remained standing to remind us of our loss; on every Appalachian mountainside the forest was marked by a kind of white varicose veining. There was no forgetting that the days were gone when, as Donald Culross Peattie wrote, the celebrated tree was "to be seen in glorious array, from the upper slopes of Mount Mitchell, the great forest below waving with creamy white Chestnut blossoms in the crowns of the ancient trees, so that it looked like a sea with white combers plowing across its surface."

Yet the Chestnut has proved extraordinarily tenacious of life. Dead from the ground up, the victims would none the less send up new shoots from the roots, then, as these were stricken and killed, further new ones. All through the Chestnut's natural range there are these evidences of its continuing viability. In the Nantahalas, where big old dead Chestnuts were still standing, vigorous and often large crown-shoots were abundant. Clearly these mountains had been hit by the blight well after others I had been in. The trail up Standing Indian passed one healthy Chestnut with a trunk six inches in diameter. To see such a tree, especially one bearing fruit, as some do, though being self-pollinated it is nearly always sterile, is almost inevitably to feel some hope for the species, even though none grows much larger than six inches in trunk diameter without contracting the fungus and with few exceptions quickly succumbing. The National Parks and Conservation Association of Washington, D. C., is promoting a program to develop a resistant strain of *Castanea dentata* "using seed from such few bearing chestnuts as remain on the fringes of original chestnut habitat and, most important, from the few forest specimens that have persisted despite repeated attacks of *Endothia*."

The Department of Agriculture, after trying unsuccessfully by hybridization to develop a blight-resistant tree with the virtues of the American Chestnut, has written off the species as doomed. Dr. Frank S. Santamour, a plant geneticist at the National Arboretum, in Washington, D. C., whom I questioned on the subject, shares its pessimism. Himself a specialist in developing trees resistant to specific pests by selective breeding, he stated that there were simply no sufficiently blight-resistant American Chestnuts to breed from with any hope of success. He saw almost no chance, moreover, that mutants would appear or could be induced that would be blight-resistant and otherwise viable: "Mutants are almost always unsuccessful." I brought up my own pet scheme: tackling the problem from the other side by finding an enemy of *Endothia*. Dr. Santamour agreed that it was virtually a natural law that every living organism would have some other preying on it. *Endothia* might well be subject to bacterial attack. But my suggestion that deliberate re-importations of *Endothia* from the Orient be tried in the hope of bringing in diseased samples he thought too dangerous: there was the possibility of bringing in a more virulent strain of *Endothia* to which other trees might succumb.

Still, as long as any leafing stems of American Chestnut survive one cannot help hoping that the greatest botanical disaster of recorded history, as the National Parks and Conservation Association calls it, may yet be reversed.

The view I had had of mountains to the east shrouded in morning cloud had recalled the time when four or five of us, being young, had set out from the side of Satulah to hike the 15 miles to Rabun's summit on a compass bearing. And that, from what I still remember, is the way to contract the feeling of wilderness: to be deep in tangled woods that are trailless. We actually reached our objective. The way down the western side of the mountain was easy, by trail to a road that came part way up it, and we got to this, and the friend who had come to pick us up in a car, tired, famished, thirsty—and scratched.

Feeling that I owed it to the past to stand again at the top of the volcano-shaped mountain, I went up the way we had come down, driving to the end of the road and walking the rest of the way up a barely Jeepable track. Something, I thought, was different from the walk I had had the day before, up another Jeep road from Patterson Gap, to the northwest, where a sign had read "3,500 FEET. CREST OF THE BLUE RIDGE." It was the same varied Southern mountain woods—but then I had it. Today the usual utter silence of the Appalachians was ruffled by a light wind in the trees. The predictable stunted Oaks that occupied most of Rabun's narrow, near 4,700-foot-high crown were Blacks, with glossy leaves. Blackberries were still green but blueberries nearly ripe. A small forestry tower, well vandalized, of course, looked out on a tremendous amphitheatre of mountains, the Nantahalas on the west, and rippling the far horizon from northwest to northeast, the Greak Smokies, Plott and Great Balsams, as I took them to be. Of the cusp of a much nearer mountain in the northeast, I was quite certain.

It was Whiteside, "the highest peak in the vicinity of Highlands; a real mountain," Bradford Torrey had written in 1898. "On the southerly side it breaks off into a huge perpendicular, light-colored cliff said to be eighteen hundred feet in depth." Forty years earlier Charles Lanman had spoken of it as "one of the most remarkable curiosities in this mountain-land. It is a granite cliff, with a smooth surface or front, half a mile long, and twelve hundred feet high and generally spoken of in this part of the country as the White-side Mountain or the Devil's Courthouse. To think of it is almost enough to make one dizzy, but to see it fills one with awe." While the mountain rises more than 2,000 feet from Whiteside Cove in less than three-quarters of a mile, the actual cliff is less than 1,000 feet high. Still, I am prepared to believe it the highest east of the Rockies, as it has been called, and to testify that Lanman is right about the effect it has on one, certainly on one climbing it. I should never have become a party to doing so, in my nineteenth year, but for a misjudgment. Three of us had hiked from Highlands to Whiteside Cove and on an impulse decided to attempt the cliff, which we had never heard of anyone's having done. Appearances were that it could be scaled without too much difficulty if one followed the bands of vegetation that seemed to zigzag up it, with one zig and one zag—an illusion, as we found. One of my companions, a lovely girl from New Orleans of constitutionally serene cheerfulness, a pre-med student, Edith—Ede—was accepted by all as of a superior species on which gravity might have been expected to act with lessened force. The other, given to representing himself as Etihw Nhoj, was a puckish Carolinian who two years later, to win a bet, was to become the first streaker, racing naked from the Harvard athletic field house across Lars Anderson bridge to his dormitory, on the way vaulting over the hood of a car waiting in bumper-to-bumper traffic at a red light. If those two had any fear they did not betray it, but there were moments, and long ones, on the way up when I was as scared as I have ever been in my life. When, unbelievably, miraculously, we gained the top my trousers were worn through at the knees and my knees abraded from the fervor with which I had pressed against that rock. We were familiar enough with Whiteside's crest and the jutting rock overhanging the precipice, which I could scarcely bear to see anyone go out on. We came up often by the easy trail from Highlands, through the primeval Hemlock forest. The view at the end was such as to move even that unexcitable New Englander, Torrey: "a boundless woodland panorama, with clearings and houses in Whiteside valley, and innumerable hazy mountains rising one beyond another in every direction. The world of new leafage below us, now darkened by cloud shadows, now shining in the sun, was beautiful far beyond any skill of mine to picture it."

I had no desire to revisit Whiteside. The virgin Hemlock forest was long ago ground up into pulp for paper, and the mountain has been "developed."

Back where I had left my bus at the end of the Rabun Bald road, a man my age was working on a house under construction. I remarked to him on all the building I had seen and how much everything around Highlands had changed in forty years. A local man, as I learned, he agreed sadly that it was so. Few farms were left and new tracts for houses had been cleared more and more in recent years. "Land that sold for three dollars an acre in the days you're talking about now brings thousands—if you can find any for sale." He had to admit, though, that things had been awfully tough back around 1930. "Nobody had no money at all until the government came in and started hiring to put people to work. That road you went up the mountain on was one of the things that was done. I worked on that one myself."

"It's only the National Forest that's saving us," Thelma Howell, for many years executive director of the Highlands Biological Station, had said. The Nantahala National Forest all but surrounds the town, although somewhat patchily and at a distance. The Appalachian National Forests are a legacy of the days, especially during the Depression, when mountain land could be had for a few dollars an acre and the Government had providently, and providentially, bought up millions of acres of it. It had not bought enough, however; only half the land within the designated boundaries of the National Forests has ever been acquired, and little is being added today.

When Clark Foreman started the Highlands Museum of Natural History in 1927 it was for the purpose of battling for Highlands' soul. Highlands, with an average elevation within the town limits of 4,119 feet, is located near the southern rim of the southernmost high plateau of the Blue Ridge, an area of high rainfall even for the southern Appalachians on a frontier between northern and southern forms of life. The Biological Station, successor to the Museum, says of it on its letterhead with appealing ardor, "The Highlands Plateau is the greatest biological asset in eastern North America." It also has great advantages as a summer resort. The question was, which set of assets would Highlands cultivate? Would it evolve in the direction of response to and appreciation and study of nature, or in the direction of the Bobby Jones Golf Course then—in 1927—about to be hewn out of the forest on the other side of town? The Museum was the impetus that Foreman and his associates in the undertaking supplied to move it in the former.

And what has been the upshot? The development of Highlands as a resort can hardly be said to have been impeded. The village has become a new, if still smaller, Blowing Rock, with motels, real estate agencies, high-toned dress- and specialty-shops and an auction gallery where practiced salesmen put glass, china, silver and jewels up for bids before a well-dressed clientele with, presumably, nothing better to do with its evenings. The blue-jeaned crowd of youths of both, and not always readily distinguishable, sexes is much in evidence on the shopping street, and motorcycles roar about. The Museum, however, has not fallen behind. Having acquired an attractive, low building with the help of the Works Progress Administration in 1940, it has become the Biological Station, supported by 14 universities and the National Science Foundation with a complex of well-equipped laboratories, library, cottages for visiting scientists and kitchen and dining-hall able to feed 50 persons.

I was made to feel at home at the Biological Station by Dr. Howell and her successor, Richard C. Bruce, introduced to the working scientists and shown some of the studies done at the station. Then, and as I walked the paths through the wonderful collection of growing wildflowers bordering the Station's six-acre lake in its 16 acres of woodland, my mind went back to my early days with the Museum, in 1928. To my lasting loss, I had arrived just too late to meet Donald Culross Peattie, who combined knowledge with eloquence in writing of the Blue Ridge as no one else has. He had come to visit the Museum fresh from a trip to the site, farther up the plateau on the east, of André Michaux's discovery of *Shortia,* the famous plant that disappeared for a century. I had had better luck with Clifford Pope, future curator of herpetology at the American Museum of Natural History. He was putting in a longer stay at Highlands, living with the Foremans, as I was. His devotion to his field, which was single-minded, must have been infectious, for, briefly, I could almost imagine salamanders competing with birds for my allegiance; the Highlands area, I might add, was more outstanding in its store of the former than of the latter. I recall today the satisfaction with which I learned that the salamander called *Plethodon jordani,* while entirely a near-black above in the southeastern Blue Ridge, had red cheeks in the Smokies and red forelegs in the Nantahalas; the signs that nature has the temperament of a collector, as I think I have, make me feel more at home on the earth. Descending from the Appalachian Trail to the Nantahala River just before my return to Highlands, I had had a small thrill in turning up a black *Plethodon* under a log and finding it had forelegs of the prescribed red; the universe was on the rails.

The compartmentalization of mountain environments, which isolates populations of less mobile organisms, like salamanders, adds to their interest to biologists. The "isolates" of *P. jordani* are now known to number about 20. "North America (including Central America)," says Roger Conant in *A Field Guide to Reptiles and Amphibians,* "has more varieties of salamanders than all the rest of the world put together." And the southern Appalachians, with (as I learn from Harry G. M. Jopson of Bridgewater College, Virginia) no less than 34 species and as many as 25 named races, all presumably evolving into separate species, is in this respect the most richly endowed area of its size in North America. I should have been highly gratified as a 17-year-old to know that the races would one day include two of *P. jordani* called respectively the Highlands Salamander and the Rabun Bald Salamander. The Plethodontidae, or Lungless Salamanders, "the largest salamander family," says Richard Highton of the University of Maryland, "has its probable center of origin in the ancient Appalachian Mountain system." (These breathe through the skin and lining of the mouth.) I should not have been as astonished as I was to learn that the Highlands Biological Station felt it could expect 30-odd Salamandarins to attend a recent conference on this amphibian wealth, for which it was host.

"And what would you say if we told you that the actual attendance reached 50?"

Apart from the very large species, salamanders are rather engaging creatures. Quite harmless, they have somewhat the facial look of bug-eyed puppies and are mostly easy to keep in captivity. One of my early duties at the Highlands Museum was catching flies for a number of them, as also for a rough-scaly, blue-throated, exceedingly swift Fence Lizard I had caught myself after an exhausting chase, persuaded that I was bringing in a species new to science. I still have a scar where I laid a finger open on the edge of a cover-glass and was put together by the grimy-nailed fingers of the local doctor, with tape, to save us both the trouble of stitches. By virtue of the salamanders, the Amphibians are one class and the only class of vertebrates you can count on finding almost everywhere in the southern Appalachians in the warm half of the year—and the Red-spotted Newt is sometimes seen in a pool swimming under a film of ice. Clifford Pope told of collecting 35 specimens of *P. jordani* in an hour in the Smokies, mostly under logs and fallen branches, and 104 of *Desmognathus f. fuscus,* or Northern Dusky Salamander, in two days on Pine Mountain, Kentucky, along streams.

Salamanders come in a variety of forms and of habitats, clear to the tops of the highest of the Southern mountains. The largest—up to a foot or more long, with a record length of over 29 inches—is the large-headed Hellbender, a seeming relic of the days when Amphibians were king. It is also one of the most aquatic, inhabiting rivers and large streams. It is the ugliest, too, so gross and appalling looking that most fishermen will cut the line when it takes their bait. The Pygmy and Cherokee Salamanders, two Dusky Salamanders of the North Carolina and Georgia Blue Ridge respectively, are only two inches long at most. At two other opposite extremes from the Hellbender, the widely distributed Marbled Salamander may be found far from water, even, under cover, on dry hillsides; and, black below and silver blotched with black above, it is a beauty. So is the Yonahlossee, a *Plethodon*—or Woodland Salamander—from the southwestern Virginia and North Carolina Blue Ridge with a bright, rust-colored back. And the rock crevices of cliffs are the home of the lichen-colored Green Salamander, a southern Appalachian endemic which may even climb up trees. Goodness! When I think about it I feel I *must get out and do something about salamanders.* But then there are the Duskies, many of which only experts can differentiate from one another or from some of the Woodlands. Most of these lurk under stones at the edge of streams, where, safe from aquatic foes, they can sprint for the water if unroofed by a terrestrial, even jumping on the way if necessary. Salamanders ordinarily come out into the open only at night, but the Black-bellied, a large, agile Dusky endemic to the main southern Appalachian massif, may climb out of a stream onto a rock during the day, even, says Conant, in the sun. And the Red Eft, the terrestrial stage of the Newt, creeps about openly by day, secure in the poison or irritant secreted by its skin when broken.

The rains from the Atlantic and Gulf that douse the Southeastern Blue Ridge Escarpment, of which the Highlands Plateau is a part, pour down from it through the gorges they have cut to form the headwaters of the Savannah and Chattahoochee Rivers, or are tumbled northwestward by tributaries of the Little Tennessee, bound for the Mississippi; the Blue Ridge Divide goes through the Highlands town limits. Since precipitation in heavy years may amount to 100 inches or even 125 very locally, the Escarpment is a place of rushing waters. The Chattooga, central branch of the Savannah forming the upper border between Georgia and South Carolina, runs through rapids rated among the most dangerous in the country for canoeists and rafters. Among the best known as well, having figured in James Dickey's novel, *Deliverance,* and the motion picture made of it, they have taken six lives.

With the rapids are falls. The road to Highlands from Franklin, which winds up the wildly, darkly beautiful gorge of the Cullasaja, faced with granite that breaks through the forest like the front of thunderclouds, takes you behind one waterfall and close by the superbly plunging, splashing Cullasaja Falls. I know of no drive in the East in which you are more in thrall to your surroundings. Even so, it cannot match the drama there was in coming upon these falls displaying their magnificence in dashing silver in the deep forest before the highway was put through here; to that I can testify. Another waterfall of outstanding beauty is formed only two miles southwest of Highlands where the East Fork of Overflow Creek cascades down rock shelved in such a way as to cause it to fan out on its way down. From below, Glen Falls are a pyramid of dashing waters that looks seventy feet high. And what rock!—a gneiss almost black, spectacularly banded in broad, wavy, flowing swaths of pure white quartz. I can stare indefinitely at falls, as who cannot? There is a recklessness and abandon in waters down-sloping into a headlong, free dive that strikes a responsive chord in the spirit.

With a botanist from the Biological Station, Bill Floyd, I went for a walk in one of the ravines below Highlands. (With a face encircled by hair, Bill may be pictured as a youthful, slight New England sea-captain.) These are moist places even for the southern Appalachians. The deeper gorges cut by the rivers in their rush to the Piedmont are even suspected of serving as flues up which the southerlies blow to have the water vapor they bear precipitated out as by condensers. The conditions created might be likened to the submarine. In the leather-leaved jungle we entered after a gentle rain had quietly begun and as quietly ended, leaving a heavy overcast, night might almost have fallen. Never have I seen such Rosebay Rhododendron

A Red Eft in the Author's hand.

and Mountain-laurel; the trunks of both were up to a foot thick. Under one stand of Rhododendron was a bed of plants a few inches high with flowers like winged maple-seeds. I should scarcely have noticed them, but they were orchids, humblest of the family: Kidney-leaved Twayblades. Bill said they grew mostly under rhododendron and that fellow botanists of his, photographing flowers in the mountains, had never come on any in the sunshine.

On the floor of the heavily-shaded hollows the law was: make do with little sunlight or none, or by hook or crook get up to where the sunlight is. A plant that did just that last was the round-leaved vine Greenbrier, an aberrant Lily, of all things. We were always having to dodge its thorny green, drawn-wire stems. Young ones were free-standing, up to five feet tall; they would sway in the breeze like cobras to a fakir's flute, waiting to be blown up against a larger plant to which they could grapple with the delicate, hooked tendrils near their tips. Best at sustaining themselves in little light were of course the liverworts—including the Three-toothed

Bazzania I had seen in the high mountains to the north—and the mosses. Rocks were completely covered by Fern Moss *(Thuidium delicatulum),* Feather Moss (the *Hypnum imponens* of Big Balsam) and the similar *Heterophyllium affine,* a Moss found only in the southern Appalachians, the Ozarks and tropical America. Lichens also did well in the moisture. Rock-tripe hung on the boulders in sheets a foot wide.

As in the ocean's depths, however, most life on the floor of the forest bottoms was dependent on the products of photosynthesis that came down from the sunlit zones above—fallen leaves and bark, nuts, fruits, branches and whole trees. A lens would have revealed an amazing fauna feeding on the detritus—the "soil decomposers," of which I had had my first, incredulous view through my young biologist daughter's microscope: copepods like shrimp; isopods, or wood-lice, like trilobites; pseudoscorpions (much resembling the real things); spiders; beetle-mites; springtails; snails; worms. Larger invertebrates—centipedes, insects, spiders—fed on these, and they in turn fed the salamanders, toads, snakes, birds and shrews.

The showiest consumers of the decaying organic matter were the mushrooms and bracket fungi. In the low, dark woods and the open woods above they were as colorful and exquisitely contrived as flowers. Paddle-shaped Conk Fungi growing out of a hemlock log were a cherry-wood red-brown and as shiny as if varnished. Growing from the bases of trees, a Berkeley's Polypore was like big stacked omelets, and a Sulphur Polypore of wavy lobes, one above another, as if sculptured of the brightest orange sherbets in bands of different shades: incredible. More truly sulphur-colored was the mushroom *Amanita flavoconia.* Growing among pine needles and oak leaves, another *Amanita*—genus of the Avenging Angel and other killers—looked as if tooled of white soap. One of the most widespread, a *Rossula,* was a white mushroom over which a cherry syrup might have been poured, settling most thickly at the center. A small *Cantharellus cinnabarinus* was of a solid, deep, intense coral- or watermelon-pink, so choice you wondered what nature had in mind.

We are apt to think of mushrooms as plants with their roots out of sight, like the green plants. In actuality, what we see is only the spore-producing body, comparable to the fruit of flowering plants. The plant body, called the mycelium and consisting of long, extensively-branched filaments, called the hyphae, which absorb the organic material the organism lives on, is entirely contained in the earth or decaying wood or whatever the mushroom is growing in. In the case of the Polypores and many other bracket fungi this is the tissue of living trees. Some mushrooms are beneficial to their hosts, however. Bill said that an *Amanita* spreads its hyphae along the roots of pines, enabling them to multiply their intake of minerals about ten times while itself probably getting nutrients somehow from the tree. Later, Dr. Santamour happened to mention to me that Long-leafed

Pines of the Deep South introduced into Puerto Rico grew only a few feet—until someone tossed some handfuls of soil from their native habitat among them, whereupon they shot up; evidently the soil contained parts of the mycelium of the fungus they depended on.

Some flowering plants have given up their chlorophyl and adopted the life of mushrooms. We came on two on higher ground. One, consisting of a small stalk of inconspicuous little brownish purple flowers, was an orchid, no less: Coralroot. The other, of equally unlikely descent—a Heath—was the rather eerie Indian-pipe, like crooks of congealed moonlight. The clump of ten must have just sprung up—as they do overnight—for it still had a pinkish cast, reminding me of wax candy containing fruit syrup I knew as a boy.

For the next stage of my travels, west through the mountains of Georgia, I left Highlands by the Dillard road. This used to be a very winding road, most so on a long, steep grade; it crossed the North Carolina/Georgia line five times on the way down. What it may be now, I do not know. The last time I saw it the highwaymen were blasting the sides out of all recognition. The idea behind the destruction of the road's attractiveness was evidently to enable motorists seeking the solace and invigoration the mountains offer to get up into them with as little awareness as possible that they were doing so.

It is unfair to the mountains of Georgia to come to them from the dark-spired cloudlands of North Carolina. They should be seen as the apex of a state that begins with Palmettos, alligators and Live Oaks hung with Spanish Moss, and the cool haven of their northerly forests and limpid, shadowed streams be approached from the hills to their south where the sun glazes the foliage of Loblolly Pine, Sweet Gum and Spanish Oak. All the same, having turned into State Highway 348, I did not feel that allowances had to be made. Called the Richard D. Russell Scenic Highway, this is like a short, displaced section of the Blue Ridge Parkway and it was nearly deserted. From Tesnatee Gap the array of mountains leading away to the north looked as sublime to me as the Great Balsams had, Brasstown Bald merging with the summer-hazy heavens. No less did they seem to speak of some lofty purpose or power in the universe beyond human conception. And the flowers! Here as in the Nantahalas every forest opening was thronged with Phlox, Black-eyed Susans, Pale Bergamot, Wild Sun-flowers, Mountain Mint, Allegheny Bluebells of delphinium azure, Fire Pinks as intense a red as Cardinal Lobelia.

There are three projections of the high Appalachians into Georgia, all largely incorporated in the 1,100-square-mile Chattahoochee National Forest. Rabun Bald is in the first, a prolongation of the eastern escarpment of the Blue Ridge. The central, a long extension of the Nantahalas to the southwest, is the principal one. The Appalachian Trail comes up this range, through Tesnatee Gap, but skirts its dominant peak, wisely. I had always looked forward to climbing Brasstown Bald, having been brought up on its oddly characterful name, but waited too long. There is now a paved road up it and, despite its being in National Forest, it is crowned with a massive and ostentatious complex of stone buildings housing a "Visitors Center" and restaurant. So I forewent it in favor of Blood Mountain, the highest in the state crossed by the Appalachian Trail.

Blood Mountain takes its name from a day of fierce fighting when the streams on its side are said to have run red. The story is that late in the eighteenth century the Creeks, invading the territory of the Cherokees, were met on the saddle between Blood and its no-less-gruesomely-named neighbor, Slaughter Mountain, and defeated. Certainly many arrowheads and spear-points have been found on the saddle. To the Cherokees Blood Mountain was the home of the Yunwee Chuns Dee, the Little Folk, whose subterranean dwellings were reached by a cave in the mountain. The Nunna-hee, who were normal sized, also abided there and came to the help of those lost in the forest. You climb from deep woods up the side of Blood Mountain as Rhododendron and Laurel multiply and, where Galax abounds, get that penetrating, mysterious, musky smell. It is much as on Rabun, except that the diminished Oaks bordering the peak are Whites instead of Blacks, as on Chinquapin, near Highlands, they are Whites and Blackjacks, as on mountains farther north they will be Reds. Over their tops you can see the Georgia Piedmont to the south and 17 miles to the southwest—30 by trail—Springer Mountain, Mile 0 on the Appalachian Trail. Perhaps being deemed unworthy, I was vouchsafed no glimpse of the spirit people of the mountain and heard no strain of the magic music for which the Yunwee Chuns Dee were known. To my delight, however, I did find a patch of Three-toothed Cinquefoil, winter associate of Snow Buntings on northern shores and on the Roan. It grew on the peak of rock capping the 4,458-foot summit, reaching to within 18 inches of the top, the first hint of the arctic, a promise of Katahdin's blizzard-flayed rocky heights 2,000 miles to the northeast.

The next day I came to recognize that if I was not becoming a compulsive walker, I easily could; it was only the thought of my family and the need to get on with my assignment that restrained me. On the trail I felt a need always to go on, and analyzing why this was, I decided the cause was an obscure but gnawing sense that if I kept going I should sooner or later come to what it was that the mountains were holding back from me.

My thoughts took this turn while I was in the Cohutta Range. The third and most westerly projection of the high Appalachians into Georgia, this is an isolated cluster of mountains of steep and intricate contours. The southern part is traversed by U. S. Highway 76, but from there for nearly

25 miles into Tennessee there are no other paved roads. To reach the interior of the range, as it were, and the campground at Conesauga Lake you make an 11-mile climb on a gravel road, up a good 2,500 feet, by my reckoning.

Woods, woods . . . with Cherry Birches replacing the Yellows of the farther north. It was late when I set out afoot from the ridge above the lake and I walked as long as I dared, telling myself that I hoped to see a beast of some kind, a Raccoon, Wildcat or Black Bear. And I did hope to, of course. But though I walked as quietly as I could, the trail around the next bend was always empty. The trees stood there in utter gravity and silence in the gathering dusk, and nothing moved. But it was not animals alone that in my heart I was looking for. What it was I had suggested to me the next day by two birds, each of a species I always associate with the sentient, attentive quality that rich woods in the brooding summer warmth seem to have. One was a yellow-bodied Kentucky Warbler, which masquerades in a black mask showing the yellow around the eyes. Surprisingly, it was almost up at the top of Bald Mountain, the last 4,000-footer to the southwest and, despite its name, entirely wooded over its dome. A male, its body carried well forward in an alert way, it twitched from side to side on its long legs to examine me, then, losing interest, darted off. The second was very like the first, only it was black of head and breast but for its wonderful gold face—a Hooded Warbler, like a gift of the tropics. Its song, clearly and emphatically whistled, seems always to take liberties with the quiet, as only a privileged intimate might. Provocative and taunting, it sounds, as if the impish singer would keep drawing you deeper into its haunted realm. The birds, I thought, had for me the character of little leaks in the immense reserve of the mountains through which teasing intimations of what was profound and withheld bubbled forth, enigmatically, to be sure, as a baiting playfulness might be permitted in the little grandchildren of the greatest and most impassive Indian chief. . . . I must be imagining that if I kept walking long enough I should come upon a clue to that secret of the mountains of which G. M. Trevelyan spoke, some revelation of it where the trail dipped or rounded the ridge, perhaps through the agency of some totemic animal. It might be that the Cherokees had expected the same lifting of the veil in the enchanted minstrelsy of the Yunwee Chuns Dee.

I had seen the Hooded Warbler in the fitting setting of the Jack's River gorge, a feature of the Cohutta range noted for its wildness and beauty. Its difficulty of negotiation was certainly to the advantage of both. While the sides lacked the extreme height of Linville Gorge's, they were closer together and, shutting out more of the sun, favored the growth of rhododendron and hemlocks, of which there were big ones. Indeed, the ravine through which the river poured in its turbulence was so narrow that the trail had to cross from side to side and back in descending it. Forewarned, I was wearing canvas shoes but had to feel my way carefully, not to go down.

Legislation expected to be passed by Congress in 1975 calls for bringing almost 50,000 acres of the Cohutta range under the protection of the Wilderness Act.

In conversation with a game official beside the road, I nodded toward a complex of ranges visible through a break in the forest. If you went up one at random, I asked, how long would you be likely to go without seeing another human being if you stayed there.

"It could be a long time," he said. "Maybe twenty years."

The Appalachians run down into Central Alabama and offer some striking gorge scenery on the way, as in the sandstone canyon of Bee Branch. But once you are more than 40 miles south of the northern border of Georgia you meet no elevations above 2,000 feet.

IX *Something About the Mammals*

Since the sketchy map of the Cohutta Wildlife Management Area on which I had been depending to take me to the Jack's River gorge omitted a key road I should probably never have found the gorge by myself. Luckily, as I was studying the map a man in a ranger-style uniform and shoulder patch of a Game Management Officer of the Georgia Game and Fish Commission came along in a Ford Bronco and stopped to see what I was about. Had I a firearm? I certainly had not!

"There's nothing wrong with firearms," I was admonished. My interrogator had a nickel-plated .38 revolver at his hip, and I dare say had reason for it.

Larry Ross, a personable, blond twenty-four-year-old, had the 90,000-acre Cohutta Wildlife Management Area to cover, with two other officers. I learned that areas so designated, of which I had been in several in National Forests, were areas in which the wildlife was under state management. Open seasons were shorter in them, the laws stringently enforced, close tabs kept on the game and range improvements undertaken. Georgia, I was glad to hear, had an advanced, progressive game-management policy. I had noticed on the Forest Service map that as much as half the Chattahoochee National Forest was in Game Management Areas.

Ross having volunteered to lead me to the gorge in his Bronco, I followed very willingly, of course, though with increasing trepidation after we had passed Dally Gap. The narrow road was what is called unimproved. We went down into holes and over sideways slopes I never thought I should see my poor little bus attempting.

At one point Ross stopped suddenly and told me to get out my camera. He had spotted a Copperhead in the road ahead—the only poisonous snake, I might say, that I saw in my travels. I took two pictures, but they were doomed by the poor light. Copperheads are handsome creatures, with their glowing browns alternating in patches of lighter and darker and coppery heads. But I never see them pictured without thinking of the time in the

Shenandoah National Park, out from Skyland on Miller's Head, when our younger daughter, then four, started to step from a pile of stones into some weeds—and would have had not Vera, acting on impulse, faster than she had time to think, put out her hand and stopped her. Then the strength drained out of us as we saw what the little girl would have landed in: three Copperheads coiled together—as many as I have seen alive, outside of zoos, in all the rest of my life. One bite she might have survived; three, never.

After two miles, in great apprehension of getting mired, turning over, or losing the transmission, I pulled the bus off into a clear space. Here, Ross following me, we had lunch before we made the rest of the trip on foot, my meal coming from my little icebox, his from his store of Army C-rations. A graduate of West Georgia College, my companion was an intelligent and interesting young man and evidently devoted to the outdoor life his occupation provided. He had gone up to Alaska in 1969 and after two other jobs had struck a bonanza in the form of work with a fire-fighting crew. For this he was paid fifty dollars a day, more than he had made in a week in a

By far the most conspicuous mammal in the Southern Mountains—the chipmunk.

textile mill in Georgia. Meanwhile the girl he was to marry was attending the University of Dijon—giving me to think how much Georgia had changed, that it could produce a couple like this in the Cohutta wilds.

In the Southern mountains generally, deer, squirrels, grouse, turkeys and bears were the principal quarry of hunters, but here, Ross said, the animals chiefly pursued were hogs. Most of these were descended from domestic stock gone wild in years past when there was free range and farmers merely marked their hogs by cutting distinctive patches out of their ears. Some were Russian Boars, originally imported into Tennessee, which had filtered south into the Cohutta range from the adjacent Ocoee Wildlife Management Area. And there were hybrids.

"There's a good deal of raccoon-hunting in the area in the open season. That's only Saturday nights in late fall and early winter. And only twenty-two-rim-fire rifles are allowed to be used against raccoons. The practice is for the coon-hunters to sit around a fire while the dogs run through the woods baying in ways that tell their masters what's going on. When the outcry indicates that they've treed a coon, the men take off after them through the woods, up the ridges, maybe tearing themselves to ribbons in a great state of excitement."

And partially anaesthetized, I added mentally, visualizing the scene around the fire. I hoped it was true that raccoons were capable of going along in a stream to lose pursuing dogs.

Charles O. Handley, Jr., of the National Museum of Natural History writes that "No other place in eastern North America can boast a mammalian fauna as diverse as that of the Appalachian highlands." And he adds, "There are more species in the southern Appalachians than in the northern (90 of the total of 93)." The great majority of the 90 are obscure rodents, moles and shrews that you will have little chance of encountering unless you run a trap-line, and bats. To count on seeing any but a few of the mammals that dwell in these mountains, certainly outside the National Parks, you would have to employ traps or hunting dogs. And it is men with traps or guns or both and often with dogs who have exterminated most of the larger beasts and reduced the numbers of most others.

The bison, which ranged from the plains across the Appalachians to their eastern foothills, were the first to go. Next were the American Elk, which had about the same range as the bison. They were killed off by the middle of the nineteenth century, leaving a variety of place-names to commemorate their former prominence: Elk River, Elk Creek, Elkview, Elk Valley, Elk Horn, Elk Park and Banner Elk. Yet there may be American Elk in Virginia today—probably are a few. Some 140 of these deer, tall as horses and proud of stance, were imported from Yellowstone National Park in 1917 and about 100 more in succeeding years. Two herds became established. One, in western Virginia, in Giles and Bland Counties, did well enough for a time to justify permitting a limited number of gunners in some years to have a chance at them. The other ranged around Peaks of Otter, on the Blue Ridge Parkway. According to the Virginia Commission of Game and Inland Fisheries, the former "has been completely extirpated during recent years" while the latter "is now reported to be at a very low population level." The last evidence of the presence of elk around the Peaks of Otter that I have been able to run down consisted of tracks that I found going most of the way up the trail to the summit of Flat-top in March 1973. The reasons for the disappearance of the elk need not be sought far. Venison is very good eating, and there are always those human types to whom getting something for nothing is the pinnacle of achievement. Moreover, the elk made enemies of the local farmers by coming down in winter and gnawing the bark from fruit trees.

That a few wolves hung on till the present century is remarkable. Every livestock keeper's hand is against them. Men who enjoy killing enjoy it more when virtue can be claimed for the act—and wolves, handsome and capable animals of admirable traits, forming an integral part of nature's economy and balance, have long been mindlessly maligned as wicked and cruel. We are brought up taking it for granted that wolves are killers of human beings, which they are not unless rabid; dogs are the homicidal canines. The last wolves reported in the mountains were one said to have been killed in Virginia in 1910 and one seen there in 1912.

River otters and beavers, aquatic epitomes respectively of svelt grace and industry, once enlivened suitable waters from our southern borders north to timberline and beyond. They were doomed in the mountains as almost everywhere else in the 48 states by their valuable pelts. But here the recital takes a more cheerful turn. Beavers are making a comeback, from the north, and their lodges are rising beside ponds of their making in Maryland and both Virginias.

If wolves are gone, foxes remain. In fact the Red Fox, which is distributed all the way around the northern hemisphere, has extended its range into the mountains in historical times, as the forest has been opened up. At the same time the southern Grey Fox has pushed north into Canada. Both are skillful hunters of rodents, especially mice, and will take a fat bird when they can, not sparing the poultry yard, but as needs be will make do with birds' eggs, insects and fruit. The Grey, of South American derivation and a different genus from other North American foxes, is more exclusively nocturnal than the Red and less canny, but when pressed can climb a small tree.

A more formidable carnivore is the Wildcat or Bobcat, which holds out probably all through the Southern mountains. Keeping hidden by day in laurel thickets, hollow logs and rock crevices, it is devilish hard to spot. It reaches 30 pounds in weight, twice a fox's size; one killed near Asheville is said to have weighed 51 pounds. It may even bring down a deer when driven by hunger to risk its quarry's deadly hooves. I have seen only two, both crossing the Blue Ridge Drive, one at dusk, the other in the morning, looking like a tawny, muzzleless dog with docked tail.

Two of the three Timber Rattlesnakes I have met with were also crossing the Drive. Rattlers are clearly apprehensive and tensely alert in man's presence. In this, and in the warning buzz they try to give before striking when they feel themselves threatened, they demonstrate their anxiety to avoid a showdown. If they and Copperheads were the aggressive menaces some persons imagine, there would be many more fatalities than there are among the religious sectarians in southern Appalachia who accept and act on the literal word of *Mark 16:18,* that true believers "shall take up serpents; . . . and it shall not harm them."

The Black Bear has meat the equal of beef and a valuable coat. It is slower than a wolf, certainly no more intelligent and presents a fairer target. It can be brought to bay by dogs, which a wolf can outrun or kill. Yet where the wolf was wiped out, the Black Bear managed to hold on until

A Black bear family in the Great Smoky Mountains National Park. *United States Department of the Interior, National Park Service Photo.*

given the protection of closed seasons. The explanation must be that bears were not pursued with such relentless ferocity as wolves. It may have been of advantage to them, too, that they are almost omnivorous and require no food at all in severe winter weather, which they drowse through, not strictly hibernating. Today their survival is ensured by the National Parks, into the campgrounds of which they saunter at nightfall to help themselves to any edibles not specially protected. So also, if not anticipated by bears, does a small, distant relative of theirs, originally from tropical America, black-masked, pointed of muzzle, of bushy, ringed tail, the most popular of our native carnivores. The Raccoon may be even more catholic in diet, consuming anything from fresh corn, berries and insects to candy bars, molluscs and red meat. A small one, which has taken to coming to our kitchen doorstep in the evening for scraps and dog food put out for her, climbed up on our porch a few nights ago and polished off half a spicy pizza pie inadvertently left there. Of all the animals I know, the Raccoon would seem to me to have the most promise of evolving into our replacement if the world's primates should all disappear. The creature is keen-witted and with enough mental flexibility to become part of a human household if taken in young. Our wild visitor quickly sized us up as innocuous and within a few days was taking food from our hands. And the Raccoon has hands itself. What other quadruped in our fauna could reach down a crayfish's burrow, feel around for the occupant, and come up with it in its clutch?

Where, along with its wiliness and adaptability, the Raccoon is assisted in maintaining itself by its appealing qualities, the skunk is assisted by its repellent. The Striped Skunk and the much less common, more silky-haired and lightly-built Spotted Skunk are alike in that. If their deterrent is ineffective against guns and motorcars, it works well against dogs, which, with cats, are prime destroyers of wildlife in the East. Skunks are frequent along the Drive, being seen most often at sundown. Early last March I met with one after another to a total of nine on a stretch of 50 miles—and in the middle of the day. One was predominantly white, two were almost black. Presumably just out of hibernation, all were ferreting single-mindedly among the grass roots and under forest debris for grubs. I found that when I stood still on the route of approach it was I, not they, who decided when they had come close enough—a dozen feet. A movement then would cause the animal to snap to attention and glare indignantly at me with white-tipped tail erect in warning. I would then withdraw, back-stepping like an obsequious functionary.

The third of the trio of middle-sized carnivores distributed generally through the mountains—this one normally in the valleys—the Opossum makes its play for survival in the size of its litters. Up to a dozen or even more young may be born at a time, and, Opossums being marsupials, these are grub-sized at birth and must be carried for two months in the mother's pouch. At least it is hard to see what, other than its fruitfulness, the slow-moving, slow-witted beast, in appearance midway between a large rat and a small pig, has in its favor. Those I have surprised, instead of feigning death as the species is supposed to in its defenselessness, have rather piteously opened their pink, tooth-lined mouths like scissors and hissed softly.

Larry Ross had spoken of the "Russian Boars," which had crossed into Georgia from Tennessee. The European Wild Boar, despite the pressures of hunting during the past nearly 40 years, appears to be a lasting addition to the Southern mountain fauna. The species, which is distributed across the whole of Europe, northern Africa and northern and central Asia, was introduced into the United States in 1912 by George Gordon Moore. For the entertainment of visiting English capitalists, whom he represented, Moore laid out a 1,500-acre game refuge on Hooper's Bald, south of the Smokies on the border of Tennessee and North Carolina. Enclosing it in a sturdy wire fence, he stocked it with bison, elk, Mule Deer from the West and Black Bears—and 14 Wild Boars from Germany. These last were further confined in an enclosure of chestnut logs. But Wild Boars are prodigiously strong and they soon broke free. The hundreds of Wild Boars in the mountains of Tennessee, North Carolina and Georgia today are their descendants. While they interbred with the free-ranging domestic hogs to the point that probably few pure-breds remained, the Wild Boar strain is so much more virile, aggressive and adapted to the wilds that the species tends to reconstitute itself; it was the ancestor of the domestic stock to begin with. Large of head and massive of shoulders, like bison, Wild Boars range in size to 400 pounds, in rare cases to 500—the size of a pretty big Black Bear. Cornered, they can be dangerous; "From the earliest times," says the *Encyclopaedia Britannica*, "owing to its great strength, speed, and ferocity when at bay, the boar has been one of the favorite beasts of the chase." It is anything but a favorite in the Great Smoky Mountains National Park, where it is destroying vegetation by its rooting, killing salamanders and the young of birds and mammals unable to elude it and making a specialty of snakes; Rattlers and Copperheads, unable to penetrate the gristle of its face with their fangs, are chomped up with as little ceremony as any others. The problem is one the University of Tennessee is trying to bring under control by baiting the males with a contraceptive drug.

Seventy years ago the naturalist William T. Hornaday, impressed by the adeptness of the Virginia or White-tailed Deer at skulking, predicted that the species will "be the last of the large hoofed animals of North America to become extinct." Its success in the East since that time, while subjected to intensive hunting as the most desired game animal the East as a whole affords, justifies Hornaday's confidence in it. Deer, which do best in

A white-tailed deer. *United States Department of the Interior, National Park Service Photo.*

open woods, have in fact benefitted from the breaking up of the forest at the white man's hands. With their major predators eliminated, they tend to multiply beyond the ability of the habitat to support them, as is well known. At least it ought to be well known; hunters are forever citing the fact as justification for shooting deer and indeed for shooting everything else. What would be to the advantage of the deer as a species would be the return of their natural predators and more culling of the herd by these with correspondingly less by indiscriminate human hunters. Such a development would be a thrilling one in itself to those of us to whom the grace, style and beauty of proportion of the great carnivores, like the grace, style and beauty of proportion of the deer—each having produced the other—are an inseparable part of what life and the earth are about. The question arises as to whether there is any possibility of this.

The predator most closely associated with deer is the Cougar—which may have something to do with its being deer-colored itself. Formerly found almost throughout the United States, this man-sized, long-tailed cat, also called the Puma, Mountain Lion, Panther and Painter, is probably the world's most adaptable carnivore. It is at home in forest, swamps, desert and high mountains, and from Alaska through the tropics to Patagonia. According to the best evidence, its extermination in the southern Appalachians was completed even well before the wolf's; it has the fatal habit of treeing readily before hunting dogs. Yet Maurice Brooks cites convincing reports of a Cougar in the West Virginia mountains in 1936 and 1962, then raises the question of why none is ever trapped or shot or treed by bear-hunters with dogs. Richard H. Manville in *The Mammals of Shenandoah National Park* states that there have been 50 purported sightings of Cougars in the Park by Rangers and tourists since 1941, but he is far from persuaded that the animal is actually there.

Since that was written in 1956, however, reports of the Cougar's presence have been accumulating. In April 1962, standing watch in the forestry tower on Shenandoah Mountain, in the Virginia Long Ridges, Charles F. Whitmore had a long look through a binocular at a large cat that walked out on the road, one "about four feet from nose to rump, six to tail-tip and"—this was startling—"a brilliant orange-yellow with dark blotches." One thinks of a tropical cat, imported and escaped, but, standing in bright sunlight, it could well have been a young Cougar. Twice in the winter of 1966–67, on the western slope of Stonyman in the Shenandoah National Park, Darwin and Eileen Lambert saw cat-tracks in the snow, about three inches across and 20 in stride, that almost certainly were those of a Cougar. Later, in June, a visitor of theirs from Tucson—Patricia Bulmer—and her two daughters, all of whom had known Cougars in the West, saw one cross the Skyline Drive north of Skyline.

Those were the first reports I heard. They were followed by others. In July 1960, on the southern side of Shenandoah Mountain, Ruby Rice of Columbia Union College saw *two* Cougars together, one of which climbed a tree. Jim Hodges, a biology student of Prof. Harry G. M. Jopson, in June 1973 while hiking the Appalachian Trail—of which he covered the full length—had a Cougar cross the trail 25 yards in front of him just north of Swift Run Gap in the Shenandoah National Park. The most astonishing encounter was reported by Joy Nicol, one of the young women employed at Skyland. She was sitting on the porch of her cabin at two o'clock in the morning when a Cougar came up onto it on the far side of a bag of trash, only four feet from her. In fleeing when it saw her, it leapt the four-foot railing to the ground eight feet below. The next morning, according to Ray Schaffner, Park Naturalist, a Cougar crossed the road in front of the car of a couple staying at Skyland. About a fortnight later, with a companion, Miss Nicol again had a brief view of a Cougar, the animal this time standing under a lamp in a parking area 20 yards off.

The Department of the Interior's Bureau of Sports Fisheries and Wildlife now accepts the presence of the Cougar in the region and has changed its status from "extinct" to "endangered"—a great event indeed. What is uncertain, according to David Marshall of the Bureau, is whether the Cougars reported belong to the eastern subspecies and have perhaps come down from Canada or up from southern Florida or are western animals released from captivity on having outgrown their appeal. The chances of their being of eastern stock seems to me enhanced by Cougar sightings in North Carolina, mostly in the coastal country but some in the Piedmont, of which Dave gave me an astonishing sheaf; Wildlife Refuge managers are quite positive about them.

That one way or another this splendid cat has returned to North Carolina and the Virginias—if it has ever been wholly absent—seems indisputable and must stir any heart responsive to wilderness. But this is gun country. It is surely true here, as an official of a northeastern Fish and Game Department wrote of his own state, that "the last Cougar, without question, would be shot without ceremony and the shooter would become a celebrity."

All the larger mammals together with grouse and Wild Turkeys are hunted legally in the mountains during open seasons except in the National and the small State Parks and posted private property. As long as they are, they will remain desperate fugitives from man and much territory they could otherwise occupy will be closed to them by its proximity to the dread enemy. At the same time the great majority of people who much prefer animals alive to animals dead will remain denied the chance to have them near enough to be seen and enjoyed. But the harassing of game animals does not stop with legal hunting. Gunners operate commonly outside the law in the southern Appalachians, out of season in the National Forests and even in the Great Smokies National Park. Pickup trucks cruise the roads, dropping off men and dogs where the coast is clear to go in after bears, deer, Wild Boars and Wild Turkeys. The driver "comes back for them at a pre-arranged time, midnight or sunup the next day," says Ed Widmer, Assistant Chief Ranger of the Great Smoky Mountains National Park in a United Press International report of December 17, 1972. "That way there's no truck around to give them away. We have indications every week that poachers are out. We'll hear shots or find kills. Or you'll see a pickup truck cruising in an area trying to locate dogs which become lost during the hunt." Some arrests are made, but successful prosecution is extremely difficult. "It's hard to get them with everything at once, the guns, the kill, the dogs," Widmer said.

The same report goes on to quote Forest Service personnel as stating that poaching in the East Tennessee area is a more serious problem than in any other area of the country. Jerry McIlwain, biologist with the Cherokee National Forest, calls it "the worst place I've ever been in."

That West Virginia is much better is doubtful. From a conversation I had there with two county game wardens—and I think I had better not be specific as to circumstances—it would hardly seem that the law exercises a very restraining influence, generally, in the mountain area. One of the wardens opened the trunk of the car they were driving and showed me some bottles of wine and whiskey they had taken from a car they had stopped, in which the driver was carrying a loaded revolver. He said that if they stopped all cars they would find eight out of ten in violation of the law. The offense that gave them most trouble was the spotlighting of deer. (Deer will stare into a bright beam of light at night and can then be shot without difficulty.) Landowners would not report violators of the strict law against this practice until too late to do any good. "You should have been around here two weeks ago," one would say. "They were spotlighting all over the place." They were afraid of making trouble for themselves, though the wardens always protected their sources. Another big problem was the illegal shooting of bears. A farmer who has suffered the depredations of one of these animals may be authorized to kill it, but he is not allowed to act on his own in the matter. A hunter who kills a bear out of season and is caught may be fined $125—and then get $123.50 for the carcass. He'll be out gunning again the next day, and the same is true of a hunter killing deer illegally. Like the bear-hunter, he'll be known to the Justice of Peace and be let off with a pat on the back by way of admonition. One trouble was that the office of Justice of the Peace was too poorly paid to attract qualified men. As an example of the difficulty of getting a conviction, one of the wardens cited the case of two men in an Ohio car caught on ———— Mountain (in the Monongahela National Forest) a few evenings before with .270 rifles, scopes and spotlights attached, and with two ice-chests in the car. But they could be taken in only on a charge of carrying uncased weapons. It was true that in this case the hunters were outsiders and were treated rough by the court—handed $400 in fines. But even they would be back. Figure the value of a few 150- or 200-pound deer at current beef prices.

Speaking of poaching in the Tennessee mountains, Captain Ray Henry of the Tennessee Game and Fish Commission is quoted by the U.P.I. as saying that the problem stems from the late start the State got in conservation education. It would take a generation, he thought, to change the East Tennesseean's philosophy about wild game, that "the good Lord put the deer there so I'm entitled to get it."

America has come a long way in respect for and protection of wildlife. It is miles ahead of, say, Italy. But ours is a gun culture, our nation second in the world in homicide rate. There is a long struggle to be waged before our behavior as a nation fully reflects the awareness we have been slowly gaining, that if our relations with our fellow creatures is one of hostility the losers will not be our victims alone.

Overleaf, a stream in the Alleghenies.

Above, Flame azalea. *Left,* Red Admiral butterfly on White snakeroot, one of the most abundant late-summer wildflowers. *Below,* a variety of lichens and mosses in a few square feet of roadside embankment at Linville Falls, N.C.

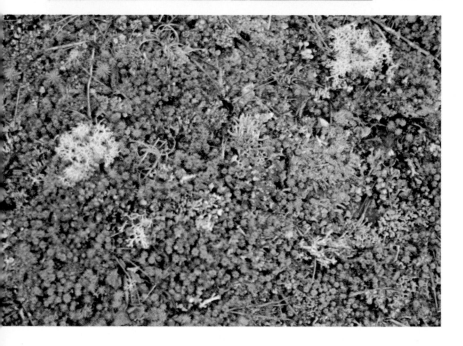

X *The Forest*

You cannot spend any time on the trails of the southern Appalachians without being mentally taken possession of by the trees. The range has indeed meant forest to those who have known it for as long as it has been known to any of us. Even today, when nearly all of it outside the fastnesses of the Smokies has been logged—and much of it two or even three times, and probably half its lower elevations lastingly cleared—a squirrel could almost certainly travel it from Pennsylvania to the decline of its spurs deep in Georgia and Alabama without descending to the ground except to cross rivers and highways. The impression it makes on you above all is of trees, trees standing bough to bough, trunks and foliage among which the view loses itself on all sides. Of a multitude of trees beyond reckoning and of the forest, an entity in itself, cohesive and enduring, forming a greater whole with the mountains it overspreads.

It seemed to me that the forest deserved to be examined as just such an entity, and I thought it might well be as an aftermath of Highlands. It was at the Biological Station there that I learned of recent, especially interesting studies of the southern Appalachian forest, and by then, too, I had seen just about all the forms that forest took.

The sense one has of the near identity of forest and mountains in the southern Appalachians is fitting. The range has been, as far as we know, the abode of forest since a time far antedating the first flowering plants, from long before trees at all resembling ours began to make their appearance. It is, moreover, the only part of North America of which this can be said. All the rest in that stretch of time have been either submerged in the sea or denuded of forest by the Ice Ages.

Not only has the southern Appalachian forest, with its wealth of herbaceous plants, ferns and mosses, antecedents that go far back into Paleozoic times, but its relationships span half the globe.

At the end of the Paleozoic era, some 200 million years ago, when the Appalachians were receiving their last major upward impetus, all the

151

continents appear to have been joined in one great assembly. To the extent that they were forested there may well have been essentially one forest in the world, though one of gradually altering character from one climate to another. Pangaea, as this world-continent has been called—from Gaea, the aboriginal earth goddess of the ancient Greeks—was of course a passing phenomenon. Early in the Mesozoic—the Age of Reptiles—it began to split apart. However, the Mesozoic produced a period of relative climatic uniformity and the forest may have been more homogeneous than before. Though the giant horsetails and giant club-mosses of the coal forests were disappearing, it would still have been an alien and fanciful realm to us, abounding in Cycads—superficially palm-like trees surviving today—and in large-leaved ferns. One tree we should have recognized was the Ginkgo, which came to our city streets from temple grounds in China and Japan; it seems not to survive in a wild state. It was the only leafy tree then existing. The latest development in trees was represented by primitive conifers, of which the Ginkgo is accounted one despite its broad leaves. The conifers we should probably have recognized as such. We should have had no doubt about the matter when trees like our pines and sequoias spread over the northern hemisphere in the mid-Mesozoic.

Pangaea had long since divided into two super-continents, a southern and a northern. The latter comprised North America and Eurasia. Enjoying a mild climate even up into what is now the Arctic, it remained united through the Mesozoic; this we know from the genera of trees common to the two landmasses today. By the end of the Mesozoic and the beginning of the Tertiary, however, a sea was widening between North America and Europe, heretofore connected by Greenland. The great age of flowering plants, birds and mammals had come. Though the Appalachians were already ancient, that was still a very long time ago—60 million years. The dinosaurs had only recently died out, for reasons not yet entirely clear. The Rocky Mountains were just beginning to rise and the Adirondacks were far in the future. Yet the plant types of the early Tertiary were not greatly dissimilar to those we are used to. Magnolias, oaks, willows, a kind of sycamore and a kind of sassafras had made their appearance, though in the southern Appalachians, at least, the vegetation was evidently more tropical than now. In the North America of that time we should certainly have felt more at home with the trees than with the mammals that grazed or browsed among them: terrier-sized proto-horses, the even smaller common ancestors of our pigs, camels and cattle, and the rhinoceros-like *Uintatheriums*, tusked and with three pairs of horns.

Coming up almost to the present—skipping all the rest of the Tertiary and most of, if not all, the Pleistocene that followed it—and imagining ourselves with the first human beings to reach the Appalachians—we should have found a forest well known to Sabre-toothed Cats, great Dire Wolves, diverse equine species, huge Moose-elk, mastodons, beavers the size of Black Bears and Ground-sloths far larger than Grizzlies; yet the forest itself we could probably not have distinguished from the virgin stands of the Smokies today. Coming, as we should have been, during the waning of the last Ice Age—10,000 years ago, at the latest—we might have encountered all the great Pleistocene beasts. None of these that we know of disappeared until they had met with man. Some undoubtedly owed their disappearance, as all may have, to the improved hunting techniques of the continent's first human invaders, who seem to have made the crossing of the Bering land-bridge about 28,000 years ago.

The southern Appalachian forest, even as we know it, goes back many million years; but it also bears conspicuously the marks of the Ice Ages of the past two million. The great glacier, overriding the mountains of New England and New York, had reached Pennsylvania and the neighborhood of the Ohio River. Behind its awesome front little life could exist, and all but far northern forms withdrew still farther before its frigid breath. Tundra spread south of it and must have occupied the high Appalachian summits down through the Great Smokies. Below the tundra came a forest of spruce and fir, sprinklings of which even penetrated the withdrawn deciduous forest as far as the coast of South Carolina, northern Florida and Louisiana. Scenes like those of Baffin Island and Greenland below the ice cap must have characterized the higher and more northerly of the southern Appalachians as recently as 15,000 years ago. Woolly Mammoths, Caribou and Musk-oxen would have browsed in winter snows on stunted birch and willow and on Reindeer Lichen and been harried by packs of giant Arctic Wolves; Gyrfalcons and Great Grey Owls would have preyed on Ptarmigan, white Arctic Foxes on Lemmings.

Four times during the Pleistocene this southward expansion of the Arctic took place with intervals of tens or hundreds of thousands of years between invasions. Four times the Eastern hardwood forest found sanctuary toward the warmer coasts and behind the shield of the mountains, and four times advanced northward again as the glacier melted back. In Europe, where the ice sheet came down to London, Leipzig and Kiev and also spread tundra before it, the hardwood forest was not so fortunate. There the mountains run east and west. The forest was forced back against the Pyrenees, the mountains of the Auvergne, the Alps, the Carpathians, the cold Black Sea and the Caucasus Mountains, and massacred. Whole genera and species by the score were wiped out, and the arboriflora of the continent left impoverished.

The ice sheet had withdrawn to about the present line of permanent ice by the time recorded history begins. However, remainders of its invasion persist in the islands of boreal forest crowning the higher Southern mountains. Elbert L. Little, Jr., of the United States Forest Service, lists eight conifers and 22 broad-leaved trees of the northern states and Canada that apparently retreated to the southern Appalachians in the Ice Ages and remained in sites favorable to them, including, in the first group, Balsam Fir, Red Spruce, Eastern White Pine and Eastern Hemlock, and, in the second, Striped Maple, Mountain Maple, Yellow Birch, the two White Birches, Pin Cherry, Bear Oak, Rosebay Rhododendron and American Mountain-ash. He considers it possible, however, that some of these species originated in the southern Appalachians and had moved north as the mountains were lowered by erosion. The northern woods are the rear guard of the Great Cold with their inhabitants, including many northern birds and not a few northern mammals. Among the latter are the Northern Flying Squirrel, Red Squirrel, Rock Vole, New England Cottontail, and Water Shrew. However, these high "refugia," as biologists term them, were not extensive enough to retain the larger mammals that had retreated down the range before the ice. Still, it is not apparent why the Grey Jay and Spruce Grouse, which had come with them, should subsequently have drawn back almost to Canada, as the Caribou and probably the Woolly Mammoth did.

While North America and Europe were growing ever farther apart, North America remained joined by the thousand-mile-wide Alaskan-Siberian land-bridge, with only two periods of separation until about four million years ago. When it went under then, it severed a forest that had been one. Since that time, the world's two greatest deciduous forests—that of temperate eastern North America and that of temperate eastern Asia—have been out of contact. The land-bridge reemerged during the Ice Ages when ocean levels fell, but the cold in the north was too great for the forests to come near to reunion. Yet even today, though they are about 5,000 miles apart at their closest, affinities persist between them. Indeed, 14 genera of trees have been found by the botanist Hiu-lin Li to exist in eastern North America and eastern Asia and nowhere else. These include the hickories, the magnolias, the tupelos, Catalpa, Witch-hazel, Sassafras and Tuliptree. Altogether, says Carrol E. Wood, Jr., of Harvard, 62 genera of plants occur exclusively in eastern North America and eastern Asia. In addition, some species of other genera, though separated by half a continent or more and the Pacific, are nearly identical: for example, our Red Maple and Mountain Winterberry Holly with Japanese equivalents.

Of the southern Appalachian species paired with Asian, none is more famous in that connection than that relative of Galax, Oconee Bells, *Shortia galacifolia*. A plant that could possibly be mistaken for a white violet at first glance, *Shortia* was destined for a role in the march of science. It had been collected by the illustrious French botanist André Michaux in 1778, and the specimen shipped to Paris with those of other plants his zeal had garnered. There, in his journal for April 8, 1839, the later famous New-

York-born botanist Asa Gray wrote, "I have discovered a new genus in Michaux's herbarium—at the end, among *plantae ignotae*. It is from that great unknown region the high mountains of North Carolina." Michaux's terse designation of the plant's origin, omitting the information that it was from a low area in the high mountains, was to mislead searchers for generations.

Claiming the right of a discoverer, Gray gave *Shortia* its name (after the Kentucky botanist Charles Wilkins Short) and its rediscovery became a special purpose of his travels in the Southern mountains, beginning in 1841. "Year after year I have hunted for that plant!" he was to declare. Friends of his, "botanizing in the mountains," he wrote, "were accosted with the question—'Found shortia yet?' " No one had so far seen its flower, Michaux's specimen bearing fruit alone. Then in 1878, exactly 100 years after its discovery by Michaux, Gray got word at third hand that it had been rediscovered by a herb-collector in North Carolina, a 17-year-old boy, George McQ. Hyams, on the banks of the Catawba near Marion. Soon he received the plant itself. "It is so," he proclaimed. "Now let me sing my nunc dimittis!" In 1886 Gray wrote to his friend Charles Sprague Sargent, who was collecting south of Lake Toxaway—part of the plateau of the southeastern Blue Ridge on which Highlands is located—"Crown yourself with glory by discovering the original habitat of *Shortia.*" The letter arrived the day Sargent returned with the leaf of a strange plant that proved to be *Shortia*. He had found it growing plentifully at little more than 2,000 feet elevation, apparently where Michaux had first discovered it.

Gray had long linked his eluder with a plant of the same genus in Japan. He had, indeed, become the first to enlarge upon the notable similarity between the flora of the southern Appalachians and that of eastern Asia. In the *American Journal of Science* in 1856 he wrote that the few genera of plants peculiar to Europe and North America "are insignificant in our flora and not to be compared . . . with the much more numerous and really characteristic genera which are shared by the eastern United States and eastern temperate Asia." The article was written partly in response to a request of Gray by Charles Darwin for a list of American alpine plants. Darwin, in reply, declared that "Nothing has surprised me more than the greater generic & specific affinity [of eastern America] with E. Asia than with W. America." Obviously he saw the relevance of the question to his own theory—which he had propounded in a letter to Gray that same year—of the evolution of species by natural selection. (The reading of the letter to the Linnaean Society in 1858, the year before the publication of *The Origin of Species,* established Darwin's priority in proposing the theory of evolution that Alfred Russell Wallace had arrived at independently.) He asked if Gray could explain the affinity. With new plant collections from Japan, Gray was already eagerly at work in pursuit of an explanation. He saw in it the chance to confound an arch antagonist and fellow professor at Harvard, Louis Agassiz. With the premise that "a species is a thought of the Creator," the Swiss-born zoölogist had no trouble accounting for the distribution of living forms. He argued that each species of plant occurs where it does because that was where it originated, thus assigning the matter "simply to the Divine will," Gray rumbled, which "would remove the whole question out of the field of inductive science."

That was certainly not good enough for Gray, least of all in the light of his discovery of 40 genera of plants endemic and confined to Japan and eastern North America. The explanation he came up with, subsequently proved correct but daring for the times, was that in the Tertiary period, when evidently warmer climates prevailed, a single flora spread unbroken across North America and Asia. As for those species which are similar but not identical between one region and the other, his explanation was even more daring. He contended that such paired forms may "in many cases be lineal descendants from a pristine stock, just as domesticated races are," that "variation in species is wider than is generally supposed, and that derivation [i.e., derivative] forms when segregated may be as constantly reproduced as their original." This assertion, with the evidence with which Gray could back it up, was powerful support for Darwin's theory of the evolution of species—foreshadowed on that day in 1839 when a *planta ignota* in Michaux's herbarium took hold of a 29-year-old botanist's imagination. *Vivat Shortia!*

Of his trip down the southern Appalachians in 1843, Gray had written that it had led "through regions which abound with the choicest botanical treasures which the country affords." The range, counting the Piedmont as part of it, has been available for colonization by plants since plants first crept ashore from the ocean. "The rich flora of the southern Appalachians," says Carroll E. Wood, Jr., "has arrived from many different directions, over a long period of time." Of flowering plants the well-favored range supports some 1,300 species, of mosses 434, or between one-third and two-fifths of all those in the whole of the continental United States and Canada. In the Great Smoky Mountains alone, according to Arthur Stupka, naturalist with the National Park Service, 230 lichens, 1,800 fungi and 50 ferns and fern allies have been counted. The diversity of the flora was signalized in 1967 when four sorts of tropical filmy-ferns were discovered by D. R. Farrar in the gorges of the southeastern escarpment of the Blue Ridge, home of Oconee Bells, only a few miles from the summits on which Arctic types of lichen are found! Just as the southern Appalachians harbor thriving relics of the invasion by the Ice Age cold of the Pleistocene, so do the filmy-ferns and the liverworts and mosses of Central and South American species growing with them in the gorges remain, as Arthur W. Cooper and James W. Hardin of North Carolina

State University observe, to witness the former continuity of the Western hemisphere's tropical and temperate-zone flora far back in Tertiary times.

Trees in the Southern mountains number about 130 species. And it is the forest that sets the conditions of existence for other living things. Where you may remain beneath their canopy for hours at a time and, in a manner of speaking, become drunk on trees, it comes to you that the tree form is one of life's most successful experiments. Its advantages became apparent more than 300 million years ago, and while trees have become far more subtly contrived since then, and are presumably capable of continuing refinement, the tree form seems unlikely to be scrapped, barring radical changes in our planet. What testifies particularly to the virtues of the arboreal idea is the diversity of plants adhering to it. Trees do not constitute a related group of plants as, say, the lilies do, or the composites. A tree cannot even be defined, except roughly and arbitrarily (a woody plant of a certain height having a single stem of a certain thickness). Conifers have no ties with other trees except as all seed-bearers have a common origin. The elms' and hackberry's bonds are with nettles and hemp *(Cannabis sativa)*—marijuana. Locusts and acacias (like Mesquite and Palo Verde) are of the pea-bean family. Hawthornes, apples and cherries are roses. Magnolias and the Tuliptree are more closely related to buttercups and anemones than to the Willow, Walnut-Hickory, Beach-Oak or Birch-Alder tribes. These in turn are less closely related to one another than the hollies, boxes, maples and buckeyes are to Poison Ivy, Crowberry and Jewelweed.

Because plants grow from small to large it is natural to assume that trees evolved from herbaceous ancestors. It is noteworthy, however, that there are no herbaceous conifers, only trees or tree-like shrubs. The trunk and main branches of all broad-leaved trees, and, for that matter, of conifers too, have the same structure: an inner core of inert, rigid heartwood is enveloped in a cylinder of sapwood and this in turn by a vital film called the cambium layer, which produces successive layers of sapwood on one side and the phelgm, or inner bark, on the other and is thus the source of the protective outer bark as well. The similarity suggests a common arboreal ancestor. In the fossil record, moreover, the remains of broad-leaved trees, even some closely akin to common types today, come well before those of herbaceous plants, though the latter, quite possibly developing on uplands where their remains were much less likely to be silted over and mineralized, could have come sooner than the fossil record suggests. On balance it would seem that trees came first—as they certainly came far ahead of grasses—and gave rise to the small perennials and annuals, as the giants of the coal forests gave rise to the little horsetails and club-mosses of today, while disappearing themselves.

What is most evident in the evolution of the flowering plants is their enormous diversification since their beginnings in the last chapter of the

Mesozoic. Among trees, if not as great as among the herbs, it has been great enough. All parts of trees' anatomy have been affected except their basic structure. Leaves have become variously adapted to differences in rainfall, light and temperature from place to place. Flowers have been modified in many ways to improve their chances of pollination by insects, birds or the wind. Fruits have been designed to disperse seed through the digestive tracts of birds and mammals, by the wind, by flotation, through the providence of squirrels, by rolling, even, in the Witch-hazel, by projection through the explosive uncoiling of a spring.

Diversification is nature's way, what it always appears to be working toward. Through diversity life's options and resources are increased. Pressed by changes in the face of the earth that could otherwise prove disastrous—inundations, ice ages, advancing deserts—life is resilient. Alternative sets of organisms are available or will be evolved as occasion offers or demands. The chance that one form of life will gain ascendancy is minimized, for all forms are beset by diverse challengers, and impregnable defense against one is likely to increase vulnerability to another. If man's success appears to demonstrate that the guarantee against predominance by a single life-form is not absolute, the final returns are not yet in. Nature hedges her bets. Modern man puts his eggs into fewer and bigger baskets. In agriculture, huge acreages are given over to a single grain, tree or animal crop. This improves yields and expands the scope of the disaster when a selective pest or disease strikes. A single, world-wide technology and civilization is replacing a multiplicity of cultures—the equivalent of putting all mankind in a single, complex and hence vulnerable super-vessel for a voyage without end on perilous seas. The way of nature, of evolution —except as it has produced man—is to put the eggs into more and more baskets. An Appalachian forest solely of American Chestnuts would have seen the mountains left treeless by *Endothia parasitica*. As it was, the forest closed over the Chestnut's place, great as it was, and remained unbroken.

There are, to be sure, considerable areas over which a forest is all or mostly of a single species. On the coastal plain of the Southeast and in the mountains of the West, uniform coniferous forests may extend for miles—though even here, in the event of the pines' or firs' destruction other vegetation would take over. When we come to think of it we may wonder why this should not be more general. For each tree there are presumably optimum conditions. In theory it might seem that where these prevailed that species would enjoy a monopoly. Yet the theory does not hold in the great Eastern deciduous forest, least of all in the epitome of that forest in the southern Appalachians. There, pure stands are very exceptional. And while the range exhibits no such diversity of floras as the Western mountains, in which you may move in half a day from low-altitude desert up through four or five quite different forest belts to alpine tundra at 13,000 feet, you can, as I believe I observed at one point, discover a variety in a 15-minute walk in the southern Appalachians that would be hard to find exceeded outside a forest of the tropics.

That this is so must be owing in part to nature's fine-tuning, in part to the long existence of the range, during which it has provided a refuge for and a source of thousands of plants. In the course of eons the many trees that have collected or evolved in it have had time to find the special set of conditions most suitable to them and to perfect their adjustment to them —have in fact been driven by competition to do so. And while the physical environments for which they compete may seem of limited range, they actually vary widely in accordance with soil, altitude, exposure and weather. This last is itself ever-varying in every location. Wind, temperature and precipitation are different, moreover, not only from day to day and season to season but from year to year and century to century. The odds for or against each plant, in other words, keep shifting. What changes them more drastically, of course, is the occasional lightning-ignited fire, which gives everything a start from scratch in the swath it clears. Man's effect has been drastic in the same way but on a much greater scale. Our species has vastly increased the incidence of fires and it clear-cuts whole mountainsides at once.

As well as of the richness of the forest in trees and other plants, the hiker in the southern Appalachians is conscious of a continuing modulation of the character of the forest in response to what he can see to be, or assumes must be, changing conditions. The distribution of the range's 130 trees and the basis for it could provide material for a lifetime's study. For those who are interested I shall recount what I have managed to learn about the pattern, repeating at the outset my confession that I am responsive to the idea of patterns in the natural world. (To reply to the poet Amy Lowell's question as to why we have to have patterns—"Christ! What are patterns for?"—I should say, to give assurance of order in the universe.) I am also, I must say, susceptible to the great personages that enact these patterns, the trees that compose the forest, as one is likely to be who has them for sole company for hours and days.

Let us take for a start a Southern mountain mean, as it might be called. It is a forested slope, moderately moist, of middling elevation, centrally located in the range. The dominant trees are likely to be Red and Chestnut Oaks, Red Maple and Sourwood. Half a century ago American Chestnut would have been among them. Trees in a subordinate role would include three Oaks—Scarlet, White and Black—three Hickories—Pignut, Red and Mockernut—Tuliptree, Mountain (Fraser) Magnolia, Eastern Hemlock, Cherry Birch, Black Tupelo, and Black Locust, while Flowering Dogwood and Witch-hazel would contribute to an understory. Mountain-laurel and Rosebay Rhododendron would probably make up a dense shrub-layer, perhaps with Smooth Hydrangea, Flame Azalea and Buckberry. For vines, Virginia Creeper and Greenbrier could be expected, among herbs two of particular attractiveness, Galax and Trailing Arbutus.

Now let us move around to a somewhat drier part of the slope—one that catches the strong southern or western sun. Tuliptree, Mountain Magnolia, Cherry Birch and Hemlock drop out. The more desiccating sunshine is not for them. The first three have wood with pores distributed throughout it rather than concentrated in the annular rings, and this seems to make for a higher rate of transpiration. Scarlet, White and Black Oaks join Chestnut Oaks as dominants, replacing the others, which lapse to second rank.

Why such a prevalence of Oaks on a typical southern Appalachian mountainside? Oaks not only have pores in their wood confined to the rings but are tough and contain, it always seems to me, a life-force as massive as their own stature. Probably no other genus of broad-leaved trees occupies as much of the earth's surface as *Quercus*. The White Oak, so called because of its pale grey bark and its comparatively pale wood—its lobed leaves are paler green than most other trees' leaves, too—reaches its maximum height of 150 feet on favorable southern Appalachian slopes, with a trunk diameter of up to eight feet. Living as much as 800 years, it is the monarch of Eastern forests, with a wood of all-around greater utility than that of any other of our trees. Oak timber is synonymous with sturdiness, and the White Oak especially, when it grows in the open, puts forth its gigantic limbs horizontally, inviting the maximum strain. (Try holding your little arms out for five minutes.) Those of the White Oak of Wye, of Maryland's Eastern Shore, stretch more than half the length of a football field. White, Scarlet and Black Oaks—three of the four dominants of the slope we are on—all have deep tap roots as part of their underground systems, which are much like mirror images of those above ground. The fourth, the Chestnut Oak; may have either a tap root or fully branching roots, furthering its growth on rocky mountainsides. Rock Oak and Mountain Oak are its other names, Chestnut Oak being suggested by the resemblance of its sharply-wavy-edged leaves to the Chestnut's toothed leaves. Reaching a girth and age comparable to the White's, it may well be the most abundant Oak of the southern Appalachians. Oaks are partly protected from insects and fungus by tannin in their inner bark, but this proved to be a deadly liability in the days before imported and synthetic tannin, when the mountains were littered with the boles of oaks stripped of their bark for the essential ingredient in the tanning of leather it yielded. The many summits from Virginia to Georgia on which Oaks—crippled by ice storms but indomitable—are almost the only trees, speak for their quality.

Hickories become more prominent as we go from the first slope to the second. Their wood is even heavier and harder than the Oaks' and has a resistance to shock that makes it supreme for the handles of axes and sledges; dropped on a rock, end on, it will ring. Structured of such wood, tap-rooted, and with thick-twigged terminal shoots as supple as whips, hickories are adapted to mountain life. As fuel, their wood is the equal of coal, cord for ton. It is ideal for smoking meats and the incense of hickory smoke, a characteristic Appalachian fragrance, belongs to that America evoked by the far-off wail of a steam locomotive. The twigs and leaves when cut or crushed are highly aromatic; one waft will take me back to my childhood in southern Georgia and the pecan groves whence come the sweetest and tastiest of all the hickory nuts. Acorns, hickory nuts and beech nuts: these make up the mast that feeds rodents, deer, bears, wild and semi-wild pigs, grouse and turkeys, and fed the Passenger Pigeon's hosts in the days when chestnuts were its most prized component.

If we proceed in the direction we have taken to the still drier environment of a ridge—though not a high, dominating ridge that would draw a large share of bounty from passing rain-clouds—we shall find that the forest canopy, already grown less dense than where we began, will thin out further. The dominants are now Scarlet Oak, with Chestnut Oak in second place, and four Pines: Shortleaf Yellow, Virginia, Pitch and Table Mountain. Scarlet Oak's leaves are deeply incised, thus reduced in expanse, and have a hard, glossy surface; in this they may resist drying sun and winds. In any event, experiments with seedlings have shown that both Scarlet and Chestnut Oaks, for unexplained reasons, make better growth in dry seasons than in wet.

The four Pines of the ridge, with their short, wiry needles and dry bark, so often misshapen in trunk and limbs from the elements, appear altogether the frugal trees they are, at one with the moss browning in the sun on the warm rocks and the torpor of a windless summer noon. In conditions most favorable to vegetation, conifers cannot compete successfully with the broad-leaved trees. It may be largely that their foliage, stiff and linear, is less efficient in those conditions. But in situations of drought, either of hot sun and low moisture or of sun, frozen earth and winter winds, it is a different matter. Their needly or scaly foliage, resinous, narrow and hard-shelled, holds transpiration to a minimum. Moreover, it does not suffer cellular destruction in temperatures even far below those lethal to maple and oak leaves. As a concession to winter's dehydrating winds, most needled conifers shed the older half of their foliage in autumn, but they are ready to get back in business in spring without having to wait to grow a wholly new suit. When fire sweeps a southern Appalachian mountain the pines with their light, wind-borne seed and thriftiness generally establish themselves on it and grow to maturity before the original forest begins to take over from them; it was the drab, threadbare Virginia Pines that reclaimed for the forest the gullied slopes of the Shenandoah Blue Ridge. With the Pines, in being first after the blaze, is Pin Cherry. A good scrounger, it has abundant, tart, light-red fruit assuring its seeds plentiful distribution by birds.

Even on the sun-soaked ridge we have reached, the Oaks we have had all along persist. So do Sourwood, Black Locust, Black Tupelo and Red Maple. And here they are joined by Serviceberry and Sassafras. One would not immediately think of a tree in this taxing environment as being the source of a honey, collected in the bee-gums of the mountain people, often pronounced the world's best. But the family *Ericaceae* is the Cinderella of the woody plants, bringing beauty out of poverty, and Sourwood, Lily-of-the-valley tree, is not only beautiful of flowers and lustrous foliage, green or scarlet, but has a nectar fit to win princes. Red Maple is an enigma, at least to me. It thrives in Appalachian bottomlands and on up slopes of almost all kinds. Why will one tree be so adaptable and another be like Yellow-wood, of smooth, grey bark and clusters of white, wisteria-like pea-blossoms, which finds so few spots anywhere acceptable it must wish it had never exchanged its home in the Orient for the southern Appalachians. The Red Maple's secret makes it at home with its roots in a Louisiana bayou or its crown in the sea-winds of Nova Scotia.

The Black Tupelo, or Black Gum, has a range comparable to the Red Maple's though it does not go so far north or quite as high up the mountains. Yet I picture it as resolutely, inflexibly holding onto survival. Well, that is how it looks with its scraggly, rather conifer-like form; its wood, if not inflexible, is virtually unsplittable; and its genus, from having once occupied all the temperate lands of the northern hemisphere, is now reduced to the eastern United States and southeastern Asia. *Nyssa sylvatica* is most at home in the southern Appalachians. A pair stood beside our first house in Virginia, so close to each other they sent up a single spreading tower of foliage—and if the Black Tupelo's structure is not of the most graceful, it is clothed summerlong in the densest mass of glossy leaves of any tree of our forest. Our Tupelos were loud with the hum of bees in spring, seldom without their thrushes in September as long as the small, oval blue-black fruit lasted, and by the time the crop had been gleaned the deep green leaves ignited in scarlet and blood-red. . . . Black Locust, originally a southern Appalachian and Ozarkian endemic, is known for its indestructibly hard wood, which will turn heavy staples (as I learned to my exasperation trying to nail barbed wire to locust posts as a boy); Serviceberry for its early white flowering, when the shad are running (hence Shadbush), and early crop of sweet rose-to-purple fruit (hence Juneberry); Sassafras, a Laurel like the trees that produce cinnamon and camphor, for its often mitten-shaped leaves and an aromatic essence particularly strong in its root bark, from which is decocted a pink tea once widely taken as all-purpose

Northern Red oak.

tonic by mountain people. With these hardy trees, three shrubs of the *Ericaceae* abound: Blueberries, Huckleberries and Mountain-laurel. Only this family produces broad-leaved evergreens able to survive in the high Appalachians. The leathery, hard-finished foliage of the Mountain-laurel fits it to endure desiccating winds, hot and cold, from the Texas border to the Gaspé peninsula. The foliage of its relatives the rhododendrons is similar. Feel the leaves of one of these in the hot summer sun and you will find it warm to the touch where the leaves of deciduous trees or shrubs next to it are tepid; the one gets rid of heat by reflection and the other by transpiration, which means water loss.

Should our ridge be very narrow with shallow soil and southern exposure the Pines are likely to make up the greater part of an open woodland with the deciduous trees reduced to an understory.

If from the Oak forest where we began, we move to a protected side of the mountain where the soil is deeper and moister, we shall find, all the way to the valley, the southern Appalachian forest at its grandest. Here in the Cove Forest, as it is called, are most of the trees we started with, but the dominants are now American Beech, White Ash, Basswood, Tuliptree, Eastern Hemlock, Red and Sugar Maples, Black Cherry, Red Oak and Cucumber Magnolia. Among the shrubs, Rosebay Rhododendron is most conspicuous, but especially along the streams, where the Hemlocks hold sway over all, it is joined by its Catawba sister, Leucothoë and Mountain-laurel. (That the evergreen *Ericaceae,* which do well on the most exposed heights, do well also in the shadowy depths is hard to understand.) Trees of record size in the virgin cove stands in the Smokies give an idea of what the Southern mountain forest once was—a Tuliptree over eight and a half feet through the trunk at breast height (exceeded by one of nearly ten in the foothills of the Virginia Blue Ridge), an Eastern Hemlock six and a third, a Cucumber Magnolia almost six feet, a Yellow Buckeye over five, even such sylvan sylphs as Allegheny Serviceberry and Sourwood as much as two feet through and a Mountain Silverbell three and three-quarters.

The flower of the Mountain Magnolia.

Between the Cove Forest and the other types, the difference is that in the former the conditions of soil, moisture and light are so favorable to vegetation that the trees' primary contention is with one another, while in the latter it is with the environment. In determining which trees will prevail in which locations, growth rates play a key part, as Arthur W. Cooper and James W. Hardin of North Carolina State University point out. To succeed in competition with other trees on protected slopes and bottom-lands, in good soil, trees must be of outstanding growth rate or capable of making do on very little sunshine. All the dominants of the Cove Forest are. None of the Oaks but the Red and White have much chance here. The Tuliptree is *the* example of a tree made for the cove environment, a dominant among dominants. Not for it the expenditure of resources on trunk and limbs of rock-like solidity. Its wood is as light as a White Pine's, less than half the weight of Hickory's. But its trunk may ascend, virtually untapering and without a branch, for seven or eight, even up to ten stories to support a broad and soaring crown another five or six stories tall. No other North American deciduous tree, even its companions, the Red and White Oaks, attains its record height of 190 feet. A Magnolia with leaves the shape of very stubby birds in flight (headless ones) or highly foreshortened fish and tulip-like flowers of orange and cream—unfortunately out of sight except on trees that have grown spreadingly in the open—*Liriodendron tulipifera* may be identified from afar in its stands by the light yellow-green of its arrowhead crown and the display of the silvered underside of its leaves in a breeze.

Silver beneath, too, is the darker foliage of the White Ash, but of compound leaves—that is, of paired leaflets growing from a central leafstalk. It is an open-crowned tree, being sparingly branched, as much light as foliage. Like all great European trees—and it is one of the tallest—the Ash is freighted with tradition. In Norse mythology man was created of an Ash—woman of an Elm—and an Ash called Yggdrasil (literally "Odin's horse") supported the universe, its roots and branches weaving through it. "England shall bide till Judgment Tide,/ By Oak, and Ash, and Thorn!" Rudyard Kipling sang. Ours is a different sort of country. Among us Ash is known chiefly for its wood. That of the White Ash is one that vast numbers of Americans know the feel and heft of, for baseball bats are made of it, and tennis racquets, hockey sticks, oars and the handles of shovels and hayforks. In its strength and resilience for its weight it stands supreme. This serves the White Ash well on the northerly slope of a mountain. So, on the sun-hungry floor of a Cove Forest, does the ability of its young to survive for years in the shade, devoting their energies to growing roots and abiding the day when age and storm will bring down a tree of the canopy above and give them their chance. Where the White Ash grows, a mass of roots underlies the surface, tending to shut out competition. The Black

Walnut, a tree superficially resembling an Ash that cannot stand shade, is said to achieve the same end by poisoning the soil with its roots.

A mat of Beech roots similarly just beneath the surface is if anything even denser and 'wider spreading than an Ash's. Above ground the beech is the antithesis of the Ash. It puts forth from its trunk a veritable burst of branches which divide and subdivide into long, fine branchlets and twigs. On these its tapering, honey-colored buds open into bluey-green lanceolate leaves, toothed like those of its relative the Chestnut; and many of these, turning a creamy fawn, remain on the tree to lighten the somber cast of the winter woods. Add to these attractions the Beech's famous smooth, blue-grey bark—a skin covering trunk, branches and roots splayed over the surface of the ground—and you have a species that Donald Culross Peattie may well call "in almost any landscape where it appears, the finest tree to be seen." In the mountains, however, its bark is so varicolored in algae and lichens as to be scarcely recognizable. What above all fits the Beech for the Cove Forest is its tolerance of shade. Only the Eastern Hemlock surpasses it in that, if it does.

Peattie writes: "When the ground has become strewn with centuries of leaf mold, and the shade so dense that other trees' own seedlings cannot compete with their parents, the Hemlock moves in. Conditions on the forest floor are then more favorable for it than any other tree. Painfully slow though the Hemlock's growth is, it will inevitably make its way above its neighbors. One by one they are eliminated, until at last only the shade-loving Beech can keep company with Hemlock. They associate together gladly, shaggy bole contrasted with smooth one; somber, motionless needles with light and flickering blades; strength with grace."

From the Blue Ridge Drive the Hemlocks may be seen standing dark among the summer hardwoods in the draws on the northerly sides of the mountains, green in winter in the leafless grey forest around them. In the wind the sleeves of foliage on the supple wands of branches weave like seaweed in the waves, rippling silver, where spruces and firs, standing stiffly, would simply quiver. From close by the highest point of the Drive in the Shenandoah National Park—3,640 feet in elevation—the White Oak Canyon Trail takes you to the "Limberlost," a grove of Hemlocks antedating the white man and incidentally affording a home to Grey and Red Squirrels and Chipmunks all together. The immense pillars of boles, irregular with age, rising to the airy skeins of minutely-leaved foliage, must in some degree, I should think, make Druids of monotheists and unbelievers alike. More of the great trees, some fallen under the weight of their antiquity, line the White Oak Canyon itself. Here they find their favorite situation, in a ravine away from the sun, cooled and humidified by a dashing brook leaping the rocks they entwine with their roots. A greater stand still is in the virgin forest protected in the 126 acres of Cathedral

Yellow birch, the predominant tree of the northern deciduous forests of the higher Appalachians.

State Park in the West Virginia Alleghenies close to the western border of Maryland.

Hemlock and Beech both climb their favored slopes to play conspicuous roles in the first of two major forest types you meet where the mountains lift you into the temperature levels of New England, lower and upper. You have reached the Northern Deciduous Forest when Yellow Birch and Beech begin to predominate in association with Hemlock, Red Oak, Red, Sugar and Striped Maples and Black Cherry and shrubs largely those of the Cove Forest. Higher still, crowning summits down to 5,000 feet in North Carolina and Tennessee, dropping northward to 4,000 in the West Virginia Alleghenies, is the Spruce-Fir Forest. The two conifers may form solid, sunless stands or have for companions, lightening the mood, Yellow Birch, Mountain Maple and American Mountain-ash. If the shade they cast is broken, Catawba Rhododendron, Scarlet Elder, Lowbush Blueberry, Round-leaf Gooseberry and Southern Bush-honeysuckle are likely to crowd the patches of sunshine. Though the trees are much lower, conditions up here where precipitation is likely to be heavy can approximate those of the Cove Forest, in that competition for sunlight darkens the forest

Beech, also an important component of the northern deciduous forests. In the high Appalachians its smooth bark is usually covered with lichens.

floor. For reasons that probably have more to do with shallowness of soil than mercilessness of exposure, conditions can also be rugged indeed, testing even the stamina of the conifers and Heaths. Spruce and Fir are equipped not only by sturdy, close, hard-shelled needles to withstand the searing winds but also with branches that, under the weight of snow, can give beneath it and let the burden slide off. The Rhododendrons emulate them in both respects. Their hard-shelled leaves can curl up in cold or drought, reducing their exposed surface, and hang down in winter, giving their forms a tented appearance. Thus the Catawba can come through the most savage mauling the highest Appalachians summits take and the Rosebay grow up into Maine.

Hiking through the mountains, daylong, the restless body's need for exertion satisfied, the circulation stimulated, the mind set free of the usual problems demanding early answers, one's thought in the harmonious atmosphere of the forest ranges like a sailing hawk buoyed on the air currents. A reflection that came to me at such a time is that man tends always to see the organization of nature and that of his own society in the same terms. In the early days of myth and fable when we ourselves were very much a part of and subject to nature, there was, indeed, no hard and fast distinction between human beings and other animals. One might be changed into the other or speak with the other's tongue, while the two might share or have similar adventures. A survival of the same turn of mind among Southern Negroes is illustrated in Joel Chandler Harris's *Uncle Remus*. On both sides, as we saw it, organization leaned toward the hierarchical—references were made to a king of beasts and king of birds—but was loose and informal. Later it tightened up. Society became more complicated and we were governed by an absolute monarch whose right was divine and who was remote from most of us. So it was with nature. We began to see its organization as more complicated. We conceived of all living things as the creatures of a distant King of Heaven obedient to him in all respects and serving his purposes.

Then in the eighteenth century human society began to be liberated. It came to us that our fellow beings of the animal kingdom were as autonomous as we by rights were autonomous and were making ourselves so in fact no less. Having won constitutional government for ourselves, we assigned it to nature as well: the Diety, if any, like a constitutional monarch, if any, respected the laws and kept hands off events. We saw that the equilibrium and order manifest in nature were, paradoxically, the outcome of the interaction, within the framework of universal laws, of countless, competing individual wills. Darwin's discovery that natural evolution came about as each living being was left free to make the most of its chances to survive, and reproduce or perish through its shortcomings, was seen as supporting the already dominant view that progress in human society would come about as human individuals were left free to do likewise.

Our way of looking at human society, and at nature, has gone on changing, however. The focus of attention has shifted away from human beings as individuals and from plants and animals as individual species. The collective whole is what we now hold to be important, and with societies more and more collectivized this should not surprise us. The chronicler of notable human lives, the historian who writes of great men, has yielded place to the analyst of society—political scientist, sociologist and economist. And the investigator of plant and animal species as such has been succeeded by the ecologist. The new specialists deal with individuals and individual species as components of a community.

So, at least until new developments in the organization of our society and our way of seeing it come to pass and change our way of looking at nature, we can expect the forest to be studied by biologists as an ecosystem. It is that, of course. It is an *oikos,* a household of many members all interrelated, each dependent on others. It can be, and has been, diagrammed in accordance with what preys on what. One model is a pyramid. In this, plants as the primary producers occupy the broad lowest level. On the next and narrower are the animals that feed on the various parts of the plants, especially insects, birds, rodents and hoofed animals. Then, the pyramid still narrowing, come the carnivores that prey on the herbivores: amphibians, other insects, raptorial birds, reptiles, the other mammals, even a few flowering plants—pitcher-plants and sundews—that have turned on their plaguers and learned to trap insects and digest them. At the apex are the eaters of carnivores—still other predatory birds, bears, raccoons, foxes, wildcats. These are limited in numbers less by natural enemies than by limitations on their food supply and by competition for *lebensraum* with their own kind.

The actual situation is of course vastly more complicated than the pyramid would indicate. Bears, raccoons and foxes at the top reach way down into it to eat fruits and grubs. The litter mate of the newly hatched Black Rat Snake that the robin feeds to its young grows up and consumes the robin's nestlings of another year. The dragonfly nymph that ingests the tadpole emerges into the winged adult only to be ingested by a frog grown from just such a tadpole. On every level plants and animals are subject to lethal attack by parasitic bacteria, fungi and protozoans—by disease. And all the remains of the losers in the battle of life—and of course all are losers in the end—are attacked by the saprophitic bacteria and fungi and the earth animalcules called soil decomposers, of which the earthworm is a very large example. They are thus reduced to nutrients available to plants for their growth. *Your worm is your only emperor for diet.* The food chain is thus a closed one.

Better to represent the complications, a diagram is constructed in which living forms are arranged in a circle and predatory relationships shown by arrows; several of these may emanate from or end in one organism and some of the arrows will be pointed at each end. What this fails to reveal, however, and what the pyramid does suggest in growing narrower at each stage of consumption, is that the *oikos* is run at a loss. A hundred pounds of plant tissue does not end up as a hundred pounds of weasels. Two would be more like it, and these two are converted finally into less than two pounds of phosphates and nitrates usable by plants. There is leakage of energy at every stage, and this the sun has to replace. Life is a sun engine. In the American Museum of Natural History, as a matter of fact, Jack McCormick has diagrammed the forest in terms of energy flow. His chart shows that of the input from the sun, plants are able to use only one per cent. Of this one per cent, 80 per cent is converted into plant tissue, 20 per cent being lost in transpiration. Of the plant tissue, about 60 per cent is retained by the plants and about 40 goes to the herbivores. Of the latter, only a quarter enters into the herbivores' tissues, the rest being dissipated into the atmosphere. And so on.

Such analyses support the authority of ecology. Yet, while conceding the crucial importance of what ecology is about, one does not feel that ecology is what nature is about—primarily. An ecosystem is a machine, and a machine functions the better the greater the stability of conditions it can rely on. But stability is not to be found in nature. The only constant in nature is change, though its processes may be underlyingly cyclical and rhythmical—spiral, perhaps one should say. The sun and moon rise and set with regularity, the seasons follow upon one another, mountains dissolve and other mountains rise of their residues, mighty as their predecessors. Yet nothing is ever the same.

If perfection of the ecosystem were nature's objective, life could have stopped with what it was eons ago. Animals could have been dispensed with and such a system, quiet and orderly, have been built on plants alone. Yet animals were evolved along with plants, to fantastic lengths, to add enormous verve and drama to life. Joy and exhilaration came with them, and thought. So also did suffering beyond contemplation. Plants were taxed to devise stratagems for defense against mobile and multiform predators. They were given the opportunity to excel over competing plants by utilizing animal organisms in propagating and dispersing their kind. Thus were called forth all the colors, fragrances and flavors of which vegetation is capable, and surely would never have been thought capable, and animal senses of appreciating—all the subtle and stunning allures of flowers and fruit.

That this has happened seems to me to bring us closer to what nature *is* about: Whatever the end may be, nature's absorbing interest appears to be in determining what inventiveness in form and function life is capable of in response to ever-shifting challenge. Certainly in this lies much of the fascination life has for us—human life, for that matter, as well as nonhuman. The inconceivable variety of living things, each a model of design, seems accountable only as the work of an inexhaustible imagination and insatiable curiosity as to what is possible and what will work. That it has come about, rather, simply as a consequence of life's driving impulse to turn every opportunity to its advantage makes it the more marvelous.

XI *Long Ridges, Cumberlands and a Valedictory*

The rocks standing a thousand feet above the Cumberland Gap offer a vantage point from which to take stock of the ranges that extend from Pennsylvania to Alabama and make up the inland strands of the Appalachians. The place is of interest in itself. Historically, anyone who has come down the Great Valley through Virginia seeking access to the fertile lands of Kentucky has been faced by a complicated mountain barrier running down through extreme western Virginia and extreme southeastern Kentucky. A major part of the barrier is the 70-mile-long ridge of Cumberland Mountain, which forms part of the border between those two states and extends on down into Tennessee. Eons ago, however, a stream by one means or another presumably ate its way through the mountain at what is now the extreme western tip of Virginia to be subsequently deflected, leaving a deep saddle in the ridge.

You are, at this point, surprisingly far west—25 miles beyond Detroit. While you have before you the anarchy of steep hills making up most of the Cumberland Mountains—with an *s*—there are passages through it leading farther westward and northward that are not too difficult of negotiation. The Cherokees, drawn by the herds of bison and deer in the Bluestem grasslands of Kentucky, regularly made use of the gap. Through it, too, passed the Warriors Path by which Indians came down through the Appalachians from the north. In 1750 the gap became known to the white settlers when Dr. Thomas Walker of Albemarle County marched with five companies of militia through the "levil" pass, which he named after the Duke of Cumberland. What the country beyond the mountains was to come to mean to landless but venturesome elements in the settled East may be glimpsed in the words set down in his journal by Walker's son, Felix, which surely evoke the explorer's rewards with an infectiousness never exceeded in so few: "As the Cain ceased, we began to discover the pleasing and Rapturous appearance of the plains of Kentucky, a New Sky & Strange Earth to be presented to our view." *A new sky and strange earth!* He goes on then to adumbrate: "So rich a soil we never saw before. Covered with Clover in full Bloom, the Woods alike abounding with wild game, turkeys so numerous that it might be said there appeared but one flock Universally Scattered in the woods." Twenty-five years after Walker's discovery of the pass, in the employ of Judge Richard Henderson, Daniel Boone and 30 axemen cut a road 208 miles long from the Great Valley through the gap to the Kentucky River. Here Henderson planned to set up a new colony on 30,000 square miles he had bought "title" to from the Cherokees. The private colony fell afoul of the pioneers' spirit of individual independence, but the Wilderness Road became a major avenue of westward migration.

A major avenue the gap has remained. Today it is flanked by the Cumberland Gap National Historical Park. The madness and roar of the traffic in the gap make you wonder what kind of park could be here. They fade out, however, in the Park's glades and on the remaining bit of the Wilderness Road that tunnels through its woods, unmarked now by wagon-wheels and the hooves of oxen but otherwise looking much as it must have long ago. And the furor of the gap is forgotten when you have wound up Cumberland Mountain on Pinnacle Road and set off on the trail to which it leads. The Ridge Trail follows the crest of the mountain for 21 miles to the northeast and you cannot walk long through the noble upland forest it threads without understanding how three-quarters of the Park's 20,000 acres can be considered qualified for designation as Wilderness. (The National Park Service has proposed only half as much, in anticipation of the gutting of the ridge forest by the Allegheny Parkway.) Two centuries of human tides swirling by it have left Cumberland Mountain in considerable part unaltered—which says something of southern Appalachian topography. To me the Park wilderness, the mountain, even the whole Appalachian range were personified in a rock structure in view above Pinnacle Overlook, at the start of the Ridge Trail. It is of sandstone, a rock that, while it lacks granite's variegated texture (though occurring sometimes in lovely hues) can be as hard as granite and seems to acquire singularly smooth and arrestingly sculptured contours through weathering. The formation, standing guard over the gateway to the West, suggested a flat-crowned, short-beaked wide-gaped bird's head and neck. Erect, it gazed across Powell Valley and away to the east, a barbaric, unappeasable, heathen bird-god. It rose among the frowning cliffs that Boone—who had lost a son to attacking Indians in the vicinity during his first attempt to reach Kentucky, and been forced to retire—found "so wild and horrid that it is impossible to behold them without terror."

Cumberland Mountain is strategically situated geologically as well as historically. From cliffs above the gap you can look to the east and south across the widely-spaced welts of the Long Ridges, here in their southward decline. In the opposite direction are the Cumberlands—choppy hills and mountains. They take their name from the Cumberland Plateau, from which they were carved. The Cumberland Plateau is the lower half of the Appalachian Plateau, of which the upper is called the Allegheny Plateau. The surface of the Appalachian Plateau is in general very far from flat, as by dictionary definitions of "plateau" it ought to be. Flat the underlying rock strata are, however.

That morning I had driven for several hours along the front of the Cumberland Plateau. The day before, I had left the Cohutta range of northern Georgia—left it reluctantly—and spent the night in a state park north of Chattanooga on Chicamauga Reservoir. This huge impoundment of the Tennessee River worms its way across more than half the state, then branches into other huge impoundments that meander northward almost to Cumberland Gap, northeastward as far as Virginia and eastward to North Carolina—a fantastic system of inland waterways. In the morning I had to drive back almost to Chattanooga to get to the other side via the monster dam by which the Tennessee Valley Authority holds back all the water in Chicamauga and exacts a tribute in the form of electric power in letting it pass. Here, rising out of the south, the Plateau first acquires stature in a remarkable tableland a dozen miles wide and 80 long. It is the only part of the Plateau I know that fits the term, being like a mesa. A rugged western wall of the valley of the flooded Tennessee, Walden Ridge, as it is called, attains an elevation of 3,000 feet near its northern end. (It was named for Elijah Walden, who explored it in 1761 with a party of long hunters he had led through Cumberland Gap.) Here and there where the face was precipitous the foundation rocks showed—course on course of blocky sandstone, as if this were a half-ruined fortress, the observer a small beetle. To me it seemed deserving of better than the commonplace housing and commercial development that I had the impression, from zigzagging up onto it and talking to several persons along the way, was likely to be its fate. Yet I heard that there were still wild parts up there, and one hopes they may be saved.

In one way Walden Ridge was like the other dominating part of the Plateau I passed on the way to Cumberland Gap, a promising-looking crumple of mountains rising from 1,000 to over 3,500 feet northwest of Oak Ridge. In both cases the map showed only a small lower corner in public ownership. Not for the first or last time in the Appalachians I was depressed by examples of the way in which we seek to realize on the attractions of the mountains and other choice spreads of nature. We divide them into lots and each grabs what he can. Thus is the value of the whole, for us all as a whole, sacrificed. Thus is a great glory dissipated in trivial individual pittances. It is not our desire to kill the wild mountain goose that provides the golden eggs of spirits regenerated; it is just that each of us wants a piece carved out of the goose for himself, and before others can beat him to it.

Once when I expressed a strong feeling for the antiquity and beauty of the granite and gneiss of the Blue Ridge, a geologist said, "I prefer sedimentary rocks. You can make out their history." So you can, of course, from the fossils they usually contain. Both the Long Ridge Mountains and the Plateau are of layered sedimentary rock: sandstones, shales, conglomerates (of pebbles embedded in finer sediments), limestones. Whereas in the former the layers are tilted, often steeply, in the latter they are level, or nearly so. If in addition the rock of the Plateau is, in my experience, anyway, less colorful than that of the Long Ridges, with its wide variety of earth shades, it contains strata of a shiny black rock for which man has acquired a fateful acquisitiveness—coal.

It will be remembered that when, between 300 and 250 million years ago, Africa and North America pressed into each other and compression of the continental crust raised the rocks of the Piedmont and Blue Ridge to presumably Alpine heights, the sedimentary rock strata that had formed at the bottom of the sea on their inland side were forced up in a succession of folds. These would have stood miles high had weathering not worn them down as they rose. The process of accordioning gave rise to the Long Ridge Mountains, though, as we have seen, their undulations do not correspond to the original folds. Wherever the edge of a thick layer of hard, resistant sandstone was turned up, as in the cliffs of Cumberland Mountain, a ridge crest developed. To picture the process we have to remember, too, that the folds of rock as they were raised snapped in long rents known as faults and the forward sides of the folds pushed out ahead, overriding the rock beneath.

All through the latter chapters of the Paleozoic era the erosion of the rising mountains continued, and vast quantities of sediment were carried to the low-lying continental interior. Periodically for millions of years this lay beneath the sea, periodically for other millions stood a little above. While above, it was the province of a boggy forest luxuriating in tropical warmth. Each time the sea advanced over it the rotting remains of the vegetation, piled deep, were buried under mud or sand spreading out over the sea-bottom from the eroding mountains. Each time it retreated the forest grew anew on the sediments it left. Thus seams of coal were created among stacked layers of shale and sandstone. You can see how it was if you have a chance to examine the raw output of a mine. With the coal are slabs of shale bearing an impress, as sharp as if cast last week, of the trunks and branches of the huge ancestors of our horsetails and club-mosses. The pattern of leaves and wood may be recognized in coal itself, showing what it is—vegetative material that has decayed under pressure of overlying deposits sufficient to force out most of the non-carbonaceous ingredients.

Then, some 190 million years ago, on the eve of the Mesozoic—the Age of Reptiles—a final compression of the two continents took place. Giving the mountains probably their greatest elevation, it slowly raised the floor of the interior basin as one might raise the edge of a sheet of plywood. The erstwhile basin gradually became a plateau sloping to sea-level at the continental midland. Being from the beginning subject to the attack of running water ferreting out the easiest paths downhill, the plateau progressively acquired a relief as acute as that of the neighboring mountains.

The younger Appalachians do not reach the heights of the Blue Ridge and Smokies. The Long Ridges, moreover, are almost all separated by broad, cultivated valleys so that any wilds they retain are in strips lacking depth. (A number are, however, highways of bird migration, the most spectacular in this respect being Hawk Mountain, a part of Kittatinny Ridge in Pennsylvania.) If they had any special quality of their own I thought I might discover it in a mountain at the rim of a curious, high, platter-like valley 130 miles from Cumberland Gap, mostly east but a bit north, just below southernmost West Virginia. Maps gave its height as 4,710 feet, which made it the highest of all the Long Ridges and the highest mountain in Virginia apart from the cluster culminating in Big Balsam, just inside the state. Yet no map I could find gave its name, even the map of the Jefferson National Forest, a prong of which extended up it. I could not resist it. I should be virtually its discoverer.

My way took me through the town of Big Stone Gap, and here I gave a ride to two boys who were going, as I was, to Norton. En route, designating the big ridges high above us, I asked my usual question: how often might you find someone up on them? They pointed to one in the north and said there was a railroad up there, the Rimrock Railroad, run just for people who wanted to ride for pleasure. Apart from that, they said, some hunters, squirrel-hunters, and some ginseng-hunters, got up on the ridges sometimes. One of the ginseng-hunters had fallen off a cliff not long before and been killed.

Norton, a town of ordinary houses, variously of clapboard, asbestos shingles and tarpaper, sprinkled over the steep hillsides, had little to distinguish it; but from its southern outskirts a road ascended an upthrust of mountains topped by High Knob, at 4,223 feet the highest for a long way around. I found the narrow road about as steep and twisting as any I had been on, 2,200 feet right on up. The top was a grassy knoll, no doubt man-made, and behind a sign saying "JOB CORPS CONSERVATION PROJECT" eight Negro boys with three older whites were putting up an octagonal, cement-block monstrosity of a tower, three stories high. The district bosses, who had been hard put to it to get through high school (I had no doubt), would have stared incomprehending if I had tried to explain to them what the objection was. One of the Negroes proudly showed me a little snake he had smashed with his shovel, a silken Ring-necked Snake, gunmetal-colored but for the orange-apricot of its belly and of the band behind its elegant small head. "It's too bad you killed it," I said to the astonished hero of the exploit. "It's harmless and it's beautiful"—in fact the most beautiful of Eastern snakes, to me. The ignorant led by ignoramuses they send to a National Forest—which is what High Knob is in—to execute the will of the uneducated on it. Or so I fumed on the way down. . . . Leaving Norton I passed a sign for "LONESOME PINE INTERNATIONAL RACEWAY." That seems to me almost worthy to rank with one that caught Vera's eye, and fancy, just north of the Smokies: "FRENCH BROAD BAPTIST CHURCH."

To get into the platter of Burke's Garden you have to surmount the rim. Coming from the north you climb Rich Mountain through hairpin turns to about 3,400 feet. Descending 600 you find yourself in a level valley of open fields. A sign tells you that it is all private property and—a welcome surprise—a wildlife refuge. Unable to identify the exalted object of my quest, I drove on and on across the valley until I came to a country store. The men inside seemed to know all about the 4,710-foot mountain. The lean, grizzled proprietor said it was called Beartown—which was odd since one of my maps showed another mountain, not a great deal lower, 35 miles to the southwest, with that name. "It's sometimes called Balsam Bear-town," he added, "because of the Balsams on it." So! It was high enough for that. I had been hoping it might be. The instructions I was given took me out a dirt road to the house and outbuildings of a modern rancher whose property went up the mountain to meet the National Forest. The inter-vening hills were in cattle range, which also extended well up Balsam Beartown's side. I had been told that the land was posted with No TRES-PASSING signs, but when the owner learned that I had no intention of hunting he said I could disregard them. He also said he drove his Jeep up the mountain every day, looking after his cattle, and thought I should be able to find the road.

The road I did find after leaving my bus at the end of the public road, and going through a gateway, soon raveled out and, to my eyes, disappeared. The range was rough, steep and partly grown up in blackberry tangles —and in flowers: the profusion of Pale Bergamot and Queen-Anne's-lace would have led you to believe that the hillside had been sowed to them. Thunder had been rumbling over the mountain before I set out. Rain soon followed. Before I had been going an hour, startling occasional Aberdeen Angus cattle, I was in one of those mountain downpours. The pellets struck like shot. Inside my rain-hood the sound was of strings of firecrackers going off all at once, unremittingly. Not inclined to climb higher, into the lightning, I turned my back to it to wait it out, like a steer in a blizzard. The silver arrows driving past my head at an angle into the ground reminded me of tracer-bullets from machine guns as they look when the battery is firing from around you.

By the time the rain had slackened off a smoky cloud had descended on the mountain and I decided to give up. Before I had gone far down, however, the sky began to brighten. So I changed my mind and started back. The early consequence was that I found myself involved in those vast blackberry brakes. With arching canes ten feet long they were nearly impassable even on cattle trails. Continually I snagged and extricated myself, found the way hopeless and backtracked to try another. I had started to struggle through toward a forested slope to the west, thinking to find an easier route up the mountain where the canopy of trees would shut out the blackberries, when the storm returned, bringing the lightning with it. Shamelessly I crouched low, on one knee. With every strike a rent shot the length of the heavens, bringing them down, by the sound of it, in a roar of rubble. The assault did subside in time, leaving the slopes streaming, and I fought my way to the woods. I even made a little distance through them. But the accumulation of fallen trees and limbs, not to mention the big rocks, made the going so circuitous I wondered if I might not end by going around the mountain rather than up it. That I should never reach the top before dark was soon clear. So I called it off and turned back once more and for good. Getting back was not as easy as I had expected, however. I had lost my way. When finally I made it down off the mountain I was lucky to be only a mile off target.

Having left my rain-trousers behind to save carrying them, I had been soaked from the hips down since the first rain, and I was tired from a long day as well. That partly answered the question of why I did not find somewhere in the valley to pull up for the night and have another go at the mountain in the morning. The rest of the answer was that I had long been away from home and had promised—myself among others—to be back the next evening. Balsam Beartown's secret, if any, would have to wait. Hungry Mother State Park, a likely refuge for the night, lay not too far to the south. But what was involved was crossing the breadth of the Long Ridges after dark. *Sic Non Juvat Transcendere Montes.* In that unwieldly little bus, too heavy for its power, I was in second gear, uphill, down and around, for 24 miles out of 25.

In their way, with broad, green valleys sweeping grandly on either side like troughs in the sea up to the wooded combers, the Long Ridges provide some of Virginia's most exhilarating scenery, as at Hot Spring they provide the background for Virginia's most luxuriously appointed resort, the Homestead. They also have a striking biological distinction. Of this I was reminded when, continuing on up the range, I arrived at a spot where early in July, returning from the West Virginia Alleghenies, I had come on a roadside bank bursting with the gorgeous yellow blooms of that otherwise homeliest of plants of the driest locations, Prickly-pear Cactus. Arid Appalachians sounds like a contradiction, but that is what these are, at least on the southeastward-facing slopes at lower elevations. Some I have seen could almost be taken for hills in New Mexico, with Virginia Pines standing in for Pinyons. They are the so-called shale barrens, and they extend up the Long Ridge Mountains from southwestern Virginia into central Pennsylvania. Rain clouds coming up from the Gulf of Mexico—the source of most summer precipitation—are intercepted by highlands to their west and they receive below 40 inches of average annual rainfall and snow-melt, less than half that at Highlands, North Carolina. On off-years they receive much less still. The slopes, moreover, steep and meagre in soil-cover, are built on highly foliated, crumbly rock in sloping layers so that whatever rain falls on them tends to drain quickly away. The rock, rich in fossils, is Devonian shale, laid down as mud upwards of 350 million years ago in the Age of Fishes, as it was of giant tree-ferns on land.

The shale barrens have their own flora. Its components are characterized

Butterfly weed—the largest plant of it I have ever seen—on a dry, lower slope of Virgina's Great North Mountain. The butterfly is a Great Spangled fritillary.

by the devices they have evolved for dealing with drought. Some have fleshy, water-retaining stems or leaves, some have deep roots. Others are skimpy in water-evaporating foliage or go into dormancy in midsummer. Having come to terms with a harsh environment, they are spared the intensity of competition their relatives must meet where living is softer. They bloom as gaily as if they had not a care in the world. In July the Large-flowered Evening-primrose displayed blossoms like saucers and in the arid soil at the foot of Great North Mountain the orange masses of Butterfly Milkweed were as large and showy as clumps of azalea. Carl S. Keener of Pennsylvania State University, an authority on the flora of the shale barrens, believes that some of the endemics evolved from common species of the surrounding country by adaptation to the barrens (for example, a Wild Onion, a Forked Chickweed, a Rock Cress, an Aster and a Goldenrod), while others migrated by one means or another from similar locations in the West—some from knolls in the upper plains (including Longleaf Clover and a Pussytoes), one from the central plains (a Milk Vetch) and some from Texas (including Showy Yellow Buckwheat, Large-flowered Evening-primrose and Swordleaf Phlox).

The highlands that cast a "rain shadow" over the barrens are those of the Appalachian Plateau. And it was to the Cumberland part of the Plateau that I first turned on leaving Cumberland Gap, before going on to Balsam Beartown. I got no farther into the Plateau, however, than U.S. 119, which I followed along the southeastern edge of Pine Mountain. This 108-mile-long ridge, which is never more than a dozen miles inside Kentucky, is well known to geologists as representing an unusually long buckling and overthrust of rock strata. Evening was bringing on a mistiness between the successive spurs of the hills, rendering each a little less substantial than its predecessor. Most wraith-like of all, and looking very high in the southeast, were Cumberland Mountain, which I had just left, and, farther along, the High Cumberlands, topped by Big Black Mountain, the highest in Kentucky. The sordid development of the valleys, rendered no more inviting as neon lights spelling the names of businesses and the floodlamps of gasoline stations and truck stops came on, was in contrast with the jungly-looking hillsides directly behind it all. The topography to the west and north was all below my limit of 3,000 feet elevation, and nothing I was passing gave me much desire to go deeper into it.

I knew the Cumberlands in that direction, in Kentucky and West Virginia, from past travels. They are a maze of steep, wooded, camel's-hump hills and mostly narrow, twisting stream-valleys. Of the latter, the more isolated are too often the scenes of rural squalor, the others too often of a mean, ugly commercialism and shabby dwellings with occasional coal tipples above a railroad track on which miles of black gondola-cars wait, and with coal trucks pounding the highway. I have asked my inveterate question here, too, and been told that of the innumerable hills, many probably see no human being near the top for years on end except an infrequent squirrel- or turkey-hunter. You look up and wonder what is there. Only you know that in fewer cases every month does it matter. More and more in recent years the coal companies have been getting the coal out by digging down to it from above and dumping the spoil down the mountainside.

Americans who think that the unbridled destructiveness we unleashed on the continent after the Civil War—before which the Passenger Pigeons, Bison, Fur Seals and the great forests were to go down like wheat before the reaper—belongs to our past should see the Cumberlands. But driving through is not enough; the havoc is not apparent from below. You must fly over. Then you will see how hills are butchered wholesale like whales drawn up the ramp of factory ships. You will grasp what strip-mining means on slopes too steep for the restoration the law requires. If you do not go where the strip-mining is, you can get the idea from the highway construction. Putting multi-lane highways through these twisting, constricted valleys is at least as destructive as strip-mining. It is just that there is more of the latter. By 1971 almost 600,000 acres of southern Appalachia had been "disturbed" by stripping. And the tempo has been accelerating ever since.

Except for being channelized and compressed by the topography, civilization in the Cumberlands does not appear as different from that elsewhere in the country as you might expect, from what you read of the poverty—though surely the difference would be greater without the welfare payments on which a large part of the population lives. Many of the houses have tarpaper roofs and asphalt siding and are run-down, some little better than shacks, a number with outhouses. The streams that run through every valley are full of cans, bottles, basins and other trash. There are junked cars everywhere, cannibalized to keep others going. But there are many new, if mostly quite modest, houses and, alas, many new mobile homes on the hillsides. Whitesburg, Kentucky, and Williamson, West Virginia, are reasonably prosperous-looking American towns. The people, whom I find more attractive in feature than the American average, are reasonably well dressed. Those I have met I have enjoyed talking to— miners young and old, shopkeepers, a farmer and his wife, hitchhiking youngsters, the English wife of a timber-cruiser in a remote "holler" (she was carrying water from a stream and must have wondered how she had ever ended here by marrying an American soldier), the owner of a repair shop for mining-machinery. There are tough characters here—as where are there not?—some quick with firearms. But I have liked all I have had any contact with, and have felt no sense of difference between us.

No, there was an exception. He was the manager of a strip-mining operation on Ferguson Creek near Pikeville, Kentucky. It was shut down for the week-end, but a grey-haired woman in the office had told me I could walk around it if I wanted to. I had done so with considerable curiosity, this being my first strip-mine. I had been distinctly impressed by the char-treuse-colored Euclid bulldozer with four-foot-high blade used to gouge out the bench, and by the augur with bits two or three feet in diameter with which the coal was drilled out of the wall above it. Also I did not overlook all the trees knocked over and partially buried, though this was a small operation—one a beautiful Beech a foot and a half through. It was when I was about to leave that I was intercepted by the manager, whose puffy face looked as if it had been bitten all over by insects. He was extremely suspicious and we had something of a session. "We've had a lot of trouble with VISTA people, and we're not taking any chances," he said. "I don't want you back here. If you want to see how a strip-mine operates, get in touch with the head of the Coal Operators Association in Pikeville on Monday." Not everyone in the Cumberlands is opposed to stripping, but among the majority that is, feelings can run very high.

Withal, how glad I invariably was to get up to the lovely woods in the passes between the valleys!—especially those, the blessed woods, as I thought of them, of the Breaks Interstate Park. On the Kentucky-Virginia border, the park is so named because here Russell Fork of the Big Sandy River breaks through Pine Mountain near its northeastern end in a canyon it has carved five miles long and up to 1,600 feet deep. From the heights of the park you look down into the gorge, much of its walls sheer and of level formations of sandstone. Here in the deep bluey chasm of the river's bend, time seemed to have been arrested and absorbed by space, and for this majesty of tranquility and for the sight of *grandeur* my soul seemed to ache. Why? The commercialism of those densely populated valleys—of au-tomobile dealers, garages, lumberyards, corner groceries, hardware stores, clothing stores, abandoned little attempts at drive-ins, eating places—was no more commercial than commercialism elsewhere in America. But here —the realization came to me—it stood out like the bones of an emaciated cow and seemed to be all life locally was *about,* except insofar as it was directed to the pursuit of ordinary individual ends, particularly those con-nected with motorcars. It was the drabness that utterly depressed my spirits, the sense of the lack of any redeeming meaning in life—simply emphasized by the bleakness of the little Baptist and Methodist churches—which called into question the point of anything.

The Cumberlands are today being torn apart by bulldozers and power-shovels. Yesterday the railroads gouged out the narrow valleys. Yesterday the priceless forests were leveled—a proposal to save a few acres being laughed down in the Kentucky legislature. The thin soil of the over-steep hills cleared for farming was being carried away by the rains.

Overleaf, early light through the mist on the North-South Trail, Cranberry, W. Va.

Upper left, Linville Gorge from Wiseman's View is an Appalachian Yosemite. *Lower left,* for the author, the most magnetic orchid of them all—the Grass pink. *Lower right,* part of the cliff of Cumberland Mountain overlooking the Gap, the sandstone hewn by the elements into the image of a strange heathen bird-god.

And it is here in the Cumberlands that something emerges which else-where is more or less concealed under the lush material prosperity of our country. It is something at least that I have come to believe: that a society cannot possess a cultural force amid scenes of the destructive exploitation of nature, of the earth. It cannot deplete its natural setting without equally depleting its own cultural content and meaning. It does not and cannot exist independently of its matrix in nature, and to the extent that its treatment of that matrix is destructive rather than creative it will destroy its own inner life and become a zombie, richly appareled, it may be, for a while, but nonetheless one of the walking dead.

I put up for the night in a motel in the town of Cumberland and the next day drove up into the mountains that had appeared as a pale shadow on the southeastern horizon the evening before. The morning was of a perfect Appalachian kind, the air clear, the breeze light, the temperature unde-tectable, the sunlight brilliant. Across the gulf that the tortuously-climbing highway was putting beneath it, every tree stood out on Big Black, the highest of the Cumberlands at 4,139 feet and the highest in Kentucky. At the crest, which is the Virginia line, I got out to walk the road to the summit, or as near as a fenced-in radar installation would permit. The northern character of the forest rather surprised me. Apart from High Knob 10 miles to the east there was no other mountain the height of Big Black for 60 miles; the Yellow Birches, Sugar Maples, Beeches and Bass-woods on the two summits must have been growing on them in isolation since the retreat of the glacier.

While I was walking, two mowing-machines came along, sickle-bars sweeping the roadside and, to my sorrow, felling swaths of blooming Wood Nettle, Pale Bergamot bearing pincushions stuck full of tiny whitish bandilleras, Jewelweed hung with little orange Phrygian caps and Tall Meadowrue with downy white flowers over my head. The men with the machines, who had their names on their helmets—Willis, Jones and Powers—stopped for a chat. One of them brought up strip-mining; there had been stripping even on Big Black. Another said what I already knew, that if I flew over the country here, especially in the fall with the leaves off the trees, I'd "really see something." How long, I asked, did they think it would take for nature to repair the damage? "Thousands of years," said one. And a second: "Maybe never." They looked, I soon perceived, with little hope on the mountains around them, and that was not new to me either. They and their fathers and grandfathers had seen too much of the power of the lumber companies and coal companies, which had taken immense wealth from the Cumberlands and left blight behind. They could not believe that any legislation strong enough to save the hills from the strippers would be enacted while there was still anything much to save.

From Big Black the descent into Virginia is long, steep and winding. Near the foot of it I came to a roadside dwelling overhung by the spoil-bank of a strip-mine. Beside it a man in his sixties resembling Gary Cooper, with fingers and thumb missing from his left hand, was working as well as he could on an old truck. Stopping to talk to him, I was so affected by his sad lot and resignation to it that I made more even than I otherwise might have of the masses of flowers in which his house was set as in a bower, among them orange sunflowers new to me and petunias overflowing from windowboxes. He had, it would seem, little else to cheer him. The strippers had cut the bench so deeply back into the hill behind his house that water collected there and in the event of a cloudburst could come pouring down, bringing the hillside with it, and take everything out of the ravine in which he lived. Much the same could happen if the stream behind the house were blocked above it by boulders tumbled down into it. This had happened before and he had had them bulldozed out, but they were piling up again. Those responsible ignored his complaints and pleas and removing them would cost more money than he had. A victim of the American way, he was one of thousands on thousands whose story has been told with almost unbearable poignancy by Harry M. Caudill in *Night Comes to the Cumberlands*.

Just north of where I had put in the evening before was the little State Park of Kingdom Come; and now before me was Big Stone Gap, the town in which the novel that the park commemorates was written, at the turn of the century. *The Little Shepherd of Kingdom Come* was one of the two immensely successful novels that John Fox wrote about the Cumberlands, the other being *The Trail of the Lonesome Pine*.

Though my concern in the mountains was with nature, I find I cannot go on with my impressions without giving more recognition than I have to the folk who have been *of* those mountains as the rest of us shall never be, or their own grandchildren either. More human beings have moved out of the southern Appalachians than ever moved into them. But many did stay, and not just in the wide, accessible valleys that differed little from the America with which they were in close communication. They stayed back in the mountains because of the hold the mountains had on their strengths or their weaknesses or on both. It is they of whom I am speaking: the Southern Highlanders, as interested outsiders call them; mountain people, as they call themselves, or called themselves, for they are mostly in the past tense now. They have never been a simple people. James Wigginton, when he went to teach high school at Rabun Gap, saw in their aging survivors in the north Georgia hills the appealing repository of vanishing skills and ways which he persuaded his students to write up on the basis of interviews; and in *The Foxfire Book*, which resulted in 1972, you may meet them as kind, patient, self-reliant, stoical, and touching. (Though Wigginton does not say so, I feel sure that "foxfire" is the mountain transliteration of "phosphorescence.") James Dickey, looking in the same hills at the same time, came up with the vicious killers of *Deliverance*.

What Wigginton did, what he dedicated in published form "to the people of these mountains in the hope that, through it, some portion of their wisdom, ingenuity and individuality will remain long after them to touch us all," was surely worthy of all the recognition it has had. After I came down from Highlands to Dillard I might have met him and I wish I had. It was on Betty's Creek, a few miles west of Rabun Gap. Wigginton had a little house here, up a short piece from the big old stone house from which Mary Hambidge had since the mid-1930's, with the local mountain people, engaged in the production of woolens, raising and shearing sheep, carding, spinning and dyeing the wool and weaving it. Wigginton passed at a distance while I was in the kitchen of the big house. But I was talking with one of the chief weavers, Margaret Norton, whom I had not seen for fifteen years, the same Margaret whose "honey cookies and cheese soufflés," along with indefatigable, grey-eyed little Mary Hambidge herself, had helped bring Wigginton back to the mountains to which he had been taken by his father as a small boy. We were talking of what she was up against in keeping the place going in Mary Hambidge's tragic final incapacitation, which meant, among other things, providing for parties up from Atlanta for lunch and for lodgers, too. Margaret lived up the road to Patterson Gap and always had. Did that mean that I, who had been on five continents, had to make allowances? Far from it! Margaret was—is—a fine, competent, intelligent and shrewd woman whose appraisal of the essential me, I felt a trifle uncomfortably, was a thoroughly realistic one, as it would be of the essential anyone else. All her life she had worked hard and now she had more on her than ever, having at home the burden of those dependent on her. But there was no complaint. She would hold whatever fort was given to her to hold, with whatever lay at hand or could be improvised. There was the mountain woman in her.

To John Fox the mountain people of his day were natural, homespun cavaliers, fearless and incorruptible. They were that, I am sure. "They have an easy and unaffected bearing and the unselfconscious manners of the well-bred," an English visitor wrote. "I have received salutations upon introductions or on bidding farewell, dignified and restrained, such as a courtier might make to his sovereign." They were also acutely touchy to their honor—the males, that is, and it was they who dominated—ferociously independent, quick to action and reckless of consequences. These qualities were never more deplorably displayed than in Hillsville, Virginia, eight miles north of Fancy Gap, through which the Blue Ridge Parkway passes, in 1912. Fred Allen was being tried for freeing two young members of the clan who had been arrested for disturbing a church meeting and, ominously, his kinsmen were on hand. Sentenced to a year in jail, the prisoner, as the W. P. A. Guide to Virginia relates it, "stood up and shouted 'I ain't a-goin'!' [and] a volley blazed 'like the crackle of mountain laurel,' a witness said. The judge, the commonwealth attorney, the sheriff, the jury foreman, and a witness for the prosecution were killed, and the clerk of the court was wounded. Then the Allens rode off into the hills." The mother of Claude Allen, one of two sentenced to death for the outrage, and the subject of a doleful ballad, had to be prevented by the authorities from inscribing on his gravestone, "Murdered by the state of Virginia."

A tradition of clan warfare among the many mountaineers of Scots descent, the inward focus of isolated communities and above all the divisive legacy of the Civil War, gave rise to the bloody mountain feuds. You catch a glimpse of how that now far-off conflict entered the lives of the mountain people in the epitaph on a gravestone in Cade's Cove recording that Russell Gregory, "founder" of Gregory's Bald (well, he found it, didn't he?) was "murdered by rebels from North Carolina." The flaring of tempers, the ambushes, surprises, sieges, shoot-outs and pitched battles that made up a feud are chillingly described by Noah M. Reynolds, a participant in one of them, in his booklet on the feuds of the Kentucky mountains, printed in Whitesburg. In it the author states that the Franch and Eversole "war," commencing about 1882, took about seventy-four lives and the Rowan County feud from eighty-five to one hundred while in the "Bloody Breathett Feud" there was never "any accurate account kept of the actual number of men killed." Horace Kephart, writing of the early years of the century in the Smoky Mountains, declared that "Homicide is so prevalent . . . that nearly every adult citizen has been directly interested in some murder case, either as principal, officer, witness, kinsman or friend."

But make no mistake: as Alberta Pierson Hannum recalls in speaking of the notorious Hatfield-McCoy feud, Devil Anse Hatfield and "Old Randall" McCoy, except to the other clan, "were as neighborly, honest, thrifty and obliging men as ever drew the breath of life." Noah M. Reynolds himself touches on this aspect of mountain society, practically evoking a mountain idyl, when he tells of his grandparents' move from Virginia to Boone Fork, a tributary of the Kentucky River: "This being a very sparsely settled section of the mountains, game was plentiful. The coves and small bottoms were fertile, bringing abundant crops of corn and garden vegetables. The neighbors being kind and generous-hearted would lend a helping hand to anything they could see their neighbors needed, without the asking, everybody going to church on Sunday and worshipping God according to the dictates of their own conscience."

Behind the killings there was characteristically pride. And pride, if it was costly to the mountain people, was what kept them going. However destitute, Kephart wrote, "they are never abject. The mordant misery of hunger is borne with a sardonic grin." Above all, the mountain man was a man. "Charity, or anything that smells to him like charity, is declined with patrician dignity or open scorn." His physical stamina matched his moral. In youth, afoot, he could easily outstrip a horse on a day's journey, Kephart declared and recalled how Long Goody, a mountain woman six feet three in height, "walked eighteen miles across the Smokies into Tennessee, crossing at an elevation of 5,000 feet, merely to shop more advantageously than she could at home. The next day she shouldered fifty pounds of flour and other groceries, and bore them home before nightfall."

Born hunters, schooled chiefly in lore and nature, quick and deadly in action, these courteous, ceremonious, self-reliant, stoic people remind one in many ways of the Indians whom they displaced. Passions that found no outlet otherwise they worked off in music and dance, like the redmen, and in emotional religious revivals not unlike the wilder of the redmen's invocations of divine favor. On a poor diet high in corn meal and hominy, they tirelessly strode their hills and tilled by hand the soil on slopes too steep to hold it. In meagre garments, often barefoot, they endured with scant shelter whatever cold the mountain winter brought. A gun, a knife, some pans and a few toolheads they needed from the outside world, with a few other necessities and luxuries, though with enough honey sugar could be done without and in dire straits parched chestnuts serve for coffee. Store-bought goods had to be paid for, which called for a product to market for cash. The forest could help but usually only partially meet the need, supplying animal hides, chestnuts (of which a family might gather two or three hundred pounds in a day at the height of the season), bark for tannin, Cherry Birch for oil of wintergreen, ginseng. The one product of their own of which they could count on a surplus above their own needs was corn. But corn was high in volume for its value and hence uneconomic to transport where roads were of the most primitive, if they existed at all. The logical expedient was to convert the corn into that which was high in value for its volume: corn whiskey. This they did—only to be told they might not sell it by a nation that otherwise disregarded them, except when it needed men to fight its wars and found in the mountain boys recruits ready and uncommonly well equipped to do so.

Independence, which was vital to the mountain people, requires versatility, and this they had. Hear Charles Lanman on the subject, for example, writing in 1848 of a trip to Alum Cave, in the Smokies: "Our first night from home we spent in the cabin of a man who treated us with the utmost kindness, and would not receive a penny for his pains. [Hospitality to the stranger was of course a matter of principle in the mountains.] . . . And now, to prove that our friend was an intelligent man, it may be mentioned that he is adept in the following professions and trades, viz., those of medicine, the law, the blacksmith, the carpenter, the hunter, the shoemaker, the watchmaker, the farmer, and he also seemed to possess an inkling of some half dozen sciences."

Given a broad-axe, an augur, an adze for squaring logs and a froe for cleaving oak into shakes (also into splits for baskets and chair-bottoms), a mountain man could raise a cabin—which he generally did in concert in a "log-rolling." The fireplace was of available rock, the chimney also, or of sticks and clay. On wheels of her husband's construction the woman spun the wool she sheered from the sheep on the hillside pasture and the flax she grew. The thread she wove on a loom handmade like the wheels. She dyed the cloth with wild plants, madder for red, walnut-shells for brown, hickory-bark for yellow, indigo for blue. Nature supplied medicines as well: "digitalis from the purple foxglove, creosote from the wood tar of the pine or beech for bronchitis and coughs, belladonna from the deadly nightshade plant for pain of inflammation and constipation, arnica from the dried flowers of the leopard's-bane for bruises and cuts, pokeroot for eczema, oil of thyme for diphtheria and typhoid, hemlock to relieve the pain of cancer, jimson root for ulcers and to help palsy, wolfbane for fevers, sassafras and boneset and snakeroot for tonics. . . ." (The pharmacopoeia is Alberta Pierson Hannum's.) But what chiefly enabled so many mountain people to reach old age was probably physical activity, light eating and the fetish they made of pure water and fresh air, to which the cabin door stood open all day even in winter. Above any other white people in North America, they were native to and belonged to their country—a country with "a softness about the wooded heights and hollows, a beauty of melting curves, of lights and shadows, of tender distances wherein the hearthsmoke is a part and the cabin is at home," as a Northern missionary-preacher, John C. Campbell, put it.

Like the Indians before them, however, the mountain people were to be overtaken by a world with little use for their aptitudes and a great deal of use for the gifts of their land. On these, outsiders have enriched themselves. "Though fabulous wealth has been generated in Appalachia, the mountaineers' share in it has been held to a minimum," Harry M. Caudill writes. Moreover, "To the industrialists who opened the coal mines, set up the great saw mills, operated the quarries, built the railroads and hauled away the resources, the population was a made-to-order source of cheap labor." The mountain people have been faced with a grinding choice. On the one hand they could assimilate themselves to the industrial order, which has meant in most cases putting themselves at the mercy of the labor market of Appalachian towns or of Chicago, Detroit, or Dayton, with all the handicaps of their background, perhaps even illiteracy. On the other they could try to hang on where and as they were, which has generally meant accepting a now ignominious poverty and the hand-outs they call "the

Welfare." As Caudill declares, "The debasement of the mountaineer is a tragedy of epic proportions."

Of course, change had to come. In contact with technological civilization, no people can hold for long to traditional ways. Change has had to come to Arabia, too, but for the Arabs it is being cushioned by oil revenues.

Nothing could have preserved the Southern Highlanders as they were —as "our living ancestors." The frontier conditions that shaped them were bound to give way before the booming national cash economy, roads, consolidated schools and electronics. Richard B. Drake in *An Appalachian Reader* tells the story in terms of one family's "evening entertainment over which the father invariably presided. Sometimes the patriarch whittled small figures; sometimes he played the banjo; and other times he put together corn-shuck figures; still others he told stories. Then one day one of the neighbors bought a television set. . . ."

But the rest may be imagined.

XII *A Prayer, and the West Virginia Alleghenies*

It is in parts of the Appalachian Plateau from which the West Virginia Alleghenies have been carved, more than anywhere else I know, that the traveler sees most to recall the earlier America of the mountains; and this affects my feeling about the region. It is here that I should have finished had I continued my way up the inland side of the southern Appalachians. Actually, as I said, it was where I began in June, though I have seen it at other times, too.

The highest part of the Appalachian Plateau, the West Virginia Alleghenies form a southern Appalachian massif second only to that which is largely contained in western North Carolina. Having originated as a nearly level uplift, the range lacks the high, dominating peaks of the major massif; however, it extends 120 miles from end to end with only minor descents below 3,000 feet and perhaps 50 crests over 4,000. Much of it is wild enough for Black Bears. No other part of the East, I suspect, has as great a potential for recreation so largely unrecognized outside it. The state itself is now waking up to its value. On highway signs inconceivable even six or seven years ago, when industrial boosterism was still the order of the day, it welcomes visitors to "WILD WONDERFUL WEST VIRGINIA." Fishing streams are abundant, the white waters of the long upper tributaries of the Potomac famous among canoeists, opportunities for hiking and horseback riding limitless, the pleasures of the eye inexhaustible. In the northern part particularly there are verdant pastoral valleys, rolling and spacious, through which the little-traveled road goes swinging, and, where the relief is steep, rangeland that swoops to deep valleys and swerves up the other side to meet the saddle-cloth of forest on the ridge. The open, spirit-releasing country gives background to West Virginia's motto: *Montani Semper Liberi*. It is here that you find the witnesses of the past—original farmhouses with fieldstone chimneys, some of clapboard, a number even of log construction, with picturesque outbuildings of logs, too, or weathered, rough-cut boards, even a few little spring-houses.

190

I cannot be here without thinking what a tremendous thing it would be if a mantle of federal protection could be extended over both the natural areas and the human landscape so long co-existent with them and, against a national future even more crowded and congested, more over-built and over-industrialized than anything we have seen yet, a National Scenic Reserve be created in these Alleghenies from which the disharmonies of our century would be excluded. Not only—as the dream goes—would generous wild areas be set aside as inviolate among forests subject to selective cutting, but the rural inhabitants be helped to keep their lands and have it made worthwhile to them to cooperate in the restoration and preservation of the old buildings, and in the gradual replacement of the now-proliferating cheap, characterless new houses and ghastly mobile homes, with dwellings more in keeping with their surroundings. Carefully structured scenic roads, judiciously located man-made lakes, facilities for sports and conforming lodges for tourists and vacationers not addicted to roughing it would not be too high a price to pay, I have thought. Then, if I had my way—and I may as well go the whole hog in this confession—a western Appalachian Trail would come through here. The idea of making two of the increasingly crowded Appalachian Trail continually came to me while I was going about in the mountains. Conceive of the present trail as in the form of a much attenuated letter H with the lower part of the right-hand upright and the upper part of the left-hand upright missing, the cross-bar being the section of the trail that crosses from the Long Ridge to the Blue Ridge Mountains just north of Roanoke. What I have had in mind is completing the H. We should then have a western trail that would be the present trail from Springer Mountain to the crossbar from which it would continue as a new trail up through the Allegheny range, then on through the Poconos, Catskills and Adirondacks. The eastern trail would start in the neighborhood of Tallulah Falls, Georgia, proceed northward over Rabun Bald, through the vicinity of Highlands and across the Balsam, Craggy and Black Mountains and so on up the seaboard escarpment of the Blue Ridge to the crossbar, whereat it would become the present trail.

Almost 1,300 square miles of the West Virginia Alleghenies are already in National Forest. But the extent of the protection this affords may be gauged from a leaflet on coal mining I took from a rack in a District Ranger Station. It pictured a strip-mined and devastated hillside (Good, I thought, that's laying it on the line!), then underneath declared, "The Monongahela National Forest is yours to enjoy—dig in!" So help me. It then went on to caution, however, that "The minerals lying under more than one-third of the Monongahela National Forest lands are privately owned." And these, as it acknowledged, the owner is at present empowered to extract regardless of damage to the surface.

There are tens of thousands of persons who stand to profit from the destructive exploitation of the Appalachians, one way or another, and whose attitude toward them is colored by that prospect. For others, to come within their magnetic field is to pray for their preservation. I must speak my mind about this, and here, before I go farther into the Alleghenies, may be as good a place as any for me to have my say, which I shall make as brief as I can.

The Forest Service, it would appear, is a house divided. Part is subservient to the lumbering, mining and grazing interests, and to the Bureau of Public Roads, thrown in for good measure. This is the Forest Service that permitted such clear-cutting in a Montana National Forest as to lead Senator Lee Metcalf of that state to exclaim, "What the once respected Forest Service let happen at the Bitterroot is appalling." It is the Forest Service that sold more than 8.75 billion board feet of timber—covering an area the size of Rhode Island, as the Sierra Club pointed out—from the Tongass National Forest in southeastern Alaska to a lumber company planning to ship it to Japan. To come closer to home, it is the Forest Service that a coalition of conservation organizations had to take to court to forestall the authorization of destructive cutting in the Monongahela National Forest in violation of a Federal Act of 1897; the Forest Service that the State of West Virginia also took to court to prevent the opening of two new coal mines in the Monongahela National Forest in noncompliance with the Environmental Protection Act of 1969. It is the Forest Service that evidently saw nothing wrong with bulldozing a destructive highway along the crest of the basin forming the Joyce Kilmer Memorial Forest, which the Service itself had declared to be "One of the most impressive remnants of our Nation's virgin wilderness." (Fortunately, conservationists got the highway relocated.) There is another Forest Service of officials and rangers who fight to prevent the very abuses I have cited, who devote themselves to extending our knowledge of trees and forest ecology, who risk their lives in fighting fires, who press to the point of endangering their careers for restraint in cutting and for the most protective classification of outstanding natural areas in the Forests.

A similar dichotomy would appear to characterize the National Park Service. Here there would seem to be less excuse for it. The National Parks were never intended for "multiple use" as were the National Forests, which were created to assure the nation a continuing supply of lumber and afford grazing, as well as to provide protection of watersheds and recreation. Unfortunately, there is a certain ambivalence in the National Park Service Act of 1916, which calls for both the enjoyment of the parks by the people and for their preservation. And plainly the more people you have enjoying the parks the harder they will be to preserve. One is inclined to be strongly critical of the authors of the Act for not having been clearer about its prime purpose—until one recalls that, if *Genesis* is to be believed, God

Himself was similarly ambivalent in His instructions to Adam for the treatment of the first National Park, Eden, which he was "to dress and to keep." If God could do no better at resolving the issue of "improvement" versus preservation, we can hardly be surprised if Congressmen and GS-15's have been tripped by it.

Be that as it may, we have, in effect, two National Park Services. One acts as if it would not appear to be doing a job unless it ran paved roads (cut-and-fill as necessary), constructed elaborate and showy visitor centers and ever-expanding campgrounds and contracted with concessionaires who operate virtual resorts in the parks with commercial shops appropriate to the Atlantic City boardwalk. It was the officials of this Service who erected a monument to themselves in that utterly incongruous observation tower on Clingman's Dome, which Anthony Wayne Smith, President of the National Parks and Conservation Association, well described as an "extravagantly expensive . . . Coney Island facility, a Steeplechase Pier feature." The other Service stands up as well as it can to the pressures for such abuses of the parks. It was of this Service as it has traditionally been that Anthony Wayne Smith wrote that "Men entered the Service and gave their lives to it because they believed in the ideals of the Service. A large measure of unselfish devotion has characterized the attitudes of Park Service personnel, from seasonal rangers to directors." Faithful to those ideals, this Service in recent years has, among other things, eliminated the "firefall" at Yosemite, in which a burning pyre was pushed off a 3,000-foot cliff, established exemplary standards for park roads, taken steps to reduce private-motorcar traffic in Yosemite Valley and in the National Seashores, and contributed admirably to a notable increase in National Parks. Its view is that expressed by the Conservation Foundation and emphatically shared by other conservation organizations, that "the parks can only be enjoyed fully if they are preserved unimpaired."

The preservation of the National Parks and the maintenance of the National Forests in a natural condition, as far as possible, depends on the strengthening of the hand of conservationists in the two Services and, most of all, on making support of conservation profitable for politicians. That this can be done, and to almost miraculously good effect, was shown by the passage of the Wilderness Act.

It is by their designation as Wilderness under this act that we can make most sure of the preservation of unspoiled areas. The nature of the act and what can be and is being done under it must be of great interest to anyone concerned for the future of the southern Appalachians. By way of explanation I think I can do no better than quote from a report of December 20, 1973, accompanying S. 316, entitled Eastern Wilderness Areas Act, by the Hon. Henry M. Jackson, Chairman, Senate Committee on Interior and Insular Affairs, as follows:

In 1964, with the passage of the Wilderness Act, the United States began a major effort to preserve its few remaining primitive areas and protect their unique value as places for wilderness experience, solitude, scientific inquiry, and primitive recreation. Although many studies remain to be done and the legislative agenda is not completed, this effort has already borne fruit. The 1964 Act designated as wilderness 54 areas covering about 9.1 million acres of land. The Act also established a procedure for designating additional areas. It requires that specific types of potential wilderness areas—primitive areas and roadless lands within parks and wildlife areas—be evaluated by the Department[s] of Agriculture and the Interior and that recommendations concerning wilderness designation be made to Congress by the President. An additional 37 areas have been added to the National Wilderness Preservation System since 1964 under this procedure, bringing the total acreage in the system to over 11 million. Studies continue, and legislative proposals are introduced for additional potential components of the Wilderness Preservation System in the national parks, forests and wildlife refuges.

This effort, however, suffers from one serious defect. This defect was emphasized by the President in his February 8, 1972, environmental message to Congress. . . . All but four Wilderness Areas in national forests are situated west of the one hundredth meridian. Thus, less than 10 percent of total area of wilderness is situated in the most populous, eastern region of our country, where 65 percent of our citizens reside.

This anomaly is due only partially to the physical fact that the East, in providing for its heavier population concentration, has developed far more land and thus deprived itself of much of its natural environment. Unfortunately, the failure to establish eastern wilderness areas has also been caused by conflicting objectives and jurisdictional disputes within both the executive and legislative branches of the Federal Government. These conflicts and disputes resulted in arguments over different resource policies—development versus protection; different interpretations of the definition of "wilderness"—both generally and specifically, as it is contained in the Wilderness Act; and different views as to who should establish eastern wilderness areas and how they should be managed. Perhaps, the highwater mark of this era of polemics was the publication of a 1971 internal report of the Forest Service, in which regional foresters for the Eastern and Southeastern regions concluded that "there are simply no suitable remaining candidate areas for wilderness classification in the [eastern] part of the national forest system."

This era, however, is now over. All parties are now united in their desire to correct the imbalance in the national effort to preserve wilderness and in their recognition that there are numerous areas in the East worthy of preservation. . . .

S. 316, as reported, would provide the truly national system of wilderness areas envisioned in the original Wilderness Act. This measure promises our eastern citizens that, after nearly a decade of waiting, wilderness protection will at least be extended to the unique unspoiled lands and natural environments in our eastern national forests.

Legislation before the 93rd Congress would incorporate in the Wilderness System over 200,000 acres of National Forest lands in the southern Appalachians in addition to the 21,200 already in the system.

Even if all the lands in the public domain in the southern Appalachians were assured of protection as natural areas, much the greater part of the range would remain assured of none at all. Only a tiny portion of it is in National Parks. Road maps on which all the land within their "boundaries" is colored green would lead you to believe that National Forests incorporate about a third of the range, including nearly all the higher parts not in the Parks. Actually, only a patchwork of tracts accounting for half of this has been brought under Federal ownership, and these holdings are not being substantially added to. The rest of the land within the so-called boundaries, like the land outside them, may be disposed of as the owners choose. Their choice, most often, is governed by the amount they are offered—and the demand for land in the mountains for commercial development and home sites is ever-growing. The bulldozers are never idle. Even from the Blue Ridge Parkway more construction is visible with every visit. Mountain-land developers are among the faithful space-buyers in newspapers. The appeal is always to come buy what, in doing so, you will be helping to destroy. A company that takes the better part of a page at a time in the Washington, D. C., papers achieves a labored pretentiousness unequalled outside this genre: "It is written [this in modified Old English type], you shall not buy the gift of immortality. But you may be among the few to see far and forever, and have visual dominion over fish and fowl and over the five millions of people whose lands stretch to the sea. In this way you shall be privileged on the Mountain, for none will be higher nor see farther than the prudent few who claim their places on this great height." Nothing is to me less accountable in the American Democracy than its willingness to leave the fate of the nation's indispensable, vital, irreplaceable resource, its land, to the schemes of gross, self-seeking men who understand nothing but money.

Colored aerial photographs of wooded mountainsides gouged in long, broad belts to the subsoil illustrate advertisements for a "$50 million ski resort and second-home development" on "5,300 acres of breathtaking natural beauty" for which the developer has the effrontery to appropriate the name of the whole, famous 50-mile-long mountain, Massanutten. "In the case of Warren County, Virginia, and very probably other areas around the Massanutten," the President's Council on Environmental Quality and the Department of Housing and Urban Development foresee "the conversion of a rural county into an urban one, not unlike those which are today the suburbs of Washington, D. C." They warn that "a proliferation of second-home subdivisions, which ultimately could saturate the rural countryside," will cost local residents "much more . . . than the loss of landscape. . . . The natural resource base" is being sold "for a short-term revenue return. . . . Today's loss of forested mountains and clean streams will be irrevocable tomorrow." The report is entitled *The Subdivision of Virginia's Mountains.* But it is not the mountains of Virginia alone that are threatened.

Without government action of a kind that is now lacking we may expect subdivisions and commercial construction to continue eating away at the southern Appalachians as a whole, with no certain barriers to their advance but the borders of the public domain. The mountains can be saved in greater part but, so long as land is regarded as the chattel of anyone with enough money to buy it, we can count on saving them only to the extent that the public authorities acquire title to them or easements to protect them. This raises the question of where the money would come from. I have felt for years that so long as the disposition of the nation's privately-owned land is left to the marketplace—in the absence, that is, of stringent public control of land use—conservation of land could best be assured through a development tax, as it might be called. Stripping the vegetative cover (whether natural or agricultural) from a parcel of land for whatever use—home site, industrial plant, commercial building, parking lot, school, church, highway—would require the payment of a substantial percentage of the parcel's value into a fund from which federal, state, county and municipal jurisdictions would draw for the purchase of land and its preservation in a natural state. Thus, the more land that was developed the more would be preserved from development. The further effect would be to enjoin a much more economical use of land, of which our wastefulness at present is wanton.

When I envision a National Scenic Reserve in the West Virginia Alleghenies—and in pleading this and other schemes for the preservation of the mountains I recognize that the only practical effect can be some satisfaction of the needs of my peace of mind—I am thinking not only of the character of their landscape, natural and human. In the West Virginia Alleghenies you can probably feel less under the pressure of people than anywhere else in the country with so many people so close around it. As of 1970, they had been losing population, as about half the southern Appalachians had been—summer people not being included in the Census Bureau's figures, however.

In contrast to the major massif of the southern Appalachians, this second massif presents its boldest front to the east. Approach it, if you will, from that direction and from near its northern end, from Petersburg, the principal town in that part of the state. You will find yourself driving up 2,500 feet in less than three straight miles: such is the Allegheny Front. It is Piedmont forest the whole way, quite unexceptional—though if you have the luck Vera and I had a recent October you will be startled by the sight of a huge fowl taking off nearly straight up, broad and large of tail, small of head and exotic-looking as a Peacock: a Wild Turkey. But rounding the brink is like turning a corner on a Virginia road and finding yourself in Newfoundland. In suddenly cool air, as if your skin had been wiped with alcohol, you have come out onto a high plateau that rises gently to a few broad domes around 4,000 feet in elevation, one that is open to distant views and clearly often windswept. A Scenic Area in the Monongahela National Forest, and now before Congress for inclusion in the Wilderness System, it bears the silly and inappropriate name of Dolly Sods. (Once, it seems, a German farmer named Dahle held land here.) Before the plateau was logged—and burned over—it was mostly in a forest of Red Spruce; you are reminded of C. F. Korstian's estimate that the Spruce forest in the southern Appalachians is now only about ten per cent of what it was at the time of the white man's arrival, though some of the shrinkage may be due to climatic warming. The Spruce is returning, however. Dark convocations of them stand about, and against them, at the end of June, the Mountain-laurel in full bloom and the Mountain-ash with it—its flat, white flower-heads like those of a giant Yarrow—are so pictorial as to appear tailored for effect by a horticulturist. The plateau is then, indeed, a festival of the Mountain-laurel, the blossoms pink as I have never known them away from the top of the Allegheny Front.

On October 20th, among patches of early snow, Vera and I nearly froze at Red Creek campground—and while freezing were astonished to hear at midnight, in the icy moonlight, what could only have been the drumming of a Ruffed Grouse. Another tenant of Red Creek told me of having been snowbound here with two fellow deer-hunters for ten days in a truck-camper. (I was sorry it had not been worse.) But even in June you are conscious of winter's bite on these highlands. For me they even conjure up the continental glacier, which for tens of thousands of years at a time stood in an arc around them, within 150 miles. At least I refuse to believe that the rock-splitting frosts of the Ice Ages were not responsible for the near-white sandstone slabs that strew the high Allegheny Front, big ones, often, collected in beds or like cakes of ice in a jam on a river.

In the evening of my arrival on my first visit, when a chill wind was bringing in clouds to efface portions of the heath and the woods, I was reminded of a photograph I had seen, taken far up in Canada, of a black frill of spruce forest behind a foreground of tundra under a sky freighted with winter. Yet amid the drizzle and the gusts of wind charging through the trees came at measured intervals, and from several points on my walk, the sweet, questing phrases, softly fluted, of that bird for which the rest of the southern Appalachians have most reason to envy the Alleghenies, the Hermit Thrush.

In the morning the sun gleamed palely through a misty sky. Dolly Sods is popular with hikers and naturalists, yet I met but three others between leaving and returning to the campground, all on the first leg, on the way to Blackbird Knob. This part of the trail is mostly in the open, through brushy country, with stands of trees and pasture; it is outside the National Forest and cattle graze here. You hobble over rocks, pull your feet out of succulent, boggy stretches. I was admiring an orange Hawkweed like a hot Aztec sun amid Bluets the shade of an early-morning sky when I saw a stocky young man approaching. His face flaming with sunburn above a close, curly beard, he needed all the evident sturdiness of his legs to carry the biggest pack I have ever seen, with much photographic equipment. He had been camping for five days beside a beaver pond a few miles away, trying to get pictures of the beavers, about which he was writing a book, but finding them strictly nocturnal. I was not surprised as I might have been to hear of beavers up here. The trail had passed an old, apparently abandoned beaver pond on a small creek, the water held back by a chevron-shaped dam pointing downstream. Beside it a Black Cherry had been gnawed neatly through its eight-inch trunk and felled, only to be left lying there.

My other encounter was with a man from Pittsburgh who was giving his four-year-old son an introduction to camping with a one-night stand on Red Creek. He had had years of backpacking and was one of those who have been caught by a sudden, unseasonable blizzard on Mount Washington of a kind in which many have died. They had had to go straight down the mountain to reach the shelter of the forest while a girl member of the party whom they were trying to help could only gasp: "I can't make it. . . . I'll never make it," though she did.

Red Creek, here 20 feet wide and having to be forded, was as delightful as only a running brook in sunny woods can be. The trail following, it soon poured down into the descending, miles-long cleft it had carved and into deep Appalachian Cove Forest. Here in the shadows the Black-throated Blue Warbler lifted a childlike voice in its brief, fuzzy song and the Canada Warbler, tilting back its head, sang with the clarity of skating on glass. And here, replacing the Hermit Thrush, the Veery ran echoing down the scales of its Pan-pipes to send unearthly fingers rippling along the nerves of one's inmost being. Most of the way down—and back—I was on a logging railroad trace, as I was much of the time in the Alleghenies. These roadbeds are of gentle gradient, which is welcome, but for that very reason become boggy where the frequent rivulets trickle down on them and spread out. I must say they stir a certain sentiment in me. It was a grisly work of destruction that spread out from them, right enough, but all that is long past as far as the railroads are concerned, as are the railroads themselves. And one looks back on the little old logging locomotives huffing and puffing up the grades, around the bends, as having been a great deal more appealing than the huge diesel trucks of today pushing deep troughs through the clay and reeking with the cloying smell of burnt oil. Then, too, in the old days the logging was done not by machines alone but by flesh and blood—men plying saws and swinging axes and horses bending to the taut traces. I find that at least less sinister than the treatment of forests as matchwood by the inhuman monsters of today.

About wet feet, whether from logging roads, dew or rain: they are chiefly disadvantageous at stream-fordings, for which there seems to be plenty of occasion in the Alleghenies. After a barefoot crossing, there is the disagreeable necessity of pulling on two pairs of wet socks afterward. Of this I had my fill, thanks to my stupidity, on my way back up Red Creek. Where the stream divided, my map showed a trail up the far branch, Fisher's Run, which would take me back to camp by a different route. "This is it," I said and set about to find the trail. I crossed and recrossed the combined branches and the branches separately, pushed through dense undergrowth along the stream bank and struggled up and around about a precipitous slope above which I thought the trail might be, an aging Tarzan half swinging from rhododendron by one hand while with the other holding my pack—slung from one shoulder to prevent its catching on branches. The waters of the streams were perishing cold, the currents swift, the rocks painful underfoot and slick, and I was constantly apprehensive of falling in, pack, binocular, camera and all. No trail could I find. It dawned on me finally that I had the wrong run, Alder instead of Fisher's. I went back the way I had come.

The West Virginia Alleghenies parallel the northern Blue Ridge at about the same latitude but are far more northerly in character. Not only is their average elevation higher, but they are much greater in breadth and farther from the moderating influence of the ocean. Northern Balsam (*Abies balsamea* as opposed to *A. fraseri*) and Larch, or Tamarack—two nearly transcontinental Canadian trees—reach their farthest south at their northern end. Cranberry bogs, likened by Maurice Brooks to Canadian muskeg—what "could be bits detached from James Bay or Minnesota north of the Red Lakes"—occur in high basins among them. There are small bogs of the kind at Dolly Sods. The main component is Sphagnum Moss, which burgeons in soft pads throughout the southern mountains where cold water comes up in springs or drips dependably down the rocks. In its capacity to soak up and retain water—rain or dew as well as the water in which it grows—Sphagnum is a sponge. It is so absorbent that, dried, it has often been used in bandages. The secret is in the large, hollow cells abundantly dispersed among the chlorophyl-bearing cells. These also give it its light color, a pale green or brassy green. Looking down at it, you might be seeing an extremely dense palm forest from an airplane. Pigeon Wheat

Moss, one of the mosses that make you think of seedling conifers, often grows with it in the bogs. To make out Cranberry's tracery of fine stems and tiny leaves you have to bend down. The fruit, the size of wild cherries, seems abnormally large for it.

The most famous of the bogs are Cranberry Glades, just within the Monongahela National Forest in the southwest, hence catercornered from Dolly Sods. Nearly ringed by spruce woods, the bogs are a hundred acres in extent. Flag Glade may be entered on a Forest Service boardwalk. Superficially it is a big field in which grow Skunk Cabbage and Wild-raisin Viburnum—also much in flower at Dolly Sods. But it is in standing water. A sign tells us that the Sphagnum-peat is three feet deep, a layer of sedge-peat beneath it four feet deep and algal ooze below that three, and that pollen from over twelve feet down is more than 10,000 years old— from the end of the last Ice Age. The Glades are noted for their orchids. In July, three of the exquisitely contrived flowers were in bloom, seeming to pose demurely for the admiration of the beholder: Rose Pogonia, its form suggested by the common name of Snakemouth; Grass Pink, which could also be conceived of as open for a bite; and Purple Fringed Orchis, resembling Yellow Fringed Orchis but violet in color. All were growing where the open bog gave way to Alder thickets and a dark bog-forest of Yellow Birch, Hemlock and Spruce. In this you almost looked for coal-forest amphibians among the enormous Skunk Cabbages, five-foot Cinnamon Fern and equally tall Indian Poke, with deeply scored leaves like sections of a football bladder. The bog-forest, too, was in standing water, and, as where the forest floor is deep in detritus, the best chance tree-seeds had to succeed seemed to be on rotting logs. One such, 50 feet long, supported 19 Hemlocks up to a foot in trunk-diameter, ten Birches and a scattering of Rosebay Rhododendrons.

The cold bogs are fascinating to botanists. Maurice Brooks, who for years taught forestry at the University of West Virginia, has found at Cranberry Glades nearly every common wildflower that grows up to timberline on Mount Washington. Dwarf Dogwood, Buckbean and Bog Rosemary here reach just about their farthest south. In *The Appalachians,* an excellent account of the range in its notable aspects, Brooks recalls camping at the Glades as a boy with his father when the latter trapped a Yellow-nosed Vole, not otherwise known south of the Catskills. The Glades are also farthest south for the Snowshoe Hare, which turns white in winter, and for the nesting of the Purple Finch, Northern Waterthrush, Mourning Warbler and Hermit and Olive-backed Thrushes.

That the bogs provide the hospitality they do for northern forms of life is owing to their functioning as refrigerators. Water is a marvellous retainer of heat or cold and moderates any climate under its influence. The bogs are not only deep in water but well insulated by Sphagnum. Chilled in winter, they release their cold but slowly through the summer—more accurately, slowly absorb heat from the overlying air. This, at over 3,000 feet elevation, is less warm to begin with than it would be below. Because the bogs are set in bowls, the air they cool, being heavier than the surrounding air, tends to remain settled where it is. Cold air at night on the rims flows down into them. Canaan Valley, located just north of Dolly Sods and site of one of the largest muskegs, sometimes experiences frosts every month of the year, according to Brooks. It is in Cranesville Swamp, a little farther north still, on the western border of Maryland, that the Northern Balsam and Tamarack take their stand below the Mason-Dixon Line. In the same swamp a White-throated Sparrow was found nesting, the first record of its breeding south of northern Pennsylvania. And the Northern Water Shrew, which can run on water, has been found in it, 200 miles south of its continuous range.

I had a great appetite for the West Virginia Alleghenies. Having no idea what to expect anywhere, I felt driven to sample as much of them as I could, from one end of the Monongahela National Forest to the other. At the northern end, beyond Canaan Valley, was the famous falls where the Blackwater River pitches 57 feet off a ledge into a deep ravine—a splendid sight but an official exhibit, accessible even to women in high heels from the nearby fancy lodge. The water is black only at a considerable depth. As it pours into the falls it is golden brown. That is the color, too, of Otter Creek, which is virtually a river and flows also through a northern part of the National Forest, one expected soon to be designated Wilderness. I was sitting having lunch at the head of the trail into it when a pickup truck pulled in to disgorge two men who proceeded to unload a pair of trail cycles—light motorcycles with small wheels and wide tires. This was my first encounter with these supercharged wheelchairs for the mentally crippled. Before they took off down the trail in a staccato roar and a cloud of blue exhaust fumes I was able to catch the eye of one of the riders with a look meant to express venomous contempt. It must have registered for I received one of equal animosity in return. I was glad to learn from a fellow hiker several miles down the trail that the cycles had been almost swamped crossing Otter Creek; I had been myself. The Otter Creek basin will make a fine, 20,000-acre Wilderness Area, the river running between the mountains in a deep wooded valley among sculptured sandstone boulders the size of motor vehicles, pouring, maple-sugar-colored, over submerged rocks to break into white rapids. What may it not contain?

The easternmost part of the National Forest is the Seneca Rocks Unit of a National Recreation Area, of which the other, the Spruce Knob Unit, is to the west across the South Branch of the Potomac. The highest point of West Virginia at 4,862 feet, Spruce Knob is the peak of Spruce Mountain, which forms the Appalachian Front south of Dolly Sods. It is accessible by road, but in order to earn it and see something of its surroundings I decided to approach it from Seneca Creek campground in the north, making a day's hike of it and camping on top. It was not to work out. Indeed, it took me half an hour even to find the beginning of the trail the Forest Service map showed taking off from a road above the camp. Even after wading Seneca Creek on the chance that it might start from the other side, as it did, I was some time in locating it. But all that was all right. It was part of the unrealized character of the range that a hiker should so often be unclear in his mind as to what was what. Once launched, I was in high fettle, as one must be in feeling well, having a day of unfamiliar trail ahead of one, over country of which one knows nothing and so well off the beaten path, by the look of things, as quite possibly to contain not another human being—as in fact it did not.

Of course, southern Appalachian vegetation—like any other—provides only so much variety. I suppose there was little novel in the dark forest of Hemlock, rhododendron and Mountain-laurel through which the trail zigzagged up the north side of the nameless mountain—nameless to me, anyway—or in the forest on top, of lichen-covered Chestnut Oaks and Table Mountain Pines and ground-cover of Blueberries and wild roses, Reindeer Lichen, Teaberry and Trailing Arbutus. But it was like the human face: there are only a few facial features, and after a hundred or so faces you might think you had seen them all, though you have made scarcely a beginning. All this was new, vistas as if never seen before by anyone, one of the vast body of Spruce Mountain between other, unknown summits, the air unbreathed—in a modest way a strange earth and new sky.... Assuming I should find streams en route I had started with an empty canteen—a mistake I was never to make again—and, finding none, was by one o'clock becoming more aware of thirst and hunger than of anything else. And behold! Against all the probabilities, way up there, I came on a little slough fed by a trickle of water.

Lunch at this benign spot turned out to be rather the high point of the day. The trail to Judy Springs veered off not far beyond and I with it, down the mountainside. Through acres of Wood Nettles it went, scarcely discernible, and, where the woods were more open, through brambles and other brush-growth soaked with rain or dew so that I was soon dripping from the thighs down, and squishing in my shoes. But what mattered was that from Judy Springs, back on Seneca Creek, the trail that was supposed to go on up Spruce Mountain was nowhere to be seen. The mountain rose

Though a plateau, the West Virginia Alleghenies have been deeply carved by streams. Here Spruce Mountain, the state's highest, is seen from the Little Allegheny Trail.

very steeply through rocky woods, where a man under a pack often had difficulty keeping his footing, to open cattle range that climbed far up its immense flank. An hour and a half I spent quartering the lower slope of Spruce Mountain trying to pick up a trail, and in vain. By then it was beginning to rain. More ominously, the patent sole of one of my new hiking shoes was beginning to peel away from the toe. A trail went back down Seneca Creek to the road where I had left the bus, and I decided I had better take it. It was the right decision. After another two miles the sole was flapping like a winded dog's tongue and had to be cut off. I had still five miles to go. It was raining the whole way through the dark gorge, the trail following the river, the river going over low falls—the level rock strata of the plateau being very productive of pictorial waterfalls—and swerving around huge detached blocks of rock that made me think of wrecked submarines. Sandstone is great, as I say, for taking imposing shapes, and my outlook may have been a trifle somber. "I am inexhaustible and indestructible," I avowed, wondering if the end of the trail would ever come and how much longer the inner sole of my shoe would hold out. When at last I reached the stream-crossing just before the road, my shoes being ruined anyhow, I could indulge myself by walking straight through, without bothering to take them off.

All this has, however, little to do with my theme, which is a simple one. As I moved on, trying to get a grasp of the essential and distinctive quality of the West Virginia Alleghenies and not succeeding—I shall have to know them much better to do so—one conclusion did come to me with increasing force: the nation is immensely fortunate in having, so close to some of its most crowded parts, this boon of still-vital mountains in which, as a nation, we have yet to discover what we have.

"You ought to go see Cheat Mountain."

I had put in for the night beside one of the outbuildings of a temporarily unoccupied 4-H Club camp just off U.S. highway 250, which cuts across the midsection of the north-and-south-running Monongahela National Forest. An employee of the State Department of Natural Resources, working in game-management, had driven up in a truck just after I had finished breakfast. I learned from him, in addition to his name—Russell Warner—that grouse and turkeys have made a good comeback in the West Virginia mountains and that bears are holding on. The worst threat to the bears is the disruption of their breeding by hunters, he said. "Some are killed by farmers. Bears will go onto private land and kill a sheep, and once they have the taste of sheep they'll keep coming back to kill more. So the farmers go after them with dogs. Without dogs there would be no finding them." Mr. Warner said he had been around this country for fifteen years and had seen a bear only three times. He also told me that the Forest

Service had begun a road through what was to have been the Cheat Mountain Roadless Area, arguing that the road was necessary in order to get the timber out, but that the sportsmen had protested and put a halt to it for the time being anyhow. "You ought to go see it."

So I did. Where U.S. 250 climbs over it, a sign reads, "ASA GRAY, FAMOUS HARVARD BOTANIST, DISCOVERED PLANTS NEW TO SCIENCE AS HE CROSSED CHEAT MOUNTAIN BY WAY OF THE STAUNTON-PETERSBURG TURNPIKE IN AUGUST 1843." Cheat Mountain runs about a third the entire length of the Monongahela National Forest; at least they call it all Cheat Mountain. I drove ten miles of it on a Forest Service road, finding most of it handsomely wooded. I also had a walk down its side through beautiful Beech woods and fields of fern and Shining Club-moss to Shaver's Creek. Of the creek, I suppose I shall always remember the shadows of Water-striders on the golden bottom, shadows not of the insects themselves but of the depressions made by their feet in the surface film. What I shall say next I can hardly account for, but here it is: Shaver's Creek, which meanders along the edge of Cheat Mountain, and the Greenbrier River, which is separated from it by Back Allegheny Mountain and then Shaver's Mountain, flow parallel to each other a few miles apart for 60 miles—and in opposite directions!

Shaver's Mountain, paralleling Cheat on the east, rises to Gaudineer Knob only a mile and a half from U.S. 250. Maurice Brooks, whose home territory this is, devotes a whole chapter of his book to the mountain, a favorite of his. Between its foot and its summit he says that twenty-two species of warblers are summer residents, "more than are known to nest on any other Appalachian peak." Gaudineer Knob itself, 4,445 feet in elevation, is entirely covered by a forest of Red Spruce, but a fire tower tops the trees. Brooks has seen Snowshoe Hares—Varying Hares—playing beneath it and Northern Flying Squirrels, which reach their farthest south at Cranberry Glades, fetch up on the scaffolding. He writes interestingly of his observations from the 60-foot structure:

> At ground level the characteristic Gaudineer birds in summer are juncos and winter wrens. A dozen feet from the ground magnolia warblers are abundant. Red-breasted nuthatches search along the higher branches, and golden-crowned kinglets hunt for tiny insects in outer twigs. The thirty-foot level is a good place for Blackburnian warblers; I found my only nest of these birds by looking squarely into it from half way up the tower. The tallest of the young spruces bear cones, these nearly always near treetop. When red crossbills are abundant, as they are some years, they feast on spruce seeds. . . .

Less for Gaudineer Knob itself, however, than for a rare preserve a mile farther along the mountain should you not fail to turn off here if you are driving past on U.S. 250. Thanks to a former supervisor of the Monongahela National Forest, Arthur Wood, a 140-acre tract of virgin forest was spared on the side of the mountain when all else was being logged. It is a lofty, deep woods having the richness and variety you find in human communities only among those that have been lived in for generations, each reworking but not destroying what it inherited. I could get my arms only two-thirds the way around a Red Spruce which was chiefly remarkable in its height—a hundred feet, I should have said. A White Ash was of equal size, and a Black Cherry, without a branch for sixty feet, I could get my arms only three-fourths the way around—and this was a very high forest, over 4,000 feet up. Among these species, Red Maples, Beeches and little Mountain Maples, the largest tree I saw was a Yellow Birch only one-half encircleable by my arms. Perhaps it was not only to measure these caryatids of high-borne domes of foliage that I felt like embracing them. You could not walk through this colonnaded, verdant sanctuary without being moved and saddened to reflect that all the Appalachians were once like it.

It is a grand drive over Cheat and Shaver's Mountains, through northern forests; you cross even the river between the two at 3,550 feet. I kept on after leaving Gaudineer Knob and at the foot of the mountain turned south on Back Mountain Road, County Road 1. This ran along the base of Back Allegheny Mountain, a steep-fronted formation some fifteen miles long. Toward the end of it my maps showed three summits, all over 4,830 feet. That is high. Yet I had never heard of them. Indeed, on no map could I find the names of any of them, except that the National Forest map identified the first as Bald Knob and showed it as half encircled by the Cass Scenic Railroad. This one and the next were the crowning elevations of Back Allegheny itself. I had my sights set on the second especially. I got as close to it as I could by car after turning off beyond Cass onto a branch road that became very rough before passing over its shoulder. For a space the wall of the unknown mountain was in view ahead looking very precipitous and fringed with the black thorns of spruces. It was clear to me that it would take far more time than I could spare from the work waiting at home to do justice to these mountains. Back in the village of Cass, I questioned a man sprawled in a chair before an ill-kept house about the mountain I had just come down from. He was elderly and rather obese and his face was grey with dirt. It was Cheat Mountain, he said. I demurred. Cheat Mountain was behind Back Allegheny, was it not? (Actually it ended in the third of the high summits.) "Well," he countered, "we're not much interested in mountains around here. We live here, so we're used to 'em." It becoming obvious that mountains were so much wasteland to him, I left him for the post office. To the nice-looking postmistress it developed that they were not very different. She said also that the mountain was Cheat and that the scenic railroad, which used an old logging line, ran up Cheat (meaning

Back Allegheny) but north of the summit I was asking about—as I knew. Two very large frame houses nearby, twins and connected, about which I was curious, had been an hotel when Cass was an important lumber-mill town.

I was sorry to leave those highlands yet glad to have their exploration to look forward to, including a ride on the railroad; I must say I feel differently about a little old narrow-gauge logging line from the way I do about a road for motorcars. But—My stars! I thought. Spruce Knob at 4,862 feet was (as I have observed) the highest peak in a 640-mile-long stretch of the Eastern mountains—no inconsiderable segment of a range that is 1,575 all the way from the tip of the Gaspé Peninsula into Alabama. Yet here were these three summits on the upper rim of the Shaver's Creek basin lacking only 30 feet or less of being as tall, and one perhaps practically as tall (4,850 feet plus or minus, says the Geological Survey map). And at least two of the three were quite disregarded by the country, even, as far as I could tell, nameless! I thought that said something about the West Virginia Alleghenies.

So, too, I think, did the next few days and a hike, when for forty-eight hours I was to see not another soul except the driver of a lumber truck the middle of the first morning.

From Cass I had gone on farther to the south and especially to the west to the Cranberry Back Country, of which over 36,000 acres has since been proposed for the Wilderness System. Starting from Cranberry campground I walked some miles south on the gravel road along the rushing, rain-swollen Cranberry River, which rises in the Cranberry Glades, farther to the south and east. My aim was to climb to the Black and Red Trail, so named, that runs the ridge lines for most of the length of this, the largest block of land in the National Forest. Lick Branch Trail, turning off to the east, promised to take me up to it. It went very sharply upward through rhododendron woods beside Lick Branch, which was roaring down the shelving rock of its bed. Stopping after a bit to fill my canteen from it, I sat for a few minutes listening to the sweet, high, lisping song of a Black-throated Green Warbler. Reflecting on the energy it took to lift two hundred pounds of human being and equipment up a few hundred feet of mountain, and seeing that stream pour an equal weight of water down the mountain about every ten seconds, I began to understand the power to be had from harnessing a waterfall.

After perhaps half a mile the trail came out onto a logging road and into the open, and I looked up the mountainside to see nothing, all the way up, but one vast, sordid, impenetrable tangle of branches and logs—the trunks of trees, and big ones, felled only to be left to rot. And this was National Forest. (A Ranger told me later that the lumberman "was only interested in pulp logs.") There was no getting through that horrifying mess, if I had been no larger than a terrier. So I went on south down the logging road to see if it would take me to the next trail up the mountain. But after a mile or so it became only a rutted, tilted, muddy track bulldozed out of the forest, extremely unpleasant to walk. Accordingly I went back the way I had come, back down to the Cranberry River and farther up it until I came to Big Rough Run Trail, which the map showed would take me where I was trying to go. Big Rough Run had a voice to match its name. Its crashing and thundering accompanied me up the trail and up the roadbed of a logging railroad the trail turned into. This I walked for half an hour. Occasionally there were still ties, and where there were you could almost, as I say, hear the chuffing of the little locomotive and the clanking of the couplings as the train came to a halt. The idea of mankind that clings to places human beings have occupied and then vacated to the assuagements of nature can be moving in a way that man in his present multitudes seldom is. A little later I came to a spot where one could almost hear the voices of the men who had swung the axes and driven the teams. This came after the trail had fetched up in a rushing stream. The stream offering the only passage through the tangles, I waded in. After a few hundred feet I came out on dry ground again. Here was a grove of spruces with clearings still on both sides. I say *still* because it was unmistakably evident that this had been a logging camp. Yet I did not see how it could have been in use less than forty years ago. Unused horseshoes were all around, a hundred or more, most of them in a pile. In addition, there were lengths of chain, a section of rail, an old agate-ware coffeepot of two-gallon size, a split axe-head and parts of a cast-iron cauldron, while beyond was a dump full of cans almost rusted away and bottles of obsolete design.

It was nearly five o'clock when I reached the crest of the ridge and, according to a Forest Service sign leaning against a tree, the Red and Black Trail. The trail I was on was supposed to join this other in a T intersection, but though I looked high and low, only one arm of the T could I find. It went off to the left, which should have been to the northwest, when it was to the southeast I meant to go. Having no choice, I set off down it. Inexplicably I soon found the sun behind me, just as if I were following the other, non-existent right arm of the T. In great puzzlement I went back and forth, the sun continuing to move around to the wrong side even after seeming inclined to go to the right one. At length I gave up and camped on top of the ridge in a spruce and hemlock forest where I had to remove a padding of damp moss from any rock I chose to sit down on.

In the morning I waked for good to the singing of a few forest birds when the sky behind the matted foliage had paled to a grey wash. By seven, when the sun appeared through the trees, I was on my way. But what way? Again I went back and forth and the sun moved with me. Finally I decided to hell with it and went off in the direction the map showed to be westerly, despite my contrary desires, and to find that the sun settled for good directly in front of me.

I spent half the day hiking the trail, seeing no sign that any other human being had been on it for months. (Not a place, I thought on the steep bits, to fall and break a leg.) On one of the rocky, brushy parts a family of Black-capped Chickadees, *dee-dee-dee*-ing in their nasal little way, came within ten feet to examine me, the young doubtless never having seen a human being before. I heard my first Olive-backed Thrush, too, on a damp mountainside among Hemlocks and Yellow Birches, its song, with that thrush quality as of another world, bubbling softly upward, gently pleading or questioning. For hours I walked through Spruce forest, the lower trunks bristling with dead branches, in places only mosses growing in the gloom but covering everything, stumps, logs, the protruding roots of the trees, rocks—all under emerald mats. A little sunlight striking through brought ferns, Wood-sorrel and Wild Lily-of-the-valley, a little more, Blueberries, more still, Mountain-laurel and Rhododendron. . . . Ordinarily the sight of a road in a wild area is nothing to rejoice in. However, the possibility had been in my mind since morning that I had been somewhere else altogether other than where I should have been at that trail intersection, and that I had been marching all day toward some kind of limbo. Hence I must confess I was relieved to have my deduction as to where I was confirmed by the opening of the woods onto a Forest Service road and a sign saying "BLACK MOUNTAIN. ELEVATION 4,600 FEET." Black Mountain: I liked that name.

The road sloped down the side, following the Left Fork, then the North Fork of the Cranberry River. After six miles it met the Cranberry River itself and joined the road paralleling it. I was to walk seven miles on this that day. Before I had gone half the distance I began to feel that my legs were giving way. But I was reaping the psychological benefits of having had to cope only with simple, physical situations for two days. The afternoon was sunny and bright. The road and the flowers visited by butterflies beside it, and the sparkling river, coursing with vigor, were all mine. I was as lighthearted as I have almost ever been, even jaunty. (One effect of being alone much of the time is that one talks aloud to oneself, may even sing.) Stopping where a rock ledge sloped into the river to create a small, calm backwash, I counted it blissful to get out of pack and clothes and take a dip in the icy water, afterward to make a cup of tea in the idyllic spot and eat graham crackers with it while air-drying on the rock and warming up again in the sun.

Every two or three miles along the river the Forest Service had built a three-sided shelter like those on the Appalachian Trail, very solid and painted dark brown. These were for fishermen; a voting bloc 26 million strong need not despair of consideration from government agencies. When the sun reached the treetops across the river I decided to call the day at an end at the next shelter. This I reached at six-thirty: Pleasant Hollow Shelter. Like the other two I had seen, it proved to be bestrewn with trash and liberally carved into with the names of anglers who had occupied it. However, I had no business with the shelter other than to remove from it, heat and consume a can of pork and beans left on a framing member. I put out my sleeping-bag on the grassy expanse between the shelter and the road. In contrast with the night before there were mosquitoes and gnats, but the new Army repellent I carried held them off very well. Another difference in the riverside site was that in place of the dead silence of the high ridge there was the rumbling, burbling and crashing of the Cranberry, sounds of the kind that lead one constantly to imagine one is hearing steps or voices among them, or animal noises. I was not much less chilly than the previous night, and, lying awake, I visualized the humanless dark wild reigning on Black Mountain. It recalled the drive I had had three evenings before in growing dusk on State Highway 39 westward of Cranberry Glades. A wooded ridge rose steeply from the other side of the river the highway followed, the North Fork of the Cherry. A dark wood it was, too, and ghostly. Each rank of trees ascending the slope stood a little dimmer than its predecessor rank yet a little darker than the greyness separating it from the rank above, to the dimmest of all, the forest silhouetted on the crest. Grey clouds were afloat above, seeming to have collected from the streamers of mist rising from the forest. Sepulchral vapors and nocturnal woods and river stampeding below, harsh of voice and heedless of the hush, white as fangs where it gnashed at the rocks—they seemed wholly inaccessible to any human plea or concern, as indeed they were. I thought how easy it is, from dabbling in it, to romanticize the wilderness. Yet if we concede nothing else to wilderness, it does for us what war does and teaches us how few and simple the ingredients of happiness are: the hearth, the company of comrades and those we love, enough to eat, books. To pile extravagances of gratification-seeking on these at the cost of so complicating our lives we cannot enjoy what we have, and, I should add, at the cost of despoiling nature, which surrounds us with beauty and inspires our creative selves to respond with beauty—this, the experience of wilderness, as of war, tells us, is a fool's bargain.

The Red and Black Trail, I hope, may provide part of the route of the western Appalachian Trail as it bears northeastward for Spruce Mountain. Spruce Mountain, if I had to name the supreme feature of the West Virginia Alleghenies as I have seen them, would be it, and not in elevation alone. If you come from the east on U.S. 33 (which passes through Swift Run Gap in the Shenandoah Blue Ridge) you will see Spruce Mountain in full before you where the highway crosses North Fork Mountain. The two are participants in an arresting confrontation. On the west is the Allegheny Front, on the east 37-mile-long North Fork, last and probably most spec-

The famous Gothic formation of Seneca Rocks of Silurian sandstone, 900 feet high, in the West Virginia Alleghenies.

tacular of the Long Ridge Mountains, sandstone of Pennsylvanian age capping the one, Silurian sandstone, half again the age of that, the other. It is exposures of this 350-million-year-old rock that give North Fork its special character. At its north end, as you will see by looking back from the road to Dolly Sods, the ancient-looking rock stands at the top in turreted formations, recalling, as Vera said, the castles high above the Rhine. A little farther south it stands as a palisade along the crest. At the mountain's midsection, Champe Rocks are a huge, saw-toothed meat-cleaver and the famous Seneca Rocks a 900-foot-high cockscomb, one of the highest cliffs in the East and much practised on by mountain climbers of the rope-and-piton kind.

On Spruce Knob, the high point to which Spruce Mountain rises inconsiderably at its south end, you are likely to be one of a score or two visitors. However, few of these are disposed to stray far from the paths between the parking aprons and the concrete observation deck, which overlooks the wizened and ragged Spruces appropriate to the lonely height. The trail that leads away is, moreover, discouragingly rocky underfoot at the start. I found it completely deserted—and on the Fourth of July!

Spruce Mountain stands above 4,500 feet for ten miles. From the dorsal trail, as it might be called, it has the semblance of a whale in a school of lesser whales. The walk is to me the grandest I know in the middle Appalachians. The trail takes you through Spruce forest tangled with blow-downs and luxuriantly upholstered over its floor with mosses of

The Dwarf cornel is a true flowering dogwood a few inches high.

concentrated green, the light picking out the little snowy bells of Wild Lily-of-the-valley, Trilliums bearing (in July) their single berry, and occasional Wild Bleeding-hearts of grey-green foliage like Grape Fern's, a Ruffed Grouse bursting off with the sound of a pyrotechnic only to regard you uncertainly from a branch. It takes you out under the open sky through thickets of Blueberries, azaleas and Southern Mountain Cranberry among which four-inch-high Dwarf Cornel displays its little dogwood blossoms in a whorl of little dogwood leaves. It takes you past massive blocks of sandstone and shambles of sandstone slabs (Vera exclaims over the impressiveness of the one and the soft, pale grey of the other) among which the Mountain-laurel blooms pink as if blushing with its own beauty. Through truncated Birch forest it goes, then out again across grassland threaded with the finely-thorned runners of glossy-leaved Dewberry, past fields of waist-high Canada Blackberry humming with bees, surveying from the mountain's broad back, beyond the ever-changing interest of the foreground, a panorama of cloud-saddled hills and a raven breasting the void for sheer adventure.

And from the top of a Spruce a Hermit Thrush sings. Its voice melodic and pensive, it sings in phrases, releasing them one by one to the wind. There is no lovelier sound. The elegiac periods, gently warbling, move up the scale, as if they would ascend to a higher realm, and fade away, the singer seeming to be drifting off into abstraction or falling silent to listen. You could believe it moved, as man may be moved, by the inexpressible.

With the Hermit Thrush singing on Spruce Mountain I should be content to rest the case for the West Virginia Alleghenies.

XIII *The Round of Seasons*

Summer in the Appalachians: the range is an archipelago of pristine, lavish-leafy green above the tatterdemalion lowlands and the mint-cool air of the heights and watered dells offers a supreme natural dispensation above the pall of heat between the Rockies and the Atlantic Ocean. That is the time, I am then persuaded, when the mountains are at their best. And it is true, I think, that at no other season have they a wider margin of superior attractiveness to their surroundings. That the mountains are more consistently enjoyable in the summer than in any other three-month period is probably equally so.

Yet there is autumn. Every passing week then brings opener views from the trails and fewer other hikers with whom to have to share them. The weather is likely to be at its clearest and brightest through October, the rains farthest apart. Then are the southern Appalachians least a range of shadow. The forest canopy takes on its brightest colors as it thins. Beneath the intense blue of a sky supremely light-filled, the mountain world is one of radiance.

With the lengthening and cooling of the nights, autumn moves down the stepping stones of the higher summits from the north, and as it touches them starts to spread down their flanks; but its advance is much subject to interruption and recession. Well before it arrives, the premonition of its coming accelerates the processes of summer. You are still thinking of the flowering season in the mountains as lagging the lowlands when it begins to move into the lead. The late-summer bloomers like the Wild Sunflowers, Goldenrod and the lavender Asters blossom in the mountains before they do below, having to make haste to mature their seed before the killing frosts. Here it should be said, however, that because cold air flows downhill, frosts come to the high valleys before they do to the slopes above them.

By late July or early August in the Shenandoah Blue Ridge, the leaves of the deciduous trees have reached their full maturity and are entering upon senescence. Photosynthesis and the production of carbohydrates and pro-

213

teins slackens. The leaves, which have been exporting sugars to the woody structure of the tree to promote its growth and that of flowers and fruit—their prime function, of course—now begin to export as well the nitrogenous compounds required for their work, so that these may be stored against the needs of spring growth. No signs of the change are apparent to the naked eye. By the time it is under way, however, some leaves will already have turned red on Virginia Creeper, Sumac and Black Tupelo.

October is the month of color. By the first, in the West Virginia Alleghenies, where the season starts in the southern Appalachians, the Red Maples are likely to be changing, varying from green and yellow through *vin rosé* to the solid burgundy of some trees. In mid-October the color is generally at its height in the two Virginias—and week-end traffic on the Skyline Drive at its heaviest. The woods then are flooded and charged with sunlight even under an overcast, and faintly redolent of what could be an aromatic tobacco. Though the Flowering Dogwoods are wine-reds and the scattered Tupelos comparable, the colors are predominantly yellow and russet. The former is that of the Tuliptrees, Hickories, Striped Maples, Chestnut shoots, vines of the Summer Grape and some oak foliage, the latter that of oaks. While the White Oak's leaves merely fade and turn a light brown, those of the Black and Red turn a deep red, those of the Scarlet a brighter and those of the Chestnut Oak yellow and then a dull orange. A soft but brighter orange is found in the foliage of the Sassafras, which, with the ovoid, dark blue berries on thick red stems makes the little tree one of the prettiest of the autumn woods.

Actually the leaves are for the most part not acquiring any color they did not have before. What happens is that the disappearance of the overwhelming green of the chlorophyl (which of course means simply "green leaf") reveals the underlying pigments. The red shades derive from anthocyanin, the yellow from carotenoid pigments. The recession of the chlorophyl does, however, stimulate the manufacture of those pigments. As Patricia W. Spencer of the University of Illinois tells us, "The production of crimson anthocyanin, in particular, requires cool autumn temperatures. A cold spell, during which anthocyanins are produced extensively in almost all tree leaves, followed by warmer weather is responsible for the beautiful colors of Indian summer."

Those do not come richer than in the lacquer colors of Sourwood and Black Tupelo, scarlet in the one, dark green to orange-yellow and blood-red in the other. Sugar Maple is superlatively brilliant in red and yellow in the southern as in the northern Appalachians. But this famous performer does not preempt mountainsides in the former as in the latter. For foliage that sets the hills on fire, those in the South admittedly take second place to the northern. At least that is true of the Virginia Blue Ridge. Some connoisseurs, however, find the North Carolina mountains, especially the Smokies, supreme. There, they say, the variety of autumnal colors is greater, the spectacle more like a stained-glass window with the sunshine pouring through myriad panes.

Autumn, I think, is best for birds in the southern Appalachians, on the high ridges of Maryland and Virginia. While no path of migration past any mountain south of it has yet been found to equal that which draws droves of observers to Hawk Mountain in Pennsylvania, the procession along a number is active enough. Wind striking the ridges is deflected upward so that a bird flying along with them is buoyed by the updrafts and spared exertion. The ridges thus form natural highways of migration. In addition, many night-flying small birds are probably intercepted by the ridges and find it convenient to drift down them by day. Through September, in any case, you meet with loose bands of the little travelers strung out through the woods, feeding as they filter southward—Vireos, Kinglets, Tanagers and especially Warblers of a score of species beautifully differentiated in bright colors and arresting patterns or almost indistinguishable in duller, feature-less autumn plumage, which makes them the delight and desperation of bird-watchers.

But it is the hawks that have the stellar role. They appear in greatest numbers on northwest winds, which strike the ridges broadside. (It is the prevailing lack of winds equally favorable to northbound flight and the diminished number of participants that make the spring migration less striking in the mountains than the autumnal.) Last fall a Red-tailed Hawk I was watching almost made the updraft visible as it turned into the wind, half erect, spread tail downbent, wings half folded, and remained so, ensconced in the air.

It was a rather eerie morning. From the Skyline Drive the Shenandoah Valley and the ridges beyond were partly hidden by long, parallel, bil-lowing grey clouds, the sky by darker clouds, and while houses and farms were conspicuous in the Valley, not a sound came from down below but the moo of a cow. One might have been seeing a dreamworld yet to be born. Seeming to confirm that this was the earth before reality had had a chance to take over, was an encounter I had with two deer. Grazing beside the road, they took no alarm as I stopped the car and got out but stood facing me with black noses, black eyes and erect, black-bordered ears, all three organs primed with curiosity. I was within about twelve feet of the motionless creatures when, to my almost unbearable enchantment, the smaller crouched low on its forelegs, its rear still high, exactly as a puppy does before bounding playfully off to lead you a merry chase. I could think of no better response than to pluck a handful of grass and advance holding this before me. At that the two went off in their rocking gait—but only to halt again no more than twenty-five feet away and munch on the leaves of a low tree.

Of a piece, too, with the morning and with the uncanny silence of the Valley was the first flight of Broad-winged Hawks, at the next overlook. The mountains put one right up among the migrants, and these circled all around me, dark above, the light underparts barred in the adults, streaked in the immature. I could think only of the portentous solemnity of the Pueblo eagle dancers circling with feathered arms outstretched. Only there was not a sound.

Broad-wings and other *Buteos*—solidly-built, soaring Hawks, by preference consumers of rodents—sail by the ridges in a steady calm. The *Accipiters*—longer-tailed, fierce-eyed bird-eaters—have to beat their shorter wings oftener, and when hungry pursue an erratic course, shooting down over the treetops and perhaps suddenly diving in a furious flutter. It is they that begin the hawk migration, in mid-August. The climax is reached in mid-September, when from a single lookout one may in a day see a score of *Accipiters,* up to a dozen each of Red-tailed and Red-shouldered Hawks— both *Buteos*—and literally hundreds of Broad-wings. There will be a few of the two small Falcons—Kestrels and Merlins—and, before DDT had done its work, a regular week-end watcher could count on a few Peregrines during a season—larger, masked Falcons on tapering, pointed wings that approached swiftly but unhurriedly. (No one who has seen a Peregrine that *was* hurrying has ever forgotten it.) Until recently, too, Bald Eagles came regularly and massively by, and only last spring a friend of mine had the rare good fortune to see two Golden Eagles in passage in West Virginia.

It is the epitome of the season, this trailing withdrawal of the winged myriads down the ridges aglow with the colors of summer's funeral pyre, borne on winds that with growing strength rip the leaves from the bending trees to send them racing, like birds themselves, over the gap. . . . The round of seasons is to me more accentuated in the mountains, as if the revolving wheel were larger than elsewhere. Summer at its lushest, fall at its most autumnal and spring (take my word for it) at its most vernal; in addition the Southern mountains may even claim superlatives of winter. "I don't think I'd do that," said a gas-station proprietor in the town of Roan Mountain when on my early March trip I said I would be driving up the mountain to spend the night there. "It could snow enough on top before morning to pile up drifts high as a house." (A northeasterly had filled the sky with cloud and I allowed myself to be persuaded.) Drifts 20 feet high and killer winds of hurricane strength are not abnormal on the Black Dome, where the temperature has dropped to 29 degrees below zero. Where you have Canadian forest you have Canadian climate.

I was spending the night of October first on Spruce Knob in West Virginia when winter struck with an advance foray. Outside my little bus it was black dark and bitter cold. Forlornly, a small bird beat against the windshield and then to the ground. A light olive, the black lines through and over its eyes identified it as a Worm-eating Warbler. It disappeared when I turned the headlamps off, soon, I hoped, to reach less alien temperatures. In the morning the Spruces stood rimed, and so did the whole top of the mountain; you could see where the sugaring of frost stopped some hundreds of feet down the side. The sun, when it finally burned through the mist, drew steam from the bare tree-trunks. No less than the night before, I could as well have been a hundred miles from the nearest motorcar as on a parking ground for several score. Wilderness may be as much a condition of time as of place.

While use of the Appalachian Trail increases sharply every year, no through-hiker has yet tackled even the southern half in winter. To do so would take hardihood of spirit no less than of body. Even when it is not a matter of trudging through snow, you can feel awfully alone when the cloud comes down on the mountaintops and the cold shadow of day's end submerges the forest below—not just alone in the woods but alone in the universe.

Well, that was true about the Appalachian Trail in winter when I first wrote it. On September 18, 1973, however, two soldiers, Specialists 4th-Class of Fort Dix, New Jersey, set out from Mount Katahdin to walk the full length of the trail. One, William H. Mason, twenty-one, had been reared on a cattle farm in the foothills of the Blue Ridge south of Roanoke and had wanted to make the trip since he had been fourteen; and the other, Pedro Villareal, Jr., twenty-four, a former college athlete from California, had proposed going with him. A new Army "Adventure Training Program" gave them their chance and arrangements were made to have them resupplied at weekly intervals en route from local Army units. On about December 2nd they crossed the Pennsylvania-Maryland line on South Mountain. By December 18th they had been hiking 92 days from sunup to sundown without a break and had gone 30 miles beyond the Shenandoah National Park. That day, after a week of snow and ice storms, "we only made eight miles and the drifts were so deep we couldn't do anything," I read of their telling a reporter from *The Washington Post.* So they quit the trail for the Blue Ridge Parkway and, on reaching a telephone, applied to Fort Dix for a week's leave, duly granted. The balance of the winter, like the one before, was unusual in being largely snowless. For that good fortune, however, after they had resumed, they paid in rain. In the Smokies, it rained consecutively for five days. Mason, when I talked to him, said that every evening they got out of wet clothes and every morning got into frozen ones. "Breaking the starch is the Army term." The remarkable thing was that they "were never sick at all." The hardest part of the entire trail was a 30-mile stretch south of the Smokies, below Fontana Dam. "It was really tough, up and down." On February 4th they reached Springer Mountain and walked the remaining eight miles to the road at Amicalola Falls State Park. All honor to two young men of stamina! And what was the chief impression the trip made on them? I asked. "Learning that you can do more than you think you can," Mason replied, and added, "It was one of the greatest things I ever did. I loved the whole hike."

I am reminded of an encounter last May 15th on Jane Bald, in the Roan group, with the only through-hikers I have met on the Appalachian Trail, Margie and Steve Skinner, as they introduced themselves. Twenty-four and twenty-seven years old respectively, they came from Schenectady and had started out from Springer on April 10th. For two years they had been working in a home for children "with emotional, behavioral problems." It had left them drained. They had needed a change of environment and a chance to think things out in perspective. The hike had turned out to be what they were looking for. "It's been a God-filled experience," Steve said.

Winter, however grim it may be, is not to be missed if you are to appreciate these mountains fully. Then their rocky structure stands revealed. Unmuffled by foliage, the rush and rumble of swollen streams carries far; you realize how plentifully watered the mountains are. Paradoxically, only when the deciduous trees stand bare does it become apparent how fully these are green hills. The copious understory of laurel and rhododendron is then unmasked. After the rains, which customarily are more frequent than snows, the lively, varied greens of the lichens spreading in wafers over almost every rock and tree-trunk make one wonder if this is truly winter in a northern sense.

Lichens come into their own in the cold months, which makes that a good time to take the notice of them they deserve. They have the field more to themselves then and can be seen to be almost everywhere. That they should be is not surprising. Sunlight and occasional rain are all they ask of life, apart from something to grow on: bark, soil too poor for other plants, or bare rock. With these, they make shift from parched deserts to Antarctic ledges on which the temperature never rises above freezing except in the sun. Some, imperceptibly spreading, may live for many hundreds of years. That a form of life having more modest requirements of the environment than almost any other is conceivably the longest-lived of all may be more than coincidental. It is certainly cause for reflection that the one thing lichens cannot endure is the air of our cities; the pollutants kill them.

When I think how much harder and harder it is in this world to get away from it all—"it all" being increasingly likely to have got there first—it seems to me that escape in the future may have to take an opposite direction. Instead of spreading ourselves over a great deal of territory we may have to narrow ourselves to very little and find under the magnifying glass a natural world too small for man to enter and hence remaining virgin and uncorrupted by him and his works. The lichens will be awaiting us on that day to unfold an exotic flora of extreme diversity. The Crustose Lichens coat rocks almost like a mineral that has condensed on them. (A half-square-foot point of rock I photographed at the very peak of Stonyman at 4,010 feet, was sheathed in Crustose Lichens of four species, from pale grey to green and yellow, all prospering under the brunt of blistering winds and sunshine.) The papery Foliose Lichens usually look as if they had come about from a thin, grey-green batter poured on a frying-pan to become ruffled and wavy in stiffening; they are the most commonly-seen kind. Designated by a word meaning "shrub-like," the Fruticose Lichens stand vertically in the form of fanciful little extrusions or, as in Reindeer Lichen, in the semblance of tiny, bleached dead trees, but may also be filamentary, like *Usnea*—Old-man's-beard—which grows from the branches of trees in grey tufts and may be long enough to be mistaken for the Spanish "moss" of the Deep South. Varied as the lichens may be they are all alike in what they are, and a most extraordinary thing that is: a combination of two wholly dissimilar plants. In each case there is a body, which is a fungus, and there are green cells enclosed in it, which are algae. The resultant creation is quite unlike either component and can live where neither, or any other plant, could. The algae, containing chlorophyl and thus being able to manufacture food from inorganic substances, supply the nourishment; they are of the same types that color the base of tree-trunks green in damp woods. The fungus, while protecting the algae from desic-cation, provides moisture, which it absorbs from water collected at its base or from rains and mists, perhaps also minerals from rocks. These its hair-like hyphae penetrate by means of an acid secretion, slowly decom-posing them—for lichens, even more than mosses, are the creators of soil for plants that cannot do without it.

Lacking these two the winter woods would seem far less alive than they do. How alive that can be I found at Linville Falls on the eve of spring. Surrounded by rhododendron tented in green leaves and the green hoar-frost of hemlock foliage, mosses everywhere of an almost virulent green, dead wood plated with Parmelia Lichens and hirsute with *Usnea*, with here and there scarlet-capped British Soldiers, a Fruticose Lichen, I thought the forest more verdant than I had seen it in many places in summer. And the sense of a living floral community was much stronger because of the lichens and mosses, which conduct their vital processes while their great neigh-bors, decked in green as they may be, are dormant. Yet even the leafless trees and shrubs seem far from dead. High up where bare forest predominates, the mountainsides can be more colorful, more subtly color-ful, anyhow, than in July as sunlight and shadow pass across them. Greys light and dark, rose grey, fawns, mauve, beige, straw, plum, muted purples and maroon: such are the hues. They are those of living tissue, of branches to which the sap begins to rise not long after midwinter, so that not a day will be lost when flowers and leaves may, on a venture, be unfurled.

Unfurled they will be, as spring seeps up the mountains, up from south to north, up from base to summit; you will have all spring simultaneously on a single mountain. While white-marble draperies of ice, dripping in the warmth, hang from the rocks where trickles from the melting snow had refrozen and now are watering vibrant green pads of moss, the pioneers of spring appear. Often they overtake winter's receding rule and must contend with a last snowfall. Red Maple breaks out its little red flowers bristling with stamens. Up through the dead leaves push the constellations of delicate, palely flushed Spring-beauties, the little lavender buttercups called Hepatica and Bloodroot, a wheel of white spokes, our native poppy. They are the precursors.

Of spring in the Southern mountains, when it comes, one must accept the demands of honesty and pronounce it, of all the seasons, the incomparable. Did I say somewhere that the best time for the Blue Ridge Drive is the second week of June? I spoke before we had traveled it in mid-May, going on to the outstanding mountains of the great massif away from the Drive: LeConte, the Roan and Big Balsam. I had expected Vera to be surprised by the abundance of flowers, and indeed she was amazed, but not to be so much so myself, having had more foretaste of it. From the very rocks of the Shenandoah Blue Ridge, Moss-pinks—a Phlox—sprouted in cushions. At intervals for hundreds of miles, and indeed all through the mountains where the forest cover was broken, trailing carpets bright yellow with Wild Mustard or orange with Golden Ragwort gave back as good as they had received from the sun. And when small flocks of Goldfinches rose floatingly from the roadside they were like yellow blossoms themselves taking wing—Yellow Hawkweed flowers. For the whole length of the Drive, too, patches of tall-stemmed, lavender-pink Wild Geranium stirred to the lightest breeze. (More than stirred; you have only to try photographing flowers in the mountains with a slow color-film to discover that none is ever still.) And the Trilliums! We passed woods flecked with the Large-flowereds, white to pale flesh tint, turning pink with age. High on Apple Orchard Mountain, where May Apples solidly covered almost half an acre with a solid sheet of shimmering, deep-green parasol leaves eight inches above the ground, Trilliums stood by the thousands in the forest. At the top of Apple Orchard the squat oaks that give it its name were as bare as in winter, while down on the James, where

A white moth in a May-apple.

the twelve-mile climb up the mountain begins, the foliage had reached summer fulness. There, too, on Otter Creek, the first Catawba Rhododendron blossoms had opened, on May 8th, nearly a week early, according to a gas-station attendant. Now, on every mountainside you saw the progress spring had made. From the valleys canopied in the Tuliptrees' vigorous, bright green foliage, it had stolen up the mountainside like an infusion or a bloom of green of many shades, growing paler and more diaphanous until it faded out in a high forest still bare. The new foliage was as exciting as the flowers, and I was almost glad we were having grey weather to see it bright nevertheless, fresh and tender against the drab, still wintry mountains. The mountainsides might have been embroidered in silk thread, emerald and sea-green and, especially where the oaks were in catkin and mouse-ear leaf, green-gold, taffy and green-silver. But then the sun came out, and how luminous then was that metallic, living beading against the sullen, brooding earth-giants! One looked, as it were, upon hills

The Tuliptree—flower and foliage.

that were piled bunches of green and honey-green grapes, translucent beneath their bloom, glowing palely. It was the virtue of the season that each tree stood out individually and, while there was green enough to guarantee that the warm months had arrived, the views were still open.

Trees and shrubs were in bloom, too. The Serviceberry's little white flowers set in new leaflets were vanilla ice cream in caramel. Dogwoods were not merely trees with white flowers but entirely white trees. Those growing in the open Vera likened to bowls of popcorn. In the forest at a distance they could have been mistaken for the spray of waterfalls behind the trees. Mountainsides they lent the appearance of having been dusted over with confectioners' sugar. Pink Azalea, abounding along the way, was so luscious one positively hungered for it, as a small boy for a mound of strawberry mousse; it was not only that delectable color but, in the open, almost as solidly so. Could any other shrub in flower be so ravishing? Fortunately the Flame Azalea came into bloom 25 miles beyond Roanoke to save me from disloyalty to itself. Seeing the two growing side by side, the Flame with larger but sparser flowers—fiery yellow-tangerine trumpet-bells pealing a stamen-tongued affirmation—one was glad not to be put to a choice but to have both. Twenty miles farther on, Mountain Magnolia began. Its flower buds resemble lemon ice cream in cones; when just opening, large, elongate yellow roses, as Vera observed. When fully extended they give the tree the appearance of a multi-branched candelabrum holding out banana-yellow or yellow-cream water-lilies. Add to their color and size, which is that of a small banana with the skin peeled back, a heavy, slightly lemon-soapy, wholly delicious and unique fragrance and you have a floral sensation.

With all this beauty we had been the only occupants of our section of the campground at Peaks of Otter, which otherwise had contained only two trailers.

Walking in the woods, one had flowers for constant company. Star Chickweed and Bluets, both of which would bloom past midsummer, were among the most dependable, Showy Orchis, with white tongue protruding from beneath pinkish-lavender cap, among the special prizes. In between were Wood Betony—a Figwort like Indian Paint-brush with a pinwheel effect when you look down on its whorl of pale yellow and subdued red florets—Dwarf Crested Iris in low, dense beds, the lavender-blue flowers with startlingly orange tongues, Carolina Spring-beauties, Squirrel-corn like Dutchman's Breeches, elegant Cut-toothwort, single starred Wood Anemone. Large-flowered Trilliums were joined by others of the courtly genus: Painted Trillium, white with magenta throat; wholly-magenta Wake Robin; white Nodding Trillium by the trail up Russell Field in the Smokies; Snowy Trillium on LeConte. Blue Loose-flowered Phacelia covered a stream-bank on Russell Field, Fringed Phacelia a slope on

The Large-flowered trillium.

Clingman's Dome and an even greater on the Roan in such profusion one thought of a green field two-thirds under newly fallen snow. But the flowers that were most of all the little floral people of the mountains were the violets. Of the blues there must have been at least ten species, of the whites and yellows four or five each. The showiest were the Bird's-foot or Pansy Violets, of dark violet upper and lavender lower petals all joined at the center in an orange button; the smallest the pale blue Wild Pansies, only half an inch long, and the little Northern White Violets on Russell Field, which would follow the moss up a tree-trunk and crowd a rotting log like a tiny audience for a fairy event. Perhaps we saw more. Arthur Stupka says there are between 40 and 50 species of violets in the southern Appalachians, a region he has treated admirably well in his *Wildflowers in Color.* All I know is that wherever we went we found them looking up at us with eager little faces.

At Linville Falls and along the Drive nearby, Carolina Rhododendron was in bloom, the first time I had seen it so. A small Catawba, its flowers are the pink of a Pink Azalea's, however, rather than orchid-pink, and, like the Azalea's, separate instead of being clustered in dense heads. Farther along where the Black Mountains suddenly come into view the Mountain Silverbell did, too, a small, slender tree with long, thin branches laden with white blossoms pendant on long stems. I had never seen it in bloom before either, and I thought the flowers were such as you might shape around the end of your finger with a piece of paper. On the heights where the foliage had scarcely made a start, the forest on the mountainsides around you looked as if composed of little heaps of pale amber or pale butterscotch froth, interspersed with little meringues; these were Serviceberries, varying from foamy tan and foamy pink to white, depending on the state of the foliage. Up in the zone of spruces, all through the mountains, were shrubs with nearly round, mat-green leaves holding out white disks of flowers, perfectly level, as if, I thought, they were poached eggs that might spill from a plate. A Viburnum, they are called Hobblebush, from the habit of their branches of bending over to root at the tip and trip the unwary, sometimes beneficently to judge by their other name of Witch-hobble.

The fecund clouds of spring, heavy and moist, alternately shut out the sun and thinned away before it, and I reflected that, with all their untimely showers, one would not wish the Appalachians other than they are. The sharpness of detail and clarity over great distances under deep blue skies that electrify the beholder in rocky Western ranges would be out of place here. They would diminish the more modest scale of these mountains and the spell they cast. In the crowded East, mountains must be elusive to retain their integrity, and that is what these are. Moody mountains, receding from view in mists and haze of their own emanation, drawing the rain-clouds about them, they speak with the mystery of the imperfectly seen and grasped. That is one of their distinctions. Another is to make one more aware, than any other part of the world I know, of the scope, oceanic yet infinitely fine in texture, of the work of creation that is spring.

We climbed LeConte by the Alum Cave Trail. At least up to the Alum Cave itself—a bluff of overhanging rock five stories high underlain by sulphurous-smelling dust—it is far from a wilderness trail. When, on our way down, one of a party of college students fell from a rock face he had been foolish enough to climb, and was painfully hurt, the force dispatched from park headquarters within an hour to his succor was larger than any he could have expected in Manhattan. Still, five and a half miles long, it is perhaps of all the trails in the Smokies the one most not to be missed. It has everything: a broad, gushing stream so limpid it is aquamarine in its depths; Cove Forest; Red Spruces that rise from far below the trail and top out high above; mountain shoulders that are heath balds; cliffs on which you are willing enough to hold on to the cable strung along the trail across them; views of high and lonely crests unaltered since the Cherokees first looked on them, dark-barbed, and their steep flanking ridges, too, with the northern conifers. Finally there is the summit of LeConte itself.

It is of an elevation evident in the distance of the lowlands below you: a sheer mile. You look down on them from the lodge between groups of spruce that at night are warrior-priests of an antique people, black cloaks around them, gazing fixedly upon the little strings and cluster of lights. By day, at the very top, the syrup-sweet incense of the balsams in the warm sun fairly melts the heart with a love independent of objective and a trust in a benevolent principle in the universe. To this emotion the high, tripping, sustained, sweet recitative of the Winter Wren contributes. No other fragrance so enchants me; no other sounds in nature stir me so deeply as the singing of the tiny Wren, the Veery and the Hermit Thrush. They seem to me no less lofty in connotations than the mute and majestic mountains in which they have their being—connotations to which the elevation of spirit they effect in one attests.

One need not be religious, in a conventional sense, to judge that human societies have as a requirement of their well-being, even of their continuing existence as such, a recognition of a higher power, a Creator, a supreme Truth, a source of all, to which we are all answerable. That at least is my thinking. And it is this common belief and a shared view of the nature of that Ultimate, and of what is owed it that, I suspect, makes a collection of people a society with a being and soul of its own, capable of lasting life, a culture. That a society lives is evidenced, I submit, by its creativity. Art, even the most secular, even when it is bitter or despairing, is in my opinion addressed not only to the human audience but over the heads of that audience to the Unknowable (as it is to me). Of that transcendent spirit, nature is the expression. A society that alienates itself from nature—must it not alienate itself from the animating spirit of Creation, from the Ever-lasting, as Hamlet called it?

The objection may be made that the religion of Western civilization is Christianity and that Christianity gives little or no recognition to nature. It is true that the New Testament is negative in that respect, but Western man until recent years lived in the greatest intimacy with nature. Nature was the medium of our existence, as the sea to fish. It imbued our con-sciousnesses. Our livelihoods depended on the most dedicated study of nature and adaptation to its processes. In Britain and Western Europe, outside the scattered towns, we lived till the nineteenth century in a landscape garden-like in natural beauty. And we celebrated nature in our poetry. In song and dance under the sky we gave expression, in harmony, to the life with which nature charged us, as boys and girls, men and women in a setting of nature have always done. The most sacred Christian an-niversaries were borrowed festivals of the changing of the seasons.

In abusing and corrupting the earth as we have since been doing, we have been abusing and denying the Creator in common recognition and honoring of whom the soul and creativity of a culture originates. In the triumph of materialism, I think we shall find—are finding—is the dissolution of society. Of this dissolution the arts again are a barometer. With its progress they become nihilistic—anti-art. We may persist with economic gain as our primary goal. We may give heed to presidential advisers—men transparently already dead within—who lay it down that the needs of the economy must, ipso facto, come first. We may continue to go through the motions of a society, building taller World Trade Centers and Sears, Roebuck headquarters, bigger nuclear reactors and more hydra-headed missiles—more hospitals, too, for that matter. We may succeed in provid-ing every family with each new electronic marvel as it appears, a tropical winter seaside and summer mountain home, three motorcars and a yacht. But the iron law remains (or so I believe) that the more we make a wasteland of the earth around us the more we shall make a wasteland of the spirit within us. Engineering and organizational skills, even the most sophisticated, are of no avail against demoralization. That is why I am content to be as old as I am, and why as troubled as I am for my children's sake. The saving grace could be that a growing perception of where our course is leading could cause us to draw back and reconcile us to the sacrifices atonement will cost. It is the signs that this may be happening, along with the grimmer anticipation that if it is not, the matter may be taken out of our hands, to the earth's salvation, that give one courage to go abroad and yield one's heart to the beauty of the mountains and of the life that envelopes them.

Appendix

SEEING THE SOUTHERN APPALACHIANS

Exploring the southern Appalachians means primarily exploring the National Parks and National Forests. These incorporate enough of the range —with most of its most rewarding parts—to keep you going for many years if you are of a mind to do so. State parks, which are identified on most highway maps with their facilities indicated, often comprise natural sites of unusual interest (as is the case of Mount Mitchell State Park in North Carolina and The Breaks on the Virginia-Kentucky border) but are of limited dimensions. Some state forests are of thousands of acres, however.

For good or ill, depending on your point of view, probably every part of the southern Appalachians to which a trail leads may be visited between comfortable nights' sleep indoors; in this the East is very different from the West. On the other hand, you can keep largely out of sight of civilization for days or weeks on end on the Appalachian Trail, and you can find challenges as serious as you wish. Try hiking the higher parts in winter, or ascending a stream or marching across country in the rougher ranges. There are intellectual challenges, too—plants and animals to learn much more about than is known. You can make a southern Appalachians excursion, within broad limits, what you would like it to be.

Lodges and Cabins

Travelers on the Skyline Drive and Blue Ridge Parkway may make the trip and linger on it for as long as they wish in comfort approaching luxury. There are five commodious, modern lodges along the way, open more or less through the snowless season. In all, reservations are advisable.

Two are on the Skyline Drive: Skyland, with restaurant, at Mile 42; and Big Meadows, with coffee shop and camping-supply (including groceries) store, at Mile 51. In addition there are cabins and a coffee shop at Lewis

229

Mountain, at Mile 57. Reservations may be made for any of the three through the Virginia Skyline Corporation, Box 191, Luray, Va., 22835.

On the Blue Ridge Parkway, the three lodges, all with restaurants, are: Peaks of Otter Lodge (P.O. Box 489, Bedford, Va., 24523), at Mile 85; Bluff's Lodge (National Park Concessions, Inc., Laurel Springs, N. C., 28644) at Mile 240; and Pisgah Inn (Route 2, Box 375A, Canton, N. C., 28716) at Mile 408. In addition there are cabins at Rocky Knob (National Park Concessions, Inc., Meadows of Dan, Va., 24120) at Mile 174.

The Great Smoky Mountains National Park, while abundantly supplied with motels along the major approaches to the Park, offers no indoor accommodations within its limits except for little Mount LeConte Lodge (Gatlinburg, Tenn., 37738), accessible only by steep trails, the shortest (via Alum Cave) 5.5 miles—but well worth the climb. Just southwest of the Park, however, Fontana Village (Government Services, Inc., Fontana Dam, N. C., 28733) offers a lodge and 300 furnished cottages.

Some mountain state parks have lodges (like the handsome ones at Blackwater Falls and Mount Chateau in West Virginia) and many have cabins and campgrounds. The department administering these has a different name in different states, but an inquiry addressed to the State Highway Department at the state capital may be expected to bring the information requested.

Campgrounds

The Shenandoah and Great Smoky Mountains National Parks and the Blue Ridge Parkway connecting them are well supplied with campgrounds and there is a campground in the Cumberland Gap National Historical Park and in Catoctin Mountain Park north of Frederick, Md. This is not to say, however, that the late-arriving traveler can by any means count on finding a space in them during the summer. But as the number of campers grows, so does the number of private campgrounds, and the Ranger on duty at a filled National Park campground will give directions to the nearer of these. In the vicinity of the Great Smoky Mountains National Park, where congestion is likely to be severest, private campgrounds are especially plentiful.

Campgrounds (as well as lodges and cabins) in the National Parks are located on small folder maps available at no charge at entrances to the Parks or in advance by mail from the following:

Superintendent, Shenandoah National Park,
Luray, Va., 22835

Superintendent, Blue Ridge Parkway,
P. O. Box 7606,
Asheville, N. C., 28807

Superintendent, Great Smoky Mountains National Park,
Gatlinburg, Tenn., 37738

Superintendent, Cumberland Gap National Park,
Box 840,
Middlesboro, Ky., 40965

Superintendent, Catoctin Mountain Park,
Thurmont, Md., 21788

The Superintendents are, of course, sources of information of all kinds on the Parks under their jurisdiction.

National Forests also offer many campgrounds, and varied, some with a spigot or two as the sole plumbing, some with elegant tiled lavatories and hot showers. These, too, are located on official maps, which also give the facilities at each, including the availability of swimming and boating. The Forest Service maps are excellent, on a scale of four miles to the inch and with contour lines. No one making serious forays in the area one covers should be without it. Usually, they are obtainable at District Ranger Stations adjacent to the National Forest or at the Supervisor's office, by mail from the latter. Addresses are:

Supervisor, Chattahoochee-Oconee National Forest,
Box 1437,
Gainesville, Ga., 30501

Supervisor, Cherokee National Forest,
P. O. Box 400,
Cleveland, Tenn., 37311

Supervisor, Daniel Boone National Forest,
27 Carol Road,
Winchester, Ky., 40391

Supervisor, George Washington National Forest,
210 Federal Building,
Harrisonburg, Va., 22801

Supervisor, Jefferson National Forest,
Carlton P. O. Box 4009,
Roanoke, Va., 24015

Supervisor, Monongahela National Forest,
Elkins, W. Va., 26241

Supervisor, National Forests in North Carolina, (for Pisgah)
P. O. Box 2750, Asheville, N. C., 28802

National Forest supervisors, like their counterparts in the National Parks, are outstanding sources of information on their jurisdictions.

An excellent, comprehensive directory of campgrounds on public and private lands in the southern Appalachians with much other useful information is offered in Jim Crain's and Terry Milne's *Camping Around the Appalachian Mountains,* a new, 95-page publication of Random House/ Bookworks with 22 maps 7½ by 9½ inches.

Trails

The trail in the Southern mountains is of course the Appalachian Trail. It offers not only a means of threading the entire range but an enjoyable hike of whatever duration you choose, wherever it is encountered. For the full length of the Skyline Drive, and for the first 100 miles of the Blue Ridge Parkway, it is never more than a few miles from the road, and crossings are frequent. Some ten guidebooks to the trail, each covering a different section of 200 to 300 miles, are available from the Appalachian Trail Conference, P. O. Box 236, Harper's Ferry, W. Va., 25425. Be advised, however, that these are dangerous reading, in the incitement they offer. In addition to large-scale contour maps and detailed information on the trail, the guides also cover interesting side trails. One of the features of the Appalachian Trail is the blue-blazed spur trails, also maintained by local members of the Conference.

Much the longest of these spurs is the Big Blue, as it is called. Outside the Great Smokies, this may well be the only trail in the southern Appalachians, apart from its parent, more than 30 miles long. Commencing at Matthews Arm campground at Mile 22 on the Skyline Drive and heading northwest, the Big Blue descends to the Shenandoah Valley, crosses both branches of the Shenandoah River and, between them, the two prongs of Massanutten Mountain's northern end; then, climbing again, follows Paddy Mountain and winds up at the village of Capon Springs, West Virginia. Here, upwards of 60 miles from its starting point, the trail is at the northern tip of the George Washington National Forest, in which, after it has left the Shenandoah National Park, its course has largely lain. The plan is to extend it about as far again northward to Hancock, on the Potomac and practically on the Maryland-Pennsylvania line. There, crossing the 186-mile-long towpath of the Chesapeake and Ohio Canal (now a National Historical Park), it would join the Tuscarora Trail, which, chiefly following the Tuscarora Ridge, will take the hiker back to the Appalachian Trail in the vicinity of Carlisle, Pennsylvania. The problem is that, for much of the way between Capon Springs and Hancock, the trail will have to cross private lands. "You get permission from fifteen landowners in a row," says the Supervisor of Trails of the Potomac Appalachian Trail Club, Raymond H. Fadner, "then the sixteenth is immovable and you have to start all over again with a different route."

There are many trails in the Shenandoah National Park. The more obvious are shown on the small folder map provided at entrances to the park, but any serious hikers should have the contour map of the park in a scale of 1:62,500, or an inch to the mile, put out in three sections by the Potomac Appalachian Trail Club, for sale by the club (at 1718 N Street, N. W., Washington, D. C., 20036) and at visitor centers in the Park. This shows all the trails. The most rewarding I know in the park, apart from the Appalachian Trail, are those to Stonyman and Hawksbill Mountains (two 4,000-footers and the highest in the Park), to Old Rag Mountain, to White Oak Canyon and to Dark Hollow Falls. All in the central section of the Park, these are unfortunately also the most popular trails, though not everyone goes all the way in each case, by any means. A good day's walk would be from Skyland down the White Oak Canyon Trail, back up the Cedar Run Trail to Hawksbill Gap, thence via the Appalachian Trail to the starting point again.

For most of its course, trails off the Blue Ridge Parkway—other than the Appalachian Trail—are brief affairs, though one of my ideas of a lovely time is to dawdle down the Parkway walking them all. Flattop and Sharptop (once thought to be the highest in Virginia) offer climbs of two or three hours round-trip, north of Roanoke; they are the Peaks of Otter (perhaps from the Cherokee for *mountains,* rendered as Ottari or Atali). But there are three notable hikes starting from the Parkway, on which I have already enlarged: the Linville Gorge Wilderness trails, the trail up to and along the crest of the Black Mountains (two of the most exciting in the southern Appalachians) and the Art Loeb Trail through the Shining Rock Wilderness. Travelers not prepared for such all-day hikes should at least make the half-hour climbs up Craggy Pinnacle at Mile 364 and up Richland Balsam at Mile 431. Good trails in the southwestern half of the Blue Ridge Parkway and to the north are shown and described on the map called *100 Favorite Trails of the Great Smokies and Carolina Blue Ridge,* prepared by the Carolina Mountain Club of Asheville and the Smoky Mountains Hiking Club of Knoxville, and for sale by The Stephens Press, Inc., 5655, Asheville, N. C., 28803, and at shops on the Parkway.

Trails in the Great Smokies can keep you going at 15 miles a day for 45 days without retracing your steps. The most popular are described in *100 Favorite Trails,* while a sheet put out by the Great Smoky Mountains National Park entitled *Favorite Hiking Trails* gives the essential data—location, length, amount of climb and degree of difficulty—for 39. (How reliable the advice is, I do not know. The Andrews Bald Trail, described as "easy," I found the worst underfoot of any trails I have walked in Southern mountains.) Within your competence you can hardly go wrong on any of the trails. Of those I know, none offers, mile for mile, as much variety and scenic drama as the ascent of LeConte via Alum Cave, starting nine miles from the visitor center at the Gatlinburg entrance up the highway to Newfound Gap: "11 miles [round trip]—strenuous—climb 2,853'." The Appalachian Trail follows the main crest of the Smokies from one end of the Park to the other, and parts of it are spectacular. Among other great mountains, it crosses the two highest of the Smokies. But to me neither Clingman's Dome nor Guyot is as thrilling as the more rugged and open LeConte.

For planning hikes in the range, there is hardly a substitute for the 32-inch by 22-inch map of *Great Smoky Mountain National Park and Vicinity,* relief-shaded and with contour lines in a scale of 1:125,000, or half an inch to the mile, prepared and for sale by the U. S. Geological Survey, Washington, D. C., 20242, and also for sale in the Park. It is a beautiful map and one carried by all knowledgeable hikers in the park. This map, somewhat reduced in scale, is contained in a newly-published Sierra Club "Totebook" that promises to be for years to come *the* guide to trails in the range: *Hiker's Guide to the Smokies,* by Dick Murlless and Constance Stallings. Pocket-sized but thorough, it covers 127 trails in 359 pages.

Between the Great Smokies and its first crossing of the Blue Ridge Parkway, the Appalachian Trail climbs to two heights that to me are outstanding, as I imagine I have already made plain. One is the crossing of the Roan group of summits on the border of North Carolina and Tennessee, the other the crossing of Big Balsam (Mount Rogers) just inside Virginia above the North Carolina line.

These are in National Forests, as is much the greater part of the Appalachian Trail in the South—as is much the greater preponderance of trails in the range. Of those in the Nantahala National Forest in southwestern North Carolina, I should like to see more of the Appalachian Trail south of the Smokies. I should like to return to Highlands and explore the gorges where the Savannah and Chattahoochee rise; as it is, I can recommend the trail down the East Fork of Overflow Creek southwest of the town in the Glen Falls Scenic Area. I should like to see if the trail to the north, over Shortoff and Yellow Mountains, would make me feel like an explorer, as it did when I walked it as a boy. Of the trails I do not know at all, my first choice would be that which ascends little Santeetlah Creek and encircles its drainage basin in that valley of the big trees protected as the Joyce Kilmer Memorial Forest, a little south of the western end of the Great Smokies.

Farther south, in the Cohutta Wilderness of central north Georgia, the trail through the gorge of Jack's River is special, but only for those who do not mind wading mountain streams.

In Virginia, one of the highest of the Long Ridges, at 4,458 feet, is Great North Mountain, which overlooks the Shenandoah Valley from the west, across from Staunton. The summit, on which the vegetation battens down against the winds—it is the highest point in the George Washington

National Forest—is partly ruined by some kind of electronics structures, but I had a grand, solitary walk up it one October day from the road that crosses near its end west of Buffalo Gap. Well-known trails also ascend Shenandoah Mountain—the next big mountain along the rim of the Shenandoah Valley to the northeast—to 4,400-foot Reddish Knob, and follow the mountain's crest. Then, farther along still, there is the Big Blue Trail: an adventure in itself, it connects with an interesting trail running along the northeastern half of 50-mile-long Massanutten Mountain, this, too, in the George Washington National Forest.

There is lastly the great Monongahela National Forest. In its easternmost projection it encompasses roughly two-thirds of North Fork Mountain, of the bold outcroppings of Silurian sandstone. A trail follows the crest for 25 miles. I have walked a little of it and mean to walk the rest. (Remember always to take water when preparing to walk a ridge crest.) Behind North Fork are Spruce Mountain and Dolly Sods.

The trail along Spruce Mountain's broad back from the road head on Spruce Knob is one I rate as highly as any in the central Appalachians. Dolly Sods is a favorite area for naturalists. The principal trail goes west from Red Creek Campground to Blackbird Knob, thence south down Red Creek. You can either turn back up Fisher Spring Run, where it joins Red Creek, and make the last leg of the return to the campground via the road, or you can continue down Red Creek to the Wildlife Manager's Station. Here you have the choice of retracing your steps or returning to the campground by the road—ten miles.

My own experience has made me highly partial to the ridge-crest trail in the Cranberry Back Country in the southwestern section of the National Forest, which runs from Redoak Knob to Black Mountain and is hence called the Red and Black Trail. But the Monongahela is over half again as large as the Great Smoky Mountains National Park and contains many trails. As well as seeking out those of known attraction, there is much to be said for making one's own discoveries; one never knows what may be around the next bend. This is true of all the National Forests. Trails in the newly-proposed Wilderness Areas incorporated in them, assuming that favorable action will be completed on them, should be worthy of special attention. These include Dolly Sods, Cranberry and Otter Creek in the Monongahela, six areas in the George Washington and Jefferson of Virginia, three in the Cherokee of Tennessee, Beaver Creek in the Daniel Boone of Kentucky and—largest of all—Cohutta in the Chattahoochee of Georgia.

Before a hike in a National Forest, it pays to stop by the nearest District Ranger Station, where often a detailed trail map of the immediate area is available. Even if simply reproduced from a hand sketch, this can be extremely helpful.

Maps

For a first introduction to a region, there is nothing like a map. Valuable special maps have been mentioned in preceding sections. There are, in addition, several general series that are worth knowing about.

The best comprehensive view of the topography of the southern Appalachians I have seen is provided by the official Sectional Aeronautical Chart, 1:500,000 (or an inch to eight miles), Cincinnati and Atlanta sheets, without overprinting. A lovely map to look at, it is sold by Distribution Division, National Ocean Survey, C 44, Riverdale, Md., 20840.

For four times as much detail, there are the topographic maps of the Geological Survey, 1:250,000-scale series. (The Forest Service maps referred to in the section on campgrounds are basically of this series.) These show contours and forest cover, in green. A dozen of them are required to cover the southern Appalachians. An index to the series (at no charge) and the maps themselves are obtainable from Map Information Office, U. S. Geological Survey, Washington, D. C., 20242. Three sheets in this series have been so composed as to have the Blue Ridge Parkway running across the center of each, North Section, Middle Section and South Section respectively. If you care to identify terrain features from the Parkway, or to know where you would get to if you started walking from it, these enable you to do so. These three maps are for sale by Eastern National Park and Monument Association, Box 1710, Roanoke, Va., and usually at visitor centers on the Parkway.

Larger-scale topographic maps put out by the Geological Survey come in 1:125,000-scale, 1:62,500-scale and 1:24,000-scale series. This last, in which one inch equals only 2,000 feet and individual buildings are shown, is as large-scale as a hiker could ask. At a pace of 2½ miles an hour you move across a map of this series at the same speed as the tip of an inch-long minute-hand of a timepiece. A day's hike of 18 miles would take you the length of two full sheets.

Equipment and Supplies

This important subject has been fully treated in a number of readily available books. Among others, Edward B. Garvey, who hiked the entire Appalachian Trail in 1970, has done so in his *Appalachian Hiker* (Appalachian Books, Oakton, Va., 22124) and his detailed discussion of the matter has to recommend it that it is directly related to Appalachian conditions.

Good hiking!

Bibliography

Brockman, C. Frank. *Trees of North America*. London: Golden Press, 1968.

Brooks, Maurice. *The Appalachians*. Boston: Houghton Mifflin, 1965.

Broome, Harvey. "The Great Smoky Mountains National Park," *National Parks Magazine*. March 1965.

Burt, William Henry. *A Field Guide to the Mammals*. Boston: Houghton Mifflin, 1952.

Byrd, Robert C. "Spruce Knob-Seneca Rocks National Recreation Area," *National Parks Magazine*. December 1966.

Calder, Nigel. *The Restless Earth*. New York: Viking, 1972.

Callahan, North. *The Smoky Mountain Country*. New York: Duell, Sloan and Pierce, 1952.

Campbell, Carlos G. *Birth of a National Park in the Great Smoky Mountains*. Knoxville: University of Tennessee Press, 1960.

Caruso, John A. *The Appalachian Frontier: America's First Surge Westward*. New York: Bobbs-Merrill, 1959.

Caudill, Harry M. Foreword to *Stinking Creek,* by John Fetterman. New York: E. P. Dutton, 1967.

Caudill, Harry M. *Night Comes to the Cumberlands*. Boston: Little, Brown, 1963.

Collingwood, G. H. and Warren D. Brush. *Knowing Your Trees*. Washington, D.C.: The American Forestry Association, 1947.

Cruickshank, Helen G., ed. *John and William Bartram's America*. Greenwich, Conn.: Devin-Adair, 1957.

Davenport, Demorest. "The Esthetics of Orchid Pollination," *Natural History*. April 1968.

Dietz, Robert S. "Geosynclines, Mountains and Continent-Building," *Scientific American*. March 1972.

Drake, Richard B. *An Appalachian Reader*. Published by Author, 1970.

Dupree, A. Hunter. *Asa Gray, 1810-1888*. Cambridge: Belknap Press of Harvard University, 1959.

Fedde, Gerhard F. "Status of Imported and Native Predators of the Balsam Woolly Aphid on Mt. Mitchell, North Carolina," Washington, D.C.: U.S. Department of Agriculture Forest Service Research Note SE-175. June 1972.

Fedde, Gerhard F. "A Parasitic Fungus Disease of Adelges piceae in North Carolina," *Annals of the Entomological Society of America.* May 1971.

Fidalgo of Elvas, A. Translated by Buckingham Smith. Bradford Club Series No. 5. New York, 1866.

Frome, Michael. *Strangers in High Places: Story of the Great Smoky Mountains.* Garden City, N.Y.: Doubleday, 1966.

Garvey, Edward B. *Appalachian Hiker: Adventure of a Lifetime.* Oakton, Va.: Appalachian Books, 1971.

Gray, Asa. *Letters of Asa Gray, 1810-1888.* Ed. by Jane Loring Gray. Boston: Houghton Mifflin, 1893.

Gulick, John. *Cherokees at the Crossroads.* Chapel Hill: University of North Carolina, 1960.

Hannum, Alberta Pierson. *Look Back With Love: A Recollection of the Blue Ridge.* New York: Vanguard, 1967.

Hatcher, Robert D. "Experimental Model for the Southern Appalachians," *Geological Society of America Bulletin.* September 1972.

Hornaday, William T. *The American Natural History.* New York: Scribner's, 1922.

Huyak, Dorothy B. "Shenandoah National Park," *National Parks Magazine.* November 1965.

Johnson, Hugh. *International Book of Trees.* New York: Simon & Schuster, 1973.

Kephart, Horace. *Our Southern Highlanders.* New York: Macmillan, 1913, 1922, 1941.

Kercheval, Samuel. *A History of the Valley of Virginia.* W. N. Grabil, 1902.

King, Philip B. *Evolution of North America.* Princeton: Princeton University Press, 1959.

King, Philip B., Robert B. Neuman and Jarvis B. Hadley. *Geology of the Great Smoky Mountains National Park, Tennessee and North Carolina.* Geological Survey Professional Paper 587. Washington, D.C. U.S. Government Printing Office, 1968.

Lambert, Darwin. "A Running Start on Earthmanship," *National Parks Magazine.* September 1968.

Lambert, Darwin. *The Earth-Man Story.* New York: Exposition Press, 1972.

Lambert, Robert S. "Logging the Great Smokies," *Tennessee Historical Quarterly.* December 1961.

Lanman, Charles. *Letters from the Allegheny Mountains.* New York: G. P. Putnam, 1849.

Manville, Richard H. "The Mammals of Shenandoah National Park," Shenandoah National Historical Association, 1956.

Mason, Robert L. *The Lure of the Great Smokies.* Boston: Houghton Mifflin, 1927.

Matoon, M. A. "Appalachian Comeback." *Trees. The Yearbook of Agriculture.* Washington, D.C.: U.S. Government Printing Office, 1949.

McCormick, Jack. *The Life of the Forest.* New York: McGraw Hill, 1966.

Palmer, E. Laurence. *Fieldbook of Natural History.* New York: Whittlesey House, 1949.

Peattie, Donald Culross. *A Natural History of Trees.* Boston: Houghton Mifflin, 1950.

Peattie, Roderick, ed. *The Great Smokies and the Blue Ridge.* New York: Vanguard, 1943.

Peterson, Roger Tory and Margaret McKenny. *A Field Guide to Wildflowers.* Boston: Houghton Mifflin, 1968.

Robinson, Benjamin Lincoln and Merritt Lyndon Fernald. *Gray's New Manual of Botany.* New York: American Book Company, 1908.

Savage, Henry, Jr. *Lost Heritage.* New York: William Morrow, 1970.

Sheppard, Muriel Earley. *Cabins in the Laurel.* Chapel Hill: University of North Carolina, 1935.

Stupka, Arthur. *Great Smoky Mountains National Park.* Washington, D.C.: National Park Service, 1960.

Stupka, Arthur. *Wildflowers in Color.* New York: Harper & Row, 1965.

Thomson, Peggy. "2,025-Mile Hike," *Modern Maturity.* August–September 1972.

Tilden, Paul M. "New Hope for the American Chestnut," *National Parks and Conservation Magazine.* July 1971.

Torrey, Bradford. *A World of Green Hills.* Boston: Houghton Mifflin, 1898.

Trevelyan, G. M. *The Call and Claims of Natural Beauty: Voices for the Wilderness.* New York: Sierra Club-Ballantine, 1969.

Wilhelm, Eugene J., Jr. "Return of the Elk to Appalachia," *National Parks Magazine.* January 1967.

In *The Distributional History of the Biota of the Southern Mountains.* Blacksburg, Va.: Virginia Polytechnic Institute and State University, 1969, 1970, 1971:

Anderson, Lewis E. *Geographical Relationships of the Mosses of the Southern Appalachian Mountains.*

Cooper, Arthur W. and James W. Hardin. *Floristics and Vegetation of the Gorges on the Southern Blue Ridge Escarpment.*

Core, Earl L. *The Botanical Exploration of the Southern Appalachians.*

Evans, A. Murray. *A Review of Systematic Studies of the Pteridophytes of the Southern Appalachians.*

Guilday, John E. *The Pleistocene History of the Appalachian Mammal Fauna.*

Hack, John T. *The Area, Its Geology: Cenozoic Development of the Southern Appalachians.*

Handley, Charles O. *Appalachian Mammalian Geography—Recent Epoch.*

Highton, Richard. *Distributional Interactions Among Eastern North American Salamanders of the Genus* Plethodon.

Hubbard, John P. *The Avifauna of the Southern Appalachians: Past and Present.*

Keener, Carl S. *The Natural History of the Mid-Appalachian Shale Barren Flora.*

Little, Elbert L., Jr. *Endemic, Disjunct and Northern Trees in the Southern Appalachians.*

Wood, Carroll E., Jr. *Some Floristic Relationships between the Southern Appalachians and Western North America.*

Index

Alder, Mountain, 88, 89

Alleghenies, 59, 190–191, 196–211

Angelica, Hairy, 112

Appalachian Mountains, Southern: Character of, 3–7, 27, 39–41, 45; Early explorations of, 10–13; Flowers of, 27–120, 135, 156, 176, 180, 183, 220, 223; Forests of, 20–21, 50, 151–154, 157–168, 170–171; Geology of, 59–72, 102–104; Mammals of, 87, 141–148, 154, 200, 201, 205; Minerals of, 59–60; People of, 184–189; Rivers of, behavior of, 102–104; Settlement of, 13–17, 56–57. *See also* Allegheny, Blue Ridge, Cumberland, Great Smoky and Long Ridge Mountains

Appalachian Trail, 28, 52–53, 80–82, 87–92, 93, 115, 119–124, 135–136, 191, 210, 217–218, 233–234; For information on, 232

Ash, White, 164, 165, 206

Azaleas: Flame, 34, 160, 223; Pink, 33, 223

Balds: Grass, 54, 85, 87–90, 112; Heath, 39, 54

Back Allegheny Mountain, 205, 206–207

Balsam Beartown Mountain, 177–178

Balsam Mountains, Great and Plott, 36, 37, 38, 44, 57, 110–117

Balsam: Southern, 43, 45, 53, 79, 85–86, 106, 108, 154, 167, 168, 177, 226; Northern, 199, 201

Bartram, John and William, 17–18, 22, 27, 74

Basswood, 74, 164

Bear, Black, 31, 46, 49, 108, 143–144, 149, 190, 204

Beaver, 142, 198

Beech, American, 36, 164, 166, 167

Bees, Bumble and Honey, 75, 77

Big Balsam Mountain, 59, 73–82, 94

Big Black Mountain, 180, 183–184

Birches: Cherry, 137, 159, 160, 187; White, 154; Yellow, 36, 50, 52, 75, 77–78, 110, 154, 167, 206

Blackberry, 88, 109, 127, 212

Black Mountains, 36, 37, 45, 53, 57, 79, 104–109, 216

Blood Mountain, 136

Blueberries and Huckleberries, 36, 100, 127, 162, 167, 209, 212

Blue Ridge Mountains, 12, 22, 24–37, 38, 59–62, 73–136, 147, 213–214; Geology of, 70

Blue Ridge Parkway, 20, 21, 24–37, 38, 62, 70, 74, 96, 109–110, 142, 229–230; Trails from, 233

Bluets, 81, 87, 198, 223

Boar, Wild, 141, 145

Boone, Daniel, 17, 173
Brasstown Bald, 120, 135
Breaks Interstate Park, 182
Brooks, Maurice, 77, 88, 147, 199, 200, 201, 205
Bryant, William Cullen, 19
Buckeye, Yellow, 39, 164
Bunting, Snow, 88
Bush-honeysuckle, 112, 167
Byrd, Col. William, 5

Cade's Cove, 56–57, 71, 186
Calder, Nigel, 68, 72
Caruso, John A., 13
Caudill, Harry M., 184, 188, 189
Cheat Mountain, 204–205, 206
Cherokee Indians, 3, 4, 11, 16–18, 38, 55–56, 58, 136, 172
Cherries: Black, 75, 164, 167, 206; Pin, 54, 109, 112, 154, 162
Chestnut, American, 124–127, 159
Chickadee, Black-capped, 42, 209
Chipmunk, 49, 120, 166
Cinquefoil, Three-toothed, 88, 120, 136
Clingman, Thomas L., 57, 106
Clingman's Dome, 37, 44, 45, 53, 56, 58, 107
Club-mosses, 79, 152, 157, 175, 205
Cohutta Mountains, 136–141, 235
Copperhead, 139–140, 143, 145
Cougar, 147–148
Craggy Mountains, 33, 34, 36, 109–110
Cranberries, 80, 81, 110, 199–200, 212
Cranberry Back Country, 207–210, 235
Cranberry bogs, 199–201
Cronquist, Arthur and Mabel, 86–87, 100
Cumberland Mountain and Gap, 17, 103, 172–173
Cumberland Mountains and Plateau, 172, 174–175; Geology of, 175–176

Deer, White-tailed, 17, 31, 77, 145–147, 149, 215–216

DeSoto, Hernando, 10
Dietz, Robert S., 68–69, 72
Dogwood, Flowering, 27, 159, 214, 223
Dolly Sods, 197–199
Dunmore, John Murray Lord, 13

Eagle, Golden, 45, 216
Eft, Red, 132
Elder, Red, 109, 167
Elk, American, 141–142

Falls, Cullasaja and Glen, 132
Fir, Fraser's. See Balsam, Southern
Ferns, 52, 79, 120, 156, 200
Foreman, Clark, 24, 129
Fox, John, 184, 185
Foxes, Grey and Red, 142
French Broad River, 10, 11, 21, 22, 110
Frome, Michael, 16, 57

Galax, 40, 100, 136
Garvey, Edward B., 86, 88, 99
Goshen Pass, 103
Grandfather Mountain, 26, 34, 71, 96
Gray, Asa, 22, 84–85, 154–156, 205
Great Smoky Mountains, 3–4, 7, 27, 34, 37, 38–58, 59, 103, 130, 215; Geology of, 71; Plants of, 156–157.
Great Smoky Mountains National Park, 7, 26, 28, 38–58, esp. 47–48, 145, 230; Hunting in, 149
Great Valley, 13, 14, 29, 33, 62, 65, 172, 173; Geology of, 71
Greenbrier, 133, 160
Grouse, Ruffed, 55, 120, 197, 204
Gum, Black or Sour. See Tupelo, Black
Guyot, Arnold Henry, 57–58
Guyot, Mount, 44, 52, 56

Hack, John T., 104
Hannum, Alberta Pierson, 186, 188
Hawk, Broad-winged, 120, 216
Hawks, migration of, 215–216

Heath Family, 100, 121, 162, 163, 164

Hemlocks: Carolina, 99–100; Eastern, 74, 98, 99, 128, 137, 154, 159, 160, 164, 166, 167, 200

Hickories, 154, 159, 160–161, 214

Highlands, N. C., and Biological Station, 18, 19, 22, 24, 124, 128, 129–131, 132

Hurricane Camille, 115

Ice Ages, 87, 153–154, 197, 200

Indian-pipe, 100, 135

Jack's River Gorge, 137–138

Joyce Kilmer Memorial Forest, 124

Junco, 50, 88, 109, 115, 205

Kephart, Horace, 5–6, 47–48, 56, 186–187

Kercheval, Samuel, 12

King's Mountain, battle of, 13–14

Lambert, Darwin, 10, 22, 31, 147

Lanman, Charles, 119, 124, 127, 187

LeConte, Mount, 7, 39–46, 94, 226, 230

Lederer, John, 10–11, 22, 103

Leek, Wild, 77

Leucothoë, 42, 100, 164

Lichens, 50, 79, 100, 134, 156, 218–219

Life zones, 36, 49, 50

Lilies, 79, 89, 109, 112

Linville Gorge and River, 96–102, 219, 233

Locust, Black, 159, 162

Long Ridge Mountains, 29, 33, 59, 65–66, 103, 173, 176–180, 211; Geology of, 71, 175

MacKaye, Benton, 28, 91

Magnolias, 27, 39, 74, 152, 154, 159, 160, 164, 223

Maples: Mountain, 154, 167, 206; Red, 100, 154, 162, 164, 167; Striped, 75,

154, 167, 214; Sugar, 39, 74–75, 93, 164, 206

Mattoon, M. A., 20–21

Michaux, André, 34, 154–155

Mitchell, Elisha, 104, 106

Mitchell, Mount. See Black Mountains

Mosses and Liverworts, 93–95, 133–134, 199–200

Mountain-ash, 79, 81, 154, 167, 197

Mountain-laurel, 32, 33, 39, 42, 45, 54, 83, 100, 133, 159, 162, 164, 197, 212

Mushrooms and other fungi, 134–135, 156

Nantahala Mountains, 116, 119–124, 126, 130

National Forests, incl. Forest Service: 20–21, 26, 86, 91, 108, 129, 139, 191–192, 194, 195, 205, 206; Poaching in, 149–150; Trails in, 234–235

National Parks, incl. Park Service, 26, 91, 144, 192–193, 195. See also individual parks

Nettle, Wood, 89, 202

New River, 11, 13, 103

Nuttall, Thomas, 21–22, 29

Oaks, 37, 119, 152, 160; Black, 127, 159, 160, 214; Blackjack, 136; Chestnut, 99, 159, 160, 161, 214; Red, 36, 136, 159, 164, 165, 167, 214; Scarlet, 159, 160, 161; White, 39, 136, 159, 160, 165, 214

Opossum, 144–145

Orchids, 31, 109, 123, 133, 135, 200, 223

Otter Creek, W. Va., 201

Peaks of Otter, 33, 142, 233

Peattie, Donald Culross, 126, 130, 166

Peattie, Roderick, 18

Piedmont, 62, 70

Pine Mountain, Ky., 180, 182

Pines: Pitch, 161; Short-leafed Yellow, 33, 161; Table-Mountain, 41–42, 100,

Pines (*cont.*)
161; Virginia, 161–162; White, 99, 154

Pope, Clifford, 130

Rabun Bald, 124, 127, 135, 136

Raccoon, 141, 144

Rattlesnake, Timber, 143, 145

Raven, 116–117, 212

Rhododendrons: Carolina, 100, 225; Catawba, 33, 42, 45, 52, 54, 81, 84–85, 109, 110, 164, 167, 222; Rosebay, 34, 49, 74, 83, 98, 132–133, 154, 159, 162, 164; Hardiness of, 162, 168

Richland Balsam Mountain, 37, 38, 44, 110

Roan Mountain, 19, 22, 33, 45, 84–95, 216

Robinson, Harold E., 93–95

Rogers, Mount. *See* Big Balsam Mountain

Ross, Larry, 138–141

Salamanders, 130–132

Sand-myrtle, 45

Sassafras, 152, 154, 162, 214

Seneca Rocks, 211

Serviceberry, 27, 88, 162, 164, 223

Shale barrens, 178–180

Shaver's Fork and Mountain, 205–206, 207

Shenandoah National Park, 24, 26, 28–31, 140, 147, 162, 166; Trails in, 232–233

Shenandoah Valley, 12–13, 18, 29–30, 65

Shining Rock Mountain and Wilderness, 110–114

Shortia, 130, 154–155

Silverbell, Mountain, 164, 225

Skunk, 114, 144

Skyline Drive, 20, 24, 26–31, 33, 62, 215–216, 229–230

Smith, Anthony Wayne, 193

Sourwood, 100, 159, 162, 164, 214

Spider, Fishing, 98–99

Spotswood, Gov. Alexander, 12

Spruce, Red, 21, 34, 36, 37, 52, 53, 79, 106, 108, 110, 154, 167, 168, 197, 206, 209, 212

Spruce Mountain, W. Va., 59, 201, 207, 210–212, 217

Squirrels, Flying, Grey and Red, 43, 166, 205

Standing Indian Mountain, 19, 119–120, 121

Sterling, Mount, 48, 50, 52

Stonyman Mountain, 30, 62, 64, 219

Thrushes: Hermit, 197, 200, 212, 226; Olive-backed, 200, 209; Veery, 49, 120, 198, 226; Wood, 49

Tilden, Paul, 125

Torrey, Bradford, 22–23, 127, 128

Trailing Arbutus, 100, 160

Trevelyan, G. M., 9, 22, 137

Trilliums, 212, 220, 223

Tuliptree, 33, 39, 99, 124–125, 154, 159, 160, 164, 165, 214

Tupelo, Black, 77, 100, 154, 159, 162, 214

Turkey, Wild, 17, 148, 173, 197, 204

Umbrella-leaf, 49

Viburnums, 120, 200, 225

Violets, 225

Vireos: Red-eyed, 75; Solitary, 42, 98

Walden Ridge, 174

Walnut, Black, 75, 165–166

Warbler: Black-throated Blue, 42, 198; Black-throated Green, 207; Canada, 40, 198; Hooded, 137; Kentucky, 137; Worm-eating, 217

Washington, George, 16, 19

Whiteside Mountain, 127–128

Wigginton, James, 184–185

Wildcat, 113, 142–143

Wilderness Act and areas under, 29, 96, 110, 138, 173, 193–195, 197, 201, 207, 234
Witch-hazel, 154, 158, 159
Wolf, Timber, 142
Woodpecker, Pileated, 49

Wood-sorrel, Mountain, 42, 52, 79, 86, 110, 209
Wordsworth, William, 19
Wren, Winter, 42, 80, 98, 115, 205, 226

Yellow-wood, 162

Scale

25   O   25   50   75   100 MILES

COPYRIGHT BY A.K. LOBECK